CHET MURPHY

Tennis Professional at Broadmoor Hotel,
Colorado Springs;
University of California, Berkeley

BILL MURPHY

University of Arizona, Tucson

TENNIS
for the Player,
Teacher
and Coach

W. B. SAUNDERS COMPANY
Philadelphia, London, Toronto

W. B. Saunders Company: West Washington Square
Philadelphia, PA   19105

12 Dyott Street
London, WC1A   1DB

833 Oxford Street
Toronto, Ontario M8Z 5T9, Canada

Library of Congress Cataloging in Publication Data

Murphy, Chester W

Tennis for the player, teacher, and coach.

Bibliography: p.

Includes index.

1. Tennis.   I. Murphy, William E., joint author.
II. Title.

GV995.M84   796.34′2′07   74–17759

ISBN 0-7216-6620-5

Tennis for the Player, Teacher and Coach   ISBN 0-7216-6620-5

Last digit is the print number: 9   8   7   6   5   4   3   2

ABOUT THE AUTHORS

CHET MURPHY

Former Tennis Coach at the University of California, Berkeley, Chet is now Coordinator of Tennis Instruction on the Berkeley Campus. He is the author of three other books, the author-consultant for the instructional loop films produced by the NCAA Film Service, long-time tennis professional at the Broadmoor Hotel in Colorado Springs, and a Master Tennis Clinician for the Lifetime Sports Foundation. He is Chairman of the Tennis Games Committee for the U.S. Collegiate Sports Council (World University Games), past President of the National Collegiate Tennis Coaches Association, and former Chairman of the AAHPER-USLTA Joint Committee for School Tennis Development. He has recently been appointed to the Educational Advisory Committee of the Junior Tennis Council (USLTA), and again to the AAHPER-USLTA Joint Committee. In his college days, Chet was runner-up for the NCAA singles and doubles tennis titles. He has coached collegiate tennis for twenty-four years (in Chicago, Detroit, Minnesota, and California). During his ten years at California, he coached five All-American players, and his teams were regularly among the strongest in the country.

BILL MURPHY

Among tennis coaches, Bill has one of the best won-lost records in the country. During the past two years, his Arizona teams have won 32 dual matches while losing only 6; in addition, both his 1973 and 1974 teams won the Western Athletic Conference Championship and finished among the top-ten teams in the country. Before coming to Arizona, he coached at the University of Michigan for nineteen years, where his teams ran up a 198-45 record, won eleven Big Ten Championships, and took one National Collegiate Championship.

Chet and Bill are regular contributors to leading tennis magazines, with many articles on tennis instruction. They have conducted numerous tennis clinics and workshops throughout the country.

In 1973, these tennis-teaching twins were jointly awarded the Education Merit Award by the National Tennis Education Foundation of the United States Lawn Tennis Association, in recognition of their contribution to the game through their publications, committee work, clinics, and workshops.

PREFACE

Tennis is one of the few sports that can be played from childhood through adulthood and into old age. It can be enjoyed by boys and girls and men and women, whether skilled or unskilled, either singly or in pairs. It is one of the few family sports in which parents and children can play together, and it does not require a great deal of expensive equipment. Quite probably all of these factors explain why equipment manufacturers, court construction firms, USLTA officials, and school authorities now claim that more people than ever are playing tennis.

Concurrent with this increase in popularity has come an awareness by school athletic officials of the necessity of providing suitable tennis instruction at all levels — elementary, intermediate, and advanced. But good programs require skilled personnel and good leadership. The responsibility for training these leaders falls on our school teacher-training programs. Even varsity coaches must be trained in teacher programs if the schools are to fulfill their obligation of providing guidance and leadership for players at all levels.

Yet, many tennis authorities feel that the schools are not meeting their responsibility in this area. The reason is that most physical education training programs attach little importance to tennis, often even relegating it to the role of a "minor" sport. Secondly, skilled athletes traditionally choose the more popular team sports when they decide to become coaches. Consequently, few graduates in physical education are capable of handling advanced tennis classes or school tennis teams. As a result, school athletic authorities must look elsewhere for their tennis coaches. Since there is seldom anyone outside the school system who is qualified and available, teachers of academic subjects are usually pressed into service as school tennis coaches.

In a number of cases, these academic teachers do not know a great deal about tennis, especially about teaching and coaching it. Many of them play, but usually not well enough to demonstrate their instruction. Because they are well-trained in educational methods, however, they can often get good results when they know the fundamentals of the subject they are teaching.

Most such teacher-coaches are concerned about the caliber of their work and want to do a creditable job in their tennis assignment. In order to organize and formulate a teaching system, they may review the recent publications concerning the game. Unhappily, they will find that not much helpful literature is available.

Most books and articles describe how the game is played, not how to teach it, and usually dwell on details of the author's playing technique. Even these works differ on many basic points, thus sometimes confusing the reader more than helping him.

There is a need, therefore, for a "how-to-teach" book — a book that describes how to teach the strokes, how to organize and conduct tennis classes, how to select the team and to manage practice, how to teach tactics and strategy, and how to do many of the other things required of a school tennis teacher or coach. This book is written to meet this need. It is an attempt to combine theory with practical matters of teaching tennis.

We feel that a knowledge of differences in form and style among good players is an essential part of any good tennis teacher's background. Accordingly, we present in our opening chapter an overview of variations in styles of playing *and teaching* seen in the game today.

We also feel that every good teacher must select and teach a playing form that is efficient, easy to learn and to teach, and undemanding of excessive time and effort. Consequently, we follow our discussion of variations with an analysis of the mechanical principles that determine good form. We then discuss some psychological aspects of tennis teaching, after which we describe methods for teaching at the various stages of development: hand tennis, paddle tennis, short-racket play, and full-scale tennis. This is teaching progression is intended for instructors of very young children, for whom the procedures described here are quite effective.

We know from experience that most school tennis teaching requires skill in handling large groups. For readers to whom group work is a new, unsettling experience, we present our theory of group tennis instruction and include diagrams and descriptions of methods that work for us and for other experienced teachers we know. We present methods for teaching strokes, tactics, and strategy to school classes, and to school teams. We list step-by-step procedures so that learners can be brought along carefully, from simple to complex moves, from easy to more difficult skills.

Our closing chapters are intended for the school coach who must establish efficient and effective procedures for (1) selecting his team, (2) providing progressive practice drills, (3) making his team physically fit to play, and (4) administering the many — and sometimes confusing — aspects of competitive inter-school play.

Our approach to the problems of teaching and learning tennis is not dogmatic. We feel there is more than one good way to hit a tennis ball. There is a range into which variations of form may fall and still be considered to be correct and efficient; we think of it as a *range of correctness*. The teacher's task is to recognize differences in physique, posture, and temperament in his students, and to orient his teaching so that variations in form are permitted, provided they fall within the range of correctness.

It is our belief that there is also more than one way to approach a learner. In our discussion of the psychology of teaching tennis, we suggest variations in teaching techniques and procedures. For maximum communication between the teacher and his students, it is often necessary to use different approaches, as described here.

We do not mean to suggest that the methods described in this book are best. They are offered because they work well for us and for many other tennis teachers we have trained. Our hope is that the descriptions of our methods will serve as a convenient reference for new *and* experienced teachers from which they can gather ideas and suggestions adaptable to their own teaching situations. We hope, too, that our opinions and points of view will engender a fuller understanding of some of the controversial points of the game and help teachers and coaches relate these controversies to their own teaching systems. Lastly, we hope that the combination of theoretical and practical matters discussed here may help our readers develop an educational and scientific approach to the problems involved in group tennis instruction and in team coaching.

Chet Murphy

Bill Murphy

ACKNOWLEDGMENTS

The writing of this book was helped along by many people. Of particular assistance were those editors who graciously released material that we had previously contributed to their journals, books, or magazines. We extend our thanks, therefore, to:

Nancy Rosenberg, of the *Journal of Health, Physical Education, and Recreation,* for permission to use in this book our material on group methods and principles of learning;

F. E. Storer, of *Tennis USA,* for permission to use in this book our material on group instruction, progressions in teaching, returning the serve, and doubles play;

John Griffith, of the *Athletic Journal,* for permission to use in this book our material on doubles play;

Mrs. Twila D. Griffith, of the William C. Brown Company, for permission to reprint Figures 1–3, 6–2, 7–1, 7–3, and 7–5, all of which appeared in *Advanced Tennis,* by Chet Murphy, and

Gladys Heldman and Ron Bookman, of *World Tennis* magazine, for permission to use in this book our material on variations in style, and our discussions of form, effectiveness, and style.

Lastly, we would like to thank Charles M. (Don) Kerr, of the Institute for the Development of Human Performance (New Orleans), for introducing us to and demonstrating the efficiency of the gravity method of movement. We are grateful also to Dr. Kooman Boycheff, of the University of California, Berkeley, for providing us with most of the photographs used in this book.

CONTENTS

Chapter One

VARIATIONS IN PLAYING AND TEACHING METHODS

Even a casual observer at top-level tennis tournaments notices that no two players hit the ball exactly alike. There are obvious differences in their swings. Sometimes the differences are a result of personal mannerisms that affect basic form only slightly. Often, however, there are major differences in swing patterns. Some players use top spin, others hit flat; some have a high circular backswing, others, a straight one; some players have tight, compact swings, while others appear to flail at the ball in a much looser pattern. Variations such as these make inexperienced teachers wonder about the kind of form to teach. Experienced teachers are likewise often led to question the validity of the form they advocate. It seems appropriate, therefore, to begin this discussion of tennis among teachers by describing differences in form and different teaching techniques found among top-flight players, teachers, and coaches. An analysis of playing and teaching methods can be useful as a foundation on which inexperienced teachers can begin to develop sound and efficient methods of their own, while for experienced teachers it may engender new ideas and techniques that will keep their teaching fresh, interesting, and up-to-date.

Most successful teachers have developed what can be called a "system," a method by which they approach the problems of instruction. After studying the styles of leading players and the methods of leading teachers, they have devised methods of their own which they feel have advantages over others. Some feel their system is easier to learn, perhaps, because anatomical checkpoints are used ("swing from the left hip," for example). Others claim theirs is best because it lends itself to group instruction ("Anyone can follow these simple instructions; turn, step, swing," and so forth). Still others claim their method makes allowances for individual differences and for that reason is superior to other methods. They say their system is simply to not have a system; instead they work around whatever natural tendencies are discernible in their students. In this way, different students develop different styles, each playing with a style best suited to his physique and temperament.

Differences in method seem to result from differences in emphasis. Some teachers want speed, others want control. Some put emphasis on strength (grip strength, for example), while others stress motion — smooth, fluid, continuous motion.

Seeing that success can be attained with several different playing styles and from several different teaching methods, an objective observer must conclude that there is no *one* correct way to play or to teach that makes all other approaches wrong. Instead, there appear to be several correct systems, several good methods of instruction *and* play. We may say that the differences noted in form — in grips, in stance, and in kinds of swings — are proper and permissible if they fall within a certain range: it may be called a "range of correctness." Any variation in a particular point of form which permits the hitter to follow the other points of form to be taught can be considered to be within this range. If, for example, a player's grip differs slightly from what the teacher prefers to see, it may not be necessary to change the grip. If the grip lets the player place his racket in the right position, and if it lets him use his arm, his hips, and his shoulders efficiently, then his grip must be considered a good one. Only in this way can one avoid being dogmatic, and only in this way can one explain the many differences that are seen to work so well for so many players and teachers.

In the discussion that follows, we isolate several points of form on the forehand and backhand. Where we feel it necessary or helpful, we include reasons for preferences by players and teachers for one method over another. No attempt is made to be definitive or dogmatic, however. We simply present an overview of several different methods, and our readers are expected to decide for themselves which are practicable for their purposes.

THE FOREHAND GROUNDSTROKE

In first-class men's tennis as it is played on fast courts today, groundstrokes are considered to be supplementary strokes, used only to return the serve and to combat an opponent's net-rushing tactics. Usually, emphasis is on the attacking game — "the big game" — in which each player follows his serve to the net and attempts to win with volleys. This is not true of beginners or intermediates, nor of many women players, however. Not all such players serve or volley well enough to play the big game. In their play, groundstrokes are the basic tools and weapons for winning tournaments.

Because every would-be tournament player must first go through the beginner and intermediate stages, most experienced teachers begin their instruction with the groundstrokes. They try to build a framework from which the learner can develop the ability to rally from the backcourt. Students are encouraged to stress net play only after they have learned to keep the ball in play reasonably well and can control the depth and direction of their groundstrokes.

The Grip

There is some difference of opinion among tennis authorities in regard to proper grips. Some prefer to see the hand behind the handle with the palm flush

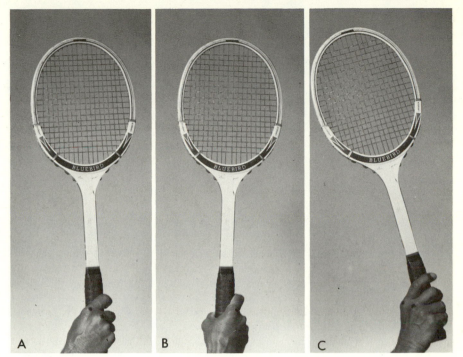

Figure 1-1   In the Eastern grip *(A)* the knuckles of the first and second fingers are directly behind the handle as shown. In the Western *(B)* they are placed more toward the bottom plane, while in the Continental grip *(C)* they are placed more toward the top plane. We feel that the Eastern grip enables most learners to relate the position of the palm to the position of the racket face, which makes it easier for them to adjust the slant of the racket face for various shots.

against the back plane of the handle. Others want the palm more toward the top plane, while still others would place it closer to the bottom plane.

For convenience in discussing terminology of grips, let us first consider the conventional "shake hands" grip. This is known as the Eastern grip. The fleshy part of the palm, which lies at the base of the first and second fingers, is placed directly behind the handle, and the heel of the hand is placed against the leather butt at the end of the handle. The fingers and thumb are wrapped around the handle, and the first and second fingers are separated to form a "trigger finger."

Most of the top American teachers advocate the Eastern grip, feeling that it allows maximum strength and control regardless of the height at which the ball is played.

In a variation of the Eastern grip the hand is moved to the left (counterclockwise) so that the knuckles are placed on the bevel between the back plane and the top plane of the handle, producing what is known as the Continental grip. The principal difference between the Eastern and Continental grips is that in the former the hand is placed more behind the racket. In the Continental grip, the wrist is more toward the top of the handle, and little or no change is required when switching from the forehand to the backhand stroke. Many top players use this grip for both shots, feeling that there isn't always time to change, and that it is not necessary to do so.

The dual usefulness of the Continental grip is considered by many to be its big advantage.

Moving the hand away from the Eastern grip in the other direction so that the knuckles are placed on the bevel between the back plane and the bottom plane (or even lower) on the handle results in the Western grip. This grip has one great disadvantage that became significant as net play and the big game grew in popularity: it requires a time-consuming change from forehand to backhand, and when an opponent is at the net, there isn't always time to make the change. For these reasons it is now not nearly as popular among teachers and players as are the other grips. Currently, it is most often seen among very young players and beginners who feel they lack the strength required to manipulate the racket when using either of the other grips.

The Hitting Stance

Most ranking players, particularly classic baseliners, prefer to hit from a sideways stance, in which the feet are placed on an imaginary line perpendicular to the net. More important than the sideways position, however, is the matter of stroking with good balance so that the body weight is transferred into the shot (toward the net) as the forward swing is begun. This is done by simply stepping with the left foot whenever possible. The step is made in whichever direction is necessary in order to reach a wide ball or in order to get away from a close ball. In fast play a wide ball often requires a step toward the right sideline. This gives the player a closed stance (Fig. 1–2). A close ball often requires a step away from the ball, toward the left net post. This hitting stance is described as an open stance.

Ideally, tennis players would like to imitate golfers or baseball batters in regard to stance when hitting. Deviations from classical stances would be made only when necessary. Players often have to hit when off-balance, or when on the move, sometimes while moving toward a sideline, and at other times even while moving away from the net. In such instances, adjustments are made in order to get maximum power when needed. Inasmuch as the body weight is not being transferred into the shot, other sources of power—the wrist, arm, or elbow motion or a body pivot—are applied more forcefully than they usually are when hitting from the conventional stance.

The Backswing

The various kinds of backswings advocated by authorities and used by leading players are generally classified as flat, slight loop, and large loop. These terms describe the manner in which the racket is carried back from the waiting position as the hitter prepares to make his forward swing.

Advocates of the flat backswing feel that it is the simplest and quickest way to get the racket back to where the forward swing is to begin. "The shortest distance is a straight line," they say. In addition, very little adjusting of the wrist or elbow is required.

Figure 1-2   When the hitter's left foot is extended toward the right sideline the stance is described as closed *(A)*. When the hitter steps toward the net the stance is described as square *(B)*. When the hitter steps toward the left sideline the stance is open *(C)*.

Figure 1-3   Julie Anthony, World Team Tennis player (Philadelphia), is shown making an adjustment often necessary in top-level play. Not having time to set herself into a good hitting stance, she hits while moving backward but uses vigorous body rotation to get the power she needs for this particular shot. (From Chet Murphy, *Advanced Tennis*, Dubuque, Iowa: Wm. C. Brown Company, 1970, p. 11.)

Observation leads one to conclude that the slightly circular backswing is more common than either of the others. Players who use it and teachers who recommend it feel that it provides a rhythm to the swing by providing continuous motion. The flat swing requires a stop-and-go motion which is considered by many to be detrimental to the stroke because it often results in a loose, sloppy wrist motion or in a stiff, jerky swing when the hitter is determined not to be "wristy."

Large, looping backswings, in which the racket and the hitting hand are carried up above the head, are not as popular now as they once were. Perhaps the emphasis on net play in the modern game, which gives the groundstroker less time to make his backswing, is the reason for the decline in the popularity of this kind of swing.

Again, in spite of the differences in backswings, there are some points of agreement. Most authorities feel that the backswing should begin early, immediately as the opponent hits the ball, so as not to be hurried and uncontrolled. Even when the player is moving to reach a ball, the backswing should begin as the moving begins; the speed of the backswing should vary, depending on the speed of the oncoming ball. If the player is making a play on a fast ball, he must make a fast backswing. If he is playing a slow ball, his backswing should be slow enough to permit him to have continuous motion.

The length of the backswing is determined by the amount of arm movement, the degree of body pivot, and the extent to which the wrist is laid back. The modern trend is toward a short backswing, one in which the racket goes back only slightly farther than a line perpendicular to the rear fence. Many experienced teachers avoid mentioning a specific length; however, they consider it to be related to certain physical qualities of the hitter (height, length of arms, firmness of grip and wrist, and so on), and as a result they permit it to vary among their students as these physical qualities vary.

The Position of the Hitting Arm

Much of the old literature in tennis stresses that the hitting arm be straight and fully extended at the end of the backswing and at contact. Modern players and teachers, however, describe the preferred arm position as "comfortably extended," neither locked straight nor cramped tight against the body. The hitter attempts to attain this comfortable position by placing himself carefully in relation to the ball. He varies and adjusts the direction of his front-foot step (the left foot, in the case of a forehand). In fast competition, however, one may not always be able to take this comfortable position. Often a hitter may have to adjust by stretching or by drawing the elbow in close to the body.

The Sources of Power

Analysis of the manner in which a hitter can generate racket speed in a stroke reveals that the arm motion is only one of several sources of power. Others are wrist action, elbow action, body rotation, and weight transfer. Some players use a great deal of wrist motion, especially on the forehand. Some rely mainly on the turning of the hips and shoulders (the body rotation), while others get most of their power by stepping toward the net and shifting their weight as they swing. Most experienced teachers feel that when a player is able to set himself for his stroke, the step and shift of weight should be the first move in the forward swing; the transfer of weight should slightly precede the turn of the hips and shoulders.

The Forward Swing

The plane in which the racket moves during the forward swing depends on the anticipated height of the ball at contact and on the kind of shot intended. If the hitter intends to hit a top spin shot, he starts his swing lower than the ball and swings in an upward plane. If he intends to slice, he starts high and swings in a downward plane. For a flat shot, his swing is flatter, with only enough rise to lift the ball to the intended trajectory.

The reasons for the use of each of these shots are stated simply: top spin helps curve the ball down and into the court after it has cleared the net; the flat shot, in which the racket is held vertically to the intended line of flight of the ball, is easy to visualize and to learn; the slice is easy to control because the ball stays on the racket longer (although this is sometimes disputed) and because some speed is taken off the ball.

Most players agree that the racket should be held firmly throughout the entire swing, and especially at contact. Some teachers, however, avoid mentioning firmness, feeling that in an attempt to be firm, a hitter might use his arm and hand muscles in a way that would restrict movement and thus prevent him from making a smooth, free swing. Other teachers suggest a fairly loose wrist at contact; they usually stress letting the racket head do the work. They suggest that the amount or degree of firmness in the forearm, hand, and wrist during the swing should be only that amount necessary to guide the racket to place it properly behind the ball and to resist the impact of the oncoming ball.

The Point-of-contact

The spot opposite the body at which the racket comes into contact with the ball is known as the point-of-contact. The basic point-of-contact, the point at which the racket meets the ball for straight ahead shots, varies among players as their grips vary. When the grip is a true Eastern, as described earlier, the point is somewhere between the left hip and the player's belt buckle. When the grip is closer to a Western, the point-of-contact is several inches in advance of the left hip; when the grip is closer to the Continental, the point is back farther than in either of the other cases.

Experienced players usually vary the placement of their shots by timing the swing so as to deliberately change the point-of-contact. A right-handed player hitting a crosscourt shot will meet the ball a little sooner (closer to the net) than he would for a down-the-line shot. He usually adjusts his timing rather than adjust the position of his wrist.

Occasionally, however, experienced players manipulate their wrists to make adjustments in the racket's position on the ball. They attain control and direction in that way rather than through the more common method of changing the point-of-contact. They use wrist action when they want to be deceptive and to disguise the direction of their shot for as long as possible. Most experienced teachers consider this wrist adjustment technique to be an advanced one, not recommended for inexperienced players.

Most teachers eventually bring advanced players to the point where both methods of placing the ball are practiced. Differences in emphasis and progression in the early stages result from different opinions about what is important.

The Function of the Wrist

There is as much difference of opinion about the use and function of the wrist as there is about the grips recommended for groundstrokes. Some players, for example, use a "laid-back" wrist, which makes the hitting hand form a 30- to 45-degree angle with the forearm throughout the entire stroke, even at contact. Others use a straighter wrist, which keeps the hitting hand in its natural position as related to the forearm. Still other players use a combination of the two positions, with the wrist laid back on the backswing and then straightening at contact. Those who stress the laid-back wrist feel that it gives better control because it permits the hitter to have his racket facing the target longer and to maintain contact with the ball longer than does any other method. Straight-wrist advocates contend that their method permits a true hit at the ball, whereas the laid-back wrist causes the hitter to push the ball. Those who prefer the combination method (laid back during the backswing and then straightened at contact) feel that their method utilizes the advantages of each of the others: it permits a hit with control.

Despite these differences, most experienced coaches and teachers agree that a firm wrist at contact results in a more accurate hit than does a loose, floppy one.

The Follow-through and Finish

Although one can argue that nothing the player does after contact can affect the flight of the ball, the follow-through (the direction in which the racket travels after contact) is considered to be an important part of the stroke. Many teachers feel that when a player tries to follow through properly — that is, along the intended line of flight of the ball — he is more likely to have his racket lined up properly and moving properly along that line at impact. A bad follow-through, on the other hand, indicates that the racket was probably moving across the line, either from inside out or from outside in, at impact. Such a swing usually results in a less effective shot than one in which the racket is moving properly along the line. The importance of the follow-through is probably best expressed in the theory that holds that if a player starts the stroke properly and also finishes the stroke properly, then what is done in between is likely (although not certain) to be performed properly.

Many coaches and teachers want their students to pose and hold the finish position for a count of two after hitting. They feel this helps the hitter attain good balance when hitting. Balance, they feel, is essential for consistent, accurate hitting; it makes the difficult matter of timing much easier. Some teachers relate the balanced finish position to footwork, which in turn is related to efficient stance and body position when hitting. "Footwork," they say, "is simply the matter of moving the body into an efficient hitting position, one in which the hitter can reach the ball comfortably and can transfer his weight into the shot."

The modern trend, with flat or only slightly topped shots for beginners, is toward a shorter follow-through than was used with excessive top spin shots. Most teachers now want their students to stop the racket short of being wrapped around the neck. Some teachers are very specific: "The racket points off 45 degrees beyond straight ahead," or, "The hand stops in front of the face." Usually when such restrictions are placed on the length of the follow-through, it is for the purpose of enabling the hitter to coach himself by checking his balance, his stance, the position of his racket, or the direction of his swing.

Many teachers avoid making specific suggestions for the length of the swing. They feel that hard hitters will swing longer than soft hitters; and that tall, rangy players will have longer swings than will short, stocky players.

Other teachers and players feel that the length of the swing depends on the hitter's intention. If he wants to hit with a great deal of force, he will make a fast and long swing. If he wants to hit softly, he will swing easier and consequently will swing shorter.

THE BACKHAND GROUNDSTROKE

Even though many ranking players have stronger backhands than forehands, most experienced teachers know that beginners usually find the backhand more difficult to learn. Although it appears to be a more natural style of swinging (because the body is naturally out of the way of the arm action, whereas with the forehand the body must first be turned out of the way), and although the arm action can be described as a simple karate-like chop, hitting from the left side is awkward for most beginners. Many say that they are unaccustomed to reaching across their body as they must do during the backswing of this stroke. Many ranking players must surely have had this same problem when they were learning to play. Very likely, however, they spent considerable time practicing this stroke and, as a result, they now feel equally comfortable and confident on forehands and backhands. Experienced teachers plan their work accordingly. They help their students overcome early preferences for forehands by spending equal time (and sometimes more) on backhands. In this way they avoid developing one-sided players with a built-in weakness on the backhand.

The Grip

Many of the factors mentioned in our discussion of the forehand grip apply to the backhand. Among top-flight players, the grips vary; probably no two players hold the racket exactly alike. It is equally probable that no two teachers teach exactly alike. But these differences are minor ones. The concept of the "range of correctness" applies here and offers consolation to many teachers uncertain about details of the grip. The concept suggests that a learner may be permitted to adjust his grip to his liking and that it may be a sound one, even if it differs from what others may use or recommend.

There are several points of agreement among players and teachers regarding the backhand grip. Almost unanimously, the typical Eastern "shake hands" grip described for the forehand is considered to be inadequate here. In it, the wrist is placed along the front plane of the handle, and as a result, the hitter can only pull the racket into the ball. Most teachers feel this grip prevents swinging with enough force to hit a strong shot. Such a grip must be changed, they say, if the hitter is to develop his stroke as something other than a weak, defensive shot.

The change most often recommended requires moving the hitting hand toward the top of the handle. The "V" between the thumb and forefinger is often used as a checkpoint. Some teachers want it directly on top of the handle, while others want it a bit to the right of the center of the top plane. Some teachers suggest using the first large knuckle as a guide, placing it on the top plane of the handle; others say to place the knuckle on the first bevel. Some instructors may be less specific; they say merely to place the fleshy part of the palm on top of the handle. The grip is then described as "palm down" in contrast to the "shake hands" position of the forehand.

There is some variation in the recommended position of the thumb. Some teachers want it wrapped around the handle, while others want it slanted diagonally across the handle. "Wrap around" advocates feel such a grip permits more flexibility in difficult situations. Those who prefer the thumb up the back of the handle feel such a grip provides firmness and solidity. But since the thumb can usually be placed in either of these positions without changing the position of the first knuckle or the palm, it seems logical for teachers to permit students to choose whichever position feels best to them. Many professionals let beginners use the thumb-up grip if the students feel that it gives them more support. Often, they are encouraged to change to a wrap-around grip at a later date, when they have developed more strength.

The Stance

There is almost unanimous agreement that both the closed stance and the square stance are better than an open stance for backhands. The slightly closed stance is preferred by most ranking players; the right foot is closer to the sideline than is the left foot. This position gets the body out of the way of the arm and permits a full, free swing. An exaggerated closed stance, in which the right foot is far over toward the sideline, is not recommended, however, because it does not permit a shift of weight into the shot. A player is often forced to hit from this position, however, to reach a wide ball.

The open stance is used only when a player cannot get away from a close ball, when he has not had time to turn sideways or does not need to, or when he hits an approach shot and wants a running start to the net.

The Backswing

We see the same variations in backswings as we see on the forehand: there are large loops, slight loops, and straight swings. With the backswing, however, the large loop is far less common than either of the other kind. Usually, at the end of the

Figure 1-4 A well-hit backhand groundstroke. The left hand supports the racket during the backswing, then releases the racket as the forward swing begins. The hitting arm is bent during the backswing and straightens for the hit. Contact occurs in advance of the front hip, and the racket is guided along the intended line of flight of the ball.

backswing, the racket is either stopped in order to permit a change of direction to the forward swing or looped a bit to provide continuous motion. Either is correct, but in advanced play the slight loop is seen more often than the stop-and-go motion.

Many top players keep the left hand on the racket's throat all during the backswing, releasing it only when the forward swing begins. Many teachers regard this as very important to the stroke, believing it encourages a full body turn during the backswing. Many free-swingers turn the body so much that their backs face the net at the end of the wind-up.

Many players slide their left hand down the handle during the backswing, bringing it to rest close to the hitting hand. This arrangement seems to permit a loose wrist at the end of the backswing and enables the hitter to generate racket speed with wrist action.

Some teachers want students to release the left hand as soon as the right-hand grip is secure. They feel that this encourages the hitter to hold the racket firmly in the right hand and thus eliminates any tendencies to use wrist action in the swing.

Regardless of whether the racket is taken back high or low, almost all players and teachers like to see it held closely against the body as the forward swing begins. A few good players keep the hitting arm straight during the backswing, but most good strokers bend it a bit. Some bend it so much that the hitting hand is brought behind the rear hip before the forward swing starts.

The Forward Swing

In all except a few unorthodox swings, the racket begins its forward motion from a point close to the body. The arm is swung from the shoulder, and the arm straightens just before contact. The body weight shifts from the rear foot to the front foot whenever possible (the hitter steps into the shot), and the hips and shoulders turn with the arm swing. Sequence photos show, however, that in the swing of most top players the shoulders are only sideways to the net at contact; they have not yet begun to face the net.

Just as it does on the forehand, the plane of the forward swing depends on the effect wanted at contact. For a top spin shot, the swing is in an upward plane. For a slice, the racket moves downward into the ball. For a flat shot, the plane is flatter, at times almost parallel to the ground.

There appears to be a natural hand movement during the backswing that affects the racket's position at the start of the forward swing. The hitting hand almost automatically turns counterclockwise, and as it does so, the racket face begins to slant skyward a bit (it opens) instead of remaining perpendicular to the ground as it was in the waiting position. A slight clockwise movement of the hand brings the racket face perpendicular again at contact, unless the hitter intends to slice, in which case the wrist position that opened the racket face is maintained.

The Point-of-contact

As in the forehand, the point-of-contact varies as grips vary. Nevertheless, the ball is always met sooner, in terms of body reference points, than it is on the forehand, because the hitting arm is closer to the net than on the forehand. Many teachers stress a specific point.of-contact (for example, opposite the right hip or opposite the shoulder socket), but many others suggest that each student should find his own point (relating it to his grip) and that he should work to perfect his timing around that point.

The Follow-through and Finish

As with the forehand, the swing will be more efficient if the racket is made to move along the intended line of flight of the ball as it passes through the contact area. Again, by attempting to follow through along that line, the hitter increases his chances of bringing the racket into the ball along that line.

To follow through properly on the backhand, the hitter must delay his body rotation so that it is somewhat slower than the movement used with the forehand. When one is hitting a forehand, the upper body should begin to face the net before contact; with a backhand, the body should be sideways at contact, and it should not begin to face the net until after the ball has been struck. Turning the hips and shoulders prematurely will cause the player to pull his racket across the line of the ball unless he adjusts his swing to avoid that fault. In either case, the result is likely to be a less efficient swing than one in which the body rotation is timed properly.

The starting position and the plane of the forward swing determine whether the finish is high or low. The position of the racket face (i.e., vertical, opened, or closed) is determined by the hitter's intention to hit either a flat shot or a shot with a spin. The amount of force applied in the swing determines whether the finish is long or short. The most typical finish on a drive is high, with the racket extended a little beyond the line of flight of the ball, and the racket face perpendicular to the ground, or nearly so.

The Two-handed Backhand

One of the more obvious variations among ranking players is the two-handed backhand. Undoubtedly there have been two-handed hitters in the game since its beginning, but the publicity offered recently to several charismatic youngsters who play in the two-handed fashion makes the style more popular now than ever before.

Most two-handed hitters admit to having started playing that way as youngsters, when they lacked the strength to control the racket adequately with one hand. Being successful with the two hands, many continued to play that way even as they grew older and stronger. Others changed to a one-handed stroke, often at the suggestion of teachers and coaches who feel the two-hand shot has definite disadvantages.

The usual procedure for the two-handed stroke is to use the right hand in its conventional Eastern forehand position and to place the left hand above it on the handle, also in a conventional forehand position. However, a few players place the right hand in an Eastern backhand grip while still using the left hand to reinforce it.

Regardless of how the hands are placed on the racket, a player's reach is restricted somewhat as he tries to keep his left hand on the racket. Many wide balls become unplayable and even the very best players must then temporarily revert to a one-handed shot. Yet this physical limitation is often less of a liability than it first appears to be. A contact point that is close to the body generally makes for a more controlled shot than is possible when the ball is met at full stretch an arm's length away. Furthermore, the use of two hands restricts the length of either the backswing or the forward swing (depending on how the hands are placed on the racket), and this too is a controlled way of stroking. Many coaches and players feel these advantages outweigh the disadvantages of the stroke and consequently continue to use it and to recommend it.

Most two-handed power hitters use a great deal of body rotation to offset the limitation in power imposed by the shortened swing. Others derive power from a sort

Figure 1-5 Chris Evert and Jimmy Connors (next page) show marked differences in stances when hitting their two-handed specialties. Evert has planted herself solidly, as she always does when time permits.

of couple effect* in which the hands are made to work against each other, the right *pushing* against the butt end of the handle to temporarily "fix" it in place, while the left causes the rest of the racket to rotate around it. The net effect of such opposing forces applied at different points on the handle is to increase the speed of the racket face.

The couple action may be applied in a diagonal plane as well, to force the racket upward quickly, thereby imparting top spin to the ball. The more common method, however, is to maintain a laid-back position of the left hand and to use it chiefly for control and support of the right hand. The hands are then moved in unison toward the target area to move the racket along the intended line of flight of the ball. The result among accomplished players is prolonged contact between the racket and the ball—the long hit—characteristic of controlled hitters.

---

*In the field of mechanics, an arrangement of two equal and opposite parallel forces is called a couple.

Figure 1-6 Jimmy Connors' two-handed swing is combined with considerable body movement. In this case, Connors has jumped upward, probably to add force with a vigorous body turn and to accentuate the upward swing of his racket.

THE SERVE

A knowledgeable observer sees many differences in style among top-flight servers. There are different kinds of swings, different grips, different stances, and even different tosses, most of which seem to work effectively for one player or another.

The Grip

The most common grip for serving is the Continental. Almost all good servers use this grip because (1) it permits maximum wrist action and (2) it allows a variety of racket positions at contact — the hitter is able to adjust his wrist position to change the placement of the racket on the ball.

Despite the strong preference for the Continental grip, however, many professionals teach beginners to use an Eastern forehand grip for serving. They know from experience that most beginners find the Continental awkward — it creates a tendency to slice too much — and since speed is not a matter of concern for a while, the Eastern forehand grip, which offers better control, is adequate. There is general agreement that the Eastern grip precludes the development of a strong serve, and for this reason players are urged to change to the Continental when they acquire experience.

Most good players place the hand down toward the end of the handle and let the butt of the handle protrude a bit beyond the palm. This is the conventional method. However, many very good servers use a longer grip: they place the center of the palm over the butt. They feel this grip gets the butt out of the way of the wrist action and gives more leverage in the swing. Consequently, they are able to generate more racket speed than they could with a conventional grip.

Most experienced teachers prefer to have players first develop racket control — and ball control — with a shorter grip, sometimes with a grip even shorter than the conventional. Players who have control but need power are encouraged to try the longer butt-covered grip. A few coaches choose one or the other of these grips for their players on the basis of calculations of hand and arm strength. These measurements are often related to age, size, and maturity. Players with insufficient strength to handle a long racket are urged to use a shorter grip than those who do have enough strength to control the full-length grip.

The Stance

The sideways stance is preferred by most top-flight players, but we see slight differences in the placement of their feet. Most coaches feel that the toes of the front foot should not be parallel to the baseline but, instead, should be placed at an angle to the line. They feel that such a stance encourages the hitter to turn his body toward the net during the forward swing and thus enables him to swing straight into the ball (as on a flat serve) rather than across it.

Nonetheless, some teachers prefer to see the front foot parallel to the baseline; they feel that such a position prevents the body from turning toward the net too soon. As a result, the hitter is able to hit across the ball and thus get effective spin on his shot. Many experienced players make these slight adjustments in their foot position during a match to vary the ball action on their serves.

Spacing and placement of the rear foot varies also. Most teachers feel that it should be placed naturally where the hitter can shift his weight to it comfortably during the swing. Some want the toes pointing in the same direction as the front foot, others want them parallel to the baseline, and still others want them pointing at an angle toward the rear fence. The selection of one of these positions is related to the amount of body turn used during the backswing. When the foot points back, the hitter is encouraged to have a great deal of body turn in that direction as he winds up to hit. Some good servers who stand this way almost turn their backs to the net during the backswing.

The Starting Position

The starting position for the serve is for the most part standardized. Almost all players hold the racket in front of the body, pointing in the direction of the shot or perhaps a little to the left of it. The ball is held in the fingers of the left hand, which is almost always held against the racket, sometimes on the strings, other times on the throat or handle. Most players appear to be "sighting" or "aiming" over the top of the racket head as they get ready to serve; they play the shot in their mind and get a mental image of the direction and placement of it.

In the "aiming" position most players have the body weight back on the rear foot and keep it there as the backswing begins. A few lean forward a bit as they aim, then shift the weight to the rear foot as they start the downward motion of the toss and the swing. In either case, the weight is usually shifted forward soon after the upward motion of the toss begins, although we occasionally see a player who doesn't shift until after the toss is made.

The Toss

The ball is usually held in the fingers — not by the fingertips nor in the palm — and the palm usually faces upward. Many professionals teach their beginners to keep the palm facing upward during the toss; they feel that this is the simplest and most efficient method. Many other servers, however, use a different hand position to release the ball. Some carry the knuckles up and flip the ball upward with a wrist motion, while others impart various kinds of sidespin to the ball at the release. Neither of these methods offers any advantage over the palm-up method, and it is for this reason we see most experienced players use the simpler toss.

Beginners are often told to toss the ball straight up (vertically) from the release point in front of them (toward the net). Many top players continue to toss in such a fashion even with their advanced swings. Some, however, move the tossing hand to the right and back a bit as they turn their hips and shoulders during the backswing. They then toss the ball forward from the release point to place it out in front of the body (toward the net) for contact.

The timing of the toss with the swing is related to the kind of backswing used. A full, long backswing takes more time than does a short, snappy one. Consequently, the ball must be tossed either later or higher than with a short backswing. Many professionals consider the sequence of moves difficult to change once a learner has established a pattern. However, experienced teachers generally stress to beginners that the ball and the racket should start down together from the "aiming" position in order to establish the rhythm of the swing. The tossing hand carries the ball down toward the left thigh while at the same time the racket moves down past the right knee. The tossing hand then carries the ball up as the racket moves up toward the top of the rear fence. A common expression used in teaching this timing is "the ball and the racket go down together, then come up together." Some teachers consider the sequence of moves difficult to teach even in this way. They feel that the timing of the swing should be allowed to develop naturally after basic instruction in the kinds of moves has been offered. They suggest that the learner simply throw the ball up, then "throw" the racket at the ball.

Movement of the Feet

The rear foot usually crosses over the front foot to make the first step into the court after contact. This step is used either to regain balance or to run to the net.

Most players simply swing the foot forward and across the baseline. Many, however, slide the foot up to the side of the front foot and use both feet as a base to provide upward body action at contact. The knees bend as the rear foot slides up to the front. Then, as the upward swing begins, the knees straighten to add body action to the swing. The rear foot then swings across after the hit. Many players jump off the ground just before contact and cross the rear foot over as they swing and jump. They land on that foot which, after contact, is in front of them. Many coaches teach the jump to the right foot because this right-foot step can then become the first step in the dash to the net; others teach it because they believe it helps generate racket speed by adding body motion to the swing.

A few players jump straight up when serving and land with the feet in almost the same position they were in when the swing began. This is not generally recommended by coaches because it does not permit a fast start to the net.

The Backswing

Backswings vary on the serve more than they do on other strokes. Some players have a long, low, full swing in which the racket dips down as low as the ankle as it goes back in the wind-up. Others lower the racket to knee height, while still others carry it back at waist height. A few very good players have a short, high wind-up in which the racket is carried back at shoulder height. These shorter swings require snappy body, elbow, and wrist action, and for a player for whom these are natural movements, these swings are recommended.

The position of the hitting hand varies during the swing as does the angle of the racket face. Most players keep the palm down throughout the downswing and backswing, letting it face skyward only as the racket begins to come up behind the back. Some strong servers turn the palm skyward as the racket goes down toward the rear knee. Many teachers feel that the first method gives better control and that the second lends itself to more power. Consequently, they encourage each pupil to use whichever method will best meet his needs.

Most good servers swing the arm down, back, up, and away from the body before bending the arm at the elbow. Some loose free-swingers raise the elbow to shoulder height before bending the arm; the arm almost appears to extend straight out, horizontally, from the shoulder socket, with the racket pointing toward the rear fence. Other players bend the arm sooner, just after the racket has begun to come up behind them. Certain players bend the arm when the racket reaches the low point of the backswing. The elbow then appears to be tucked in against the side, and the racket appears to travel up the player's side during the forward swing.

The Forward Swing

Regardless of the differences in the kinds of backswings, all good players draw the racket in close to their backs by raising the upper arm and bending it at the elbow before starting the upward, forward motion into the ball. As the elbow bends,

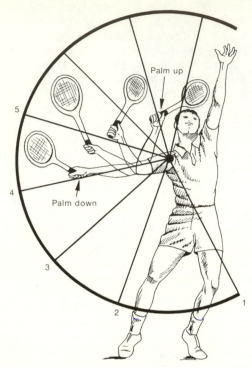

Figure 1-7   Sketch shows possible variations when serving. Servers can raise their arms and bend their elbows at various points during the backswing — 1, 2, 3, 4, or 5. Here the hitter's hand is shown in the palm-down position at point 4. It changes to the palm-up position as he draws his racket forward to place it in the conventional back-scratching position.

the wrist is flipped back to permit the racket head to drop behind the back. This "back-scratching" position is one of the most common points of form among good servers.

Most coaches and players feel that the racket should be in continuous motion during the swing. It is not unusual, however, to see top-flight players pause momentarily at various places in the backswing before drawing the racket toward the back. Such an action used to be called a "hitch" and was considered detrimental to effective serving. Some professionals now permit it in their pupils' swings if the hitters are still able to generate sufficient racket speed. A few even consider it necessary to enable the hitter to gather balance for the power thrust into the ball.

Most good servers crouch a bit just before the hit by bending their knees as they draw the racket into the back-scratching position. Then, as the racket goes up to meet the ball, the knees are straightened to add to the racket's speed.

During the upswing from the back-scratching position, the body is turned toward the net. The timing of this action varies among players. Most professionals consider it to be a difficult point to teach, just as is the turn on the backswing. For this reason they encourage a natural motion here. This body motion is probably related to the hitter's stance, to the movement of his feet, and to the placement and timing of his toss. As these vary among players, so does the timing of the body motion.

Contact

Most good servers meet the ball at a point slightly forward of the body. The exact point-of-contact varies among players as their heights vary. Very tall players toss and meet the ball farther in front of their bodies than do very short players. Flat serves are met farther forward than are overspin serves.

Regardless of these differences, there appears to be one point of agreement among experienced coaches and players. At the moment of impact, the shoulder of the hitting arm should be behind the ball (farther from the net than is the ball). Many coaches consider this position of the shoulder in relation to the ball to be the most vital aspect of serving. If the shoulder leads, the hitter is forced to pull the racket forward into the ball and he therefore deprives himself of maximum power on the hit.

The contact point usually changes a bit either to the left or to the right of straight ahead, depending on the kind of serve to be hit. On a flat serve, the ball is generally tossed straight ahead and the hitting arm is then extended upward and forward a bit, but not angled to either the left or right from the shoulder socket. For the flat hit, the wrist is in a natural position at contact to put the forearm and racket handle in a fairly straight line. For top-spin serves, the ball is usually tossed a bit to the left of the body. The hitter then bends backward and reaches in that direction to meet the ball. At contact, the racket handle forms an angle to the forearm. For slice serves, the ball is usually tossed a bit to the right of the body, and the hitter reaches in that direction to meet the ball.

Many modern servers, however, toss consistently to one place—the same place all the time—and vary the direction and spin of the ball by changing only the position of the wrist at contact. This technique offers the advantage of not giving away the server's intentions and makes it more difficult for the opponent to anticipate the kind of serve to be hit.

The height of the ball at contact varies in different kinds of serves. On flat and slice serves, the better players hit with the arm fully extended at contact; they are stretching upward to the full extent of their reach. On top-spin serves, the contact point is lower than the point of the player's maximum reach. To put spin on the ball, the racket must to some extent brush the ball at contact. This cannot be done if the arm is fully extended. Most good spin servers have a slight bend in the arm at contact, and the wrist is cocked to the left a bit. The arm and wrist straighten during the hit and are in a straight line immediately after contact. The upward carry of the ball occurs during the straightening process.

The Follow-through and Finish

From the contact point, the racket follows various paths, depending on the kind of serve. On a flat hit, it travels along the line of the ball's flight as far as the outstretched arm permits. On a top-spin serve, it travels across the line of flight from left to right. On a slice serve, it moves across the line of flight in the opposite direction — from right to left.

On extreme overspin serves such as the American Twist, the momentum of the racket as it moves from left to right carries it out to the player's right side. The swing usually ends behind the player's right knee, especially if he remains in the backcourt after serving. Many players bring the racket in toward the center of their body, however, either from force of habit from earlier training on other kinds of serves or from a desire to get a quick start to the net.

On flat and sidespin serves, the racket eventually moves down toward the left knee and finishes either in front of it or to the left and rear of it. Some players bend from the waist so much as to permit the racket to come up along the left side of the body. Most coaches do not specify a definite finish point; they usually allow the hitters to develop a loose, natural finish. They feel that the direction of the follow-through and finish positions is a function of the arm and body action used in the strokes; the positions are determined, to a large degree, by the amount of racket momentum generated in the swing.

Chapter Two

MECHANICS OF TENNIS

New students of tennis who review the literature of the game find little material in which authors treat the game scientifically. Most of the better-known books and periodicals merely describe strokes of top performers without offering a mechanical explanation of why these players stroke as they do. Readers are told to do such-and-such and to swing thus-and-so, and they are led to infer that because such techniques worked for the various authors, they will also work for the reader.

Despite such inexact reasoning, inexperienced teachers with little knowledge of the mechanics involved in stroking often accept the form described in such books as the ideal, the model to follow and to teach to their pupils. They often simply imitate, copy, and parrot what is described in the literature. As a result, the techniques they advocate are not usually based on scientific principles and are not always defensible.

We feel new reference material is needed to help inexperienced teachers establish a scientific basis for their tennis teaching. We have written this chapter to help fill this need. In it we discuss objectively some principles of mechanics that relate to tennis strokes. We feel that knowledge of mechanical principles can help teachers distinguish between efficient and inefficient movement, and between correct and incorrect technique. We feel it can enable them to judge the validity of the form they teach and to make allowances for variations in form when necessary. Other things being equal, such a scientific approach is more likely to result in effective teaching than is a system based on the more limited empirical approach.

Readers are cautioned to remember, however, that many aspects of body mechanics cannot be measured or analyzed precisely. It is often difficult to determine the amount of force applied by a particular segment or joint of the body, or even the direction in which the force is being applied. Furthermore, because humans differ in strength, flexibility, leverage, power, and stamina, what applies and appears to work for one player may not apply to or work with another. Lastly, mechanical principles applied to fixed structures and moving systems in a laboratory cannot always adequately explain stroke patterns of tennis players whose behavior is also governed by biological and psychological principles. Consequently, teachers may have to settle for something less than mechanical perfection and may have to search for whatever other positions and movements appear to work best for each individual.

In the discussion that follows, we do not intend to prove that one kind of swing or another is right or wrong. We intend only to show how human mechanics work in the tennis swing, leaving each reader to conclude for himself which stroke patterns and which combinations of positions and movements are appropriate for his students.

WHAT HAPPENS AT IMPACT

When analyzed as a mechanical problem, the result of the impact between the racket and the ball is easy to explain and predict. The flight of the ball off the racket is determined by the combined effects of the following factors: (1) the position of the racket on the ball; (2) the direction in which the racket is moving; (3) the speed at which the racket is moving; (4) the angle at which the ball approaches the racket; (5) the kind and amount of spin on the oncoming ball; and (6) the amount of grip pressure applied by the hitter to support the racket against the force of the oncoming ball. Immediately as the ball leaves the racket, however, wind, gravity, and spin may begin to alter its flight.

For convenience in discussing those factors that a hitter may control, we will use the following terms to describe the positions and movements of the racket during the swing. When the racket face is perpendicular to the ground, it is called *flat*. When the hitting surface is slanted skyward, it is *open*; when the hitting face slants toward the ground, it is *closed*.

If at contact the hitting surface faces directly toward the intended target, it is *square* to the target, square to the intended line of flight of the ball. When it faces to either the left or right of that line, it is *angled* in the left or right direction.

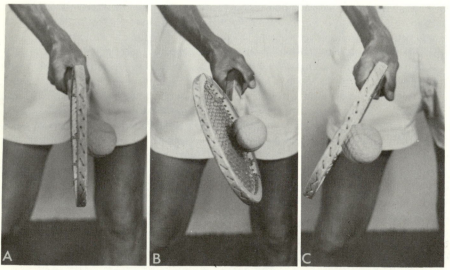

Figure 2–1   When the racket face is perpendicular to the ground as in *A*, we say that the racket is "flat." When the face slants skyward as in *B*, we say the hitter has "opened" it; when it slants down toward the ground as in *C*, he has "closed" the face.

The direction in which the racket is traveling in the contact area with respect to the intended line of flight of the ball is called the *line* of the swing. A hitter may swing his racket along the line, or, either intentionally or inadvertently, he may swing it across the line to either his right or left.

The direction in which the racket is moving during the forward swing lies within a *plane* that can be either upward, downward, or parallel to the ground. When a hitter starts his swing below a waist-high ball, swings up to meet it, and finishes above his waist, he has swung in an upward plane. When he starts his swing above the ball and finishes below it, he has swung in a downward plane. A flat plane is one in which the racket moves parallel to the ground.

A player must consider these four variables—the slant and angle of the racket, and the plane and line of the swing—on every shot. Whether he is swinging quickly or slowly, whether he is serving, volleying, or hitting groundstrokes, he must somehow manage to bring his racket into the ball with these variables set properly for the direction, trajectory, and ball action he wants.

In elementary instruction, building the pattern of the stroke is only one aspect of a player's training. In addition, he should be given practice and instruction in adjusting these variables in the swing. One way of doing this is to let him hit several shots from a fixed location, his baseline, for example, while aiming at a target placed perhaps five feet inside the opposite baseline. After he develops reasonable skill at this, he may be required to hit from various locations in his court while aiming at the same target. With such practice he will begin to recognize the changing conditions of play: his distance from the net and from the target, the height of the ball at contact, the speed of the oncoming ball, the force with which he must swing, and the trajectory he must choose to place his shot to the target. Experienced players react and adjust to these conditions almost subconsciously, but this ability comes only after experience or practice such as we have described.

If the hitter intends to hit a flat drive, he must adjust the slant and angle of his racket and the plane of his swing according to the height of the ball at contact and according to the intended force and trajectory of his shot. For a knee-high ball, his racket must be opened, and his swing must be in more of an upward plane than it should be for a chest-high ball. The same is true if he intends that his shot clear the net by a large rather than scant margin. Furthermore, if he hits hard, he must aim lower than when hitting softly because there will be less time for gravity to bring the ball down and into the court after it has cleared the net.

The racket face may be opened for low forehands simply by rotating the wrist and forearm in a clockwise direction from whatever positions they are in when hitting with a flat racket. For high balls, the racket face may be closed by rotating the wrist and forearm in the opposite direction, or the elbow may be raised at contact. On the backhand the action is reversed: the wrist and forearm may be rotated counterclockwise to open the racket face and clockwise to close it. When specific practice at controlling the up-and-down direction of the ball is provided, the learner is likely to develop this ability sooner than if he were left alone to discover his own best methods for ball control.

Control of direction comes from skillfully adjusting the timing of the swing. To hit to his left, a player must hit the ball sooner in terms of its flight toward him than he would for straight-ahead shots. To make contact sooner, he may simply swing his arm sooner, shift his weight sooner, or twist his trunk sooner. He may even simply flick his wrist a bit to bring the racket head through the contact point slightly ahead

of his hitting hand. Any of these methods or any combination of them will enable the player to make contact with his racket face angled slightly to his left. As a result, the ball will be deflected to his left.

By delaying the movements in a shot—by meeting the ball later in terms of its flight—the player can manage to hit while his racket is angled slightly to his right. On the backhand the same techniques of timing apply, except that the hitter has the option of making an additional adjustment to steer the ball to his left. Normally, for straight-ahead shots, his arm should be straight at contact. But if it is bent slightly at the elbow, the racket head will be lagging behind the hitting hand slightly, and as a result the racket can be placed a bit toward the near side of the ball. From such a position the ball will be deflected to the hitter's left.

The Aerodynamics of Tennis

The position of the racket and the direction in which it is traveling at contact determine not only the direction of the shot but also the kind and amount of spin on the ball. Although not necessary in elementary play, spin is needed for the controlled speed and the variety of shots required in intermediate and advanced play. An understanding of how spin can be applied and used to a player's advantage is essential for effective teaching and coaching.

Each kind of spin makes the ball curve in flight in a specific way. One useful and popular spin is top spin, which makes the ball curve downward and drop sooner than it would from the force of gravity alone. It is most useful against a net man when the groundstroker wants to drive low to his feet. It is also useful for full-length drives because it enables the player to hit extremely hard and with some degree of safety: the spin helps keep the ball in the court.

Top spin is applied by hitting the ball a glancing blow when the plane of the swing is upward from the plane in which the racket face is facing.

On a top-spin shot, the top surface of the ball rotates forward and downward while the bottom surface rotates backward. The bottom surface drags a certain amount of the air near the front of the ball around with it, and the effect is to speed up the flow of air there relative to the speed of flow over the top surface of the ball. The faster flowing air exerts less pressure against the ball than does the slower moving air at the top surface. The net result of this difference in pressure is the downward curve characteristic of all top-spinning balls.*

When the ball is hit a glancing blow and the plane of the swing is downward from the plane in which the racket is facing, backspin is imparted to the ball. Backspin acts in precisely the opposite manner of top spin and causes the ball to stay in flight longer. The lift provided by backspin neutralizes the pull of gravity somewhat and makes the ball appear to "sail" or "float" until it loses momentum. On a backspinning ball, the top surface moves backward, and in so doing drags some of the nearest air around with it. The faster moving air exerts less pressure than does the slower moving air at the bottom surface of the ball. The greater air pressure

---

*This is in accord with the principle formulated by Daniel Bernoulli, the eighteenth-century Swiss scientist, which states that the pressure in a fluid decreases with increased velocity of the fluid.

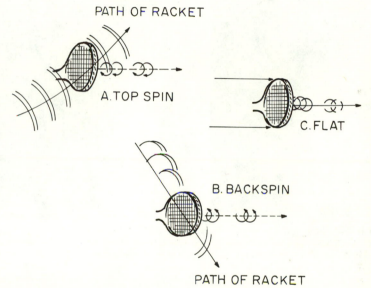

Figure 2-2   An upward glancing blow imparts top spin *(A)*, a downward glancing blow, backspin *(B)*. A head-on blow makes the ball travel a flat path *(C)*.

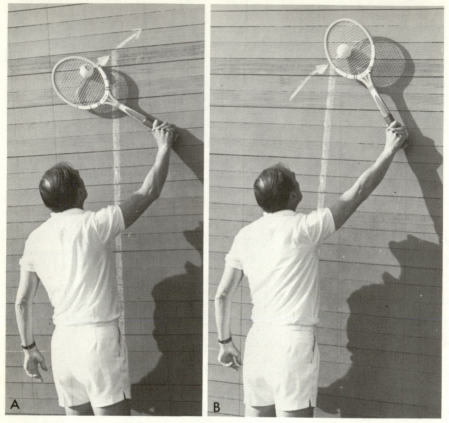

Figure 2–3 An effective way to demonstrate the kind of spin on an American Twist serve. The player presses a ball between his racket and the backboard, then rolls the ball upward and to his right by moving his racket in the direction of the arrow.

against the bottom surface causes the lift that is characteristic of cuts, chops, and slices.

Experienced players slice or chop certain shots for the purpose of gaining added control. This is done most frequently on the backhand by players who cannot drive confidently and consistently from that side. The glancing downward blow enables them to soften somewhat the force of impact between the racket and ball, and for many of them this is a more accurate way of hitting than is a crisply driven shot.

Sidespin is imparted to the ball when it is hit a sideward glancing blow (as when the racket moves across the intended line of flight of the ball at contact). The ball spins in the opposite direction from the path that the racket is traveling and curves in flight toward the direction in which it is spinning.

Another useful and common kind of spin is the combination of top spin and sidespin applied on the American Twist serve. The ball is struck an upward glancing blow in a left-to-right direction. The upward direction of the racket imparts the top spin, the sideward direction, sidespin. The top spin gives the ball an exaggerated downward curve in flight, and the sidespin curves it to the left. The combination of spins makes the ball bounce fast and high to the receiver's left.

Several fundamental facts of spin must be kept in mind by teachers as they analyze the cause-and-effect relationships that occur at contact:

1. The kind and amount of top spin is determined by (a) the size of the angle formed by the plane of the swing and the slant of the racket and (b) the force of the swing.

2. Assuming that other factors are equal, the more spin imparted to the ball, the less speed it will have (in a glancing blow only a part of the racket's energy is being used to propel the ball).

3. A spinning ball tends to curve in flight toward the direction in which its front surface is spinning.

4. Top spin makes the ball bounce faster and farther. Backspin makes it bounce lower if the ball has been hit in a low trajectory, and higher and slower if it has been hit in a lofted, curved trajectory.

5. A heavily topped drive tends to deflect upward off a volleyer's racket; a heavily chopped ball tends to deflect downward. A volleyer, however, can reduce the effect of spin off his racket by hitting crisply with a firm grip to make the force of his swing dominant over the force of the spinning ball. The direction of the rebound off his racket will be the result of the two forces and will be closer to the direction of the dominant force.

FORCE AND MOTION

Although the position, speed, and direction of the racket at impact determine the direction and characteristics of the flight of the ball, the teacher must analyze the entire stroke to determine how the racket is to be swung to ensure proper contact. This requires an understanding of various principles of force and motion, elements that determine the effectiveness and efficiency of performance in all physical activity.

In tennis, as in all athletics, motion is the result of muscle action. The entire body and various segments of it are used to move the racket during the swing. Speaking in terms of mechanics, the motion used to move the body and the racket is either linear (in a straight line) or angular (in an arc or a circle). Sometimes both kinds of motion are applied simultaneously. At other times, they are applied in sequence. As a player steps into a groundstroke and transfers his weight, he is applying linear motion. As he pivots and turns his shoulders, he is applying angular motion. For best results, these two must be blended smoothly; his shift of weight must be coordinated with his pivot and with his arm and wrist action. The effective force for moving the racket will be the sum of these forces if they are applied in the right direction, in the right sequence, and with proper timing.

The Grip

A logical starting point for a discussion of force in the swing is the grip. It is the link between the hitter's body (from which force originates) and the racket (through which force is applied to the ball). To prevent loss of force generated at the start of the swing, the grip should be firm enough to permit only a minimum of recoil at contact. If the wrist and grip are firm, there will be very little recoil, and most of the force of the swing will be transferred to the ball.

In order to insure firmness at impact, the position of the hand on the racket must sometimes be adjusted according to the strength in the hitter's hand, wrist, and forearm. The hand should be placed in a manner that permits the racket to best withstand the force of impact. Theoretically, the Eastern forehand grip, in which the "meat" of the hand is placed behind the handle is best for "weak" players. Many youngsters and women find it difficult to control the racket with such a grip, however. For them, the Western grip, with the palm under the handle, is more comfortable and efficient, at least until they develop strength enough to hold the recommended Eastern. Teachers must understand this preference for the Western among young players and should be careful and patient when recommending a change from it. Physical readiness is a factor here; the pupil should not be required to hold the racket in a prescribed manner until he has acquired strength enough to do so.

Resistance to the oncoming ball is only one of the requirements of a good grip. The grip should also provide the player with sufficient amounts of "touch" and "feel" to enable him to sense the position of his racket and to adjust its slant and angle accurately throughout his swing. Holding the racket "in the fingers," as many teachers say, is more likely to provide this sensitivity than is a club-like grip by the entire hand. But here again, individual differences in strength must be considered, and the decision on how best to place the hand for both force and control should be made only after observing what appears to work best for each individual.

The concept of *a range of correctness* is a useful one when judging grips for appropriateness and efficiency. Certain variations among grips may all be considered good, provided they permit the player to handle the racket skillfully and accurately without requiring unusual and awkward movements or postures. Bad grips are those that require complicated movements in the swing in order to allow efficient motion and that prevent the player from developing the sensitivity necessary for accurate placement of the racket.

Despite the advantages of a firm grip, it is not unusual to see players, particularly youngsters, hit reasonably well with a loose grip. Many of them swing with such force that the speed of their racket is sufficient to overcome the force of the oncoming ball. With their loose grips and forceful swings, however, they are not able to control the position or direction of the racket, and as a result they are not usually steady or accurate hitters. This is a common problem with youngsters under 12 or 13 years of age, many of whom do not have strength enough to make what can be described as a controlled swing. Experienced teachers have learned not to expect much in the way of controlled hard hitting until these youngsters gain hand and forearm strength. When that time comes, the teacher's job is to convince the player that control of the ball comes from control of the racket, and that this depends in part on the degree of firmness in the grip and wrist. The grip must be firm enough to control the speed of the racket, the direction in which it is moving, and the position in which it is placed (its slant and angle) as it comes into the ball. All of these are determinants of force and placement and require the attention of the players and the teacher.

When working on the backhand, teachers often are faced with a specific problem. Many students express a preference for placing the thumb along the back of the handle. They say that the thumb gives them a feeling of security and that they can use it as a brace against the force of the ball. Other players, however, prefer wrapping the thumb around the handle. They maintain that such a grip enables them to hold the racket more firmly and thus provides more control in their swings. A logical conclusion is that either grip is correct. Whether a player should use one or the other becomes a matter of individual preference usually decided after comparing the results obtained with each.

The problem of deciding which grip to recommend becomes more acute when teaching intermediate players to volley. Play at this level is often too fast to permit the changing of grips for forehands and backhands that is taught to most players when they are beginners. Instead, intermediate players must learn to use a "no-change" grip — the Continental. Many of them find this difficult to do because of the strength needed to hit a backhand volley with such a grip. Often the transition to the grip must be a gradual one. The student may have to be encouraged to move his hand toward the Continental grip by degrees as he gradually develops strength enough to handle the racket efficiently after each slight change.

Wrist Action

A discussion of strokes should include an explanation of wrist action, for the wrist also plays a part in placing the racket on the ball properly and in transmitting momentum from the body and arm to the racket and ball. This is not to imply that the wrist is used consciously on every stroke. Instead, we suggest that a hitter must sometimes prevent wrist action from entering into the swing. He can do this simply by holding the racket firmly. As he squeezes his grip, he will automatically restrain his wrist, because the tendons in the forearm that close the fingers and those that bend the wrist restrict each other's movements.

In tennis, a player's wrist movement is often related to his grip strength. A player with strong hands can grip relatively less tightly than an individual with weak hands and still maintain adequate racket control and resistance to the oncoming ball. Moreover, as he squeezes less tightly, he is able to have freer wrist movement. Of course, players differ in the degree of suppleness at the wrist joint. We must conclude, therefore, that there is no one specific amount of wrist action that will work effectively for everyone. Instead, various amounts of mobility at the wrist can be used effectively by different players. As teachers, we should help our students experiment to find their own best combination of grip pressure and wrist mobility.

Two terms are generally used in tennis to describe the positions of the wrist. When the right arm hangs normally at the side of the body, the palm of the hand faces the right thigh. When the wrist is in this position, we say it is *straight*. When a person uses wrist action to move his palm away from his thigh so that it faces the ground, we say that his wrist is *laid back*. These same moves and positions can be seen when the hitter extends his racket opposite his body to place it at the point of contact. It is to this point that we now direct our attention.

In a mechanical sense, hitting with a laid-back wrist position is more efficient than a straight wrist, especially for inexperienced players. The laid-back wrist, when combined with arm and body action that guides the racket along the intended line of flight of the ball, lets the hitter hold his racket face perpendicular to that line as his

Figure 2-4   A good example of the laid-back wrist at contact.

racket passes through his hitting area. As a result, he is likely to hit more accurately than with a straight wrist.

In the kind of swing described here, the wrist is laid back during the backswing and is held firmly that way until the finish of the stroke. Some teachers even use the term "locking" to apply to the degree of firmness at the wrist joint. There is a good deal to be said for this method, especially among beginners, because it reduces the number of variables in the swing: the hitter has only to time his arm swing accurately to meet the ball in the proper contact area. Furthermore, if he swings along the line of flight of the ball (in a manner that we shall describe later) rather than in a circular path across that line, he can lengthen his hitting area and provide a margin of safety at the contact point.

Intermediate and advanced players, who must often hit with a great deal of force, use a slight amount of what can be called "controlled hand action." The wrist is laid back during the backswing and is made somewhat straighter at contact. The movement of the wrist increases the momentum of the racket and adds speed to the shot.

The amount of wrist action varies among individuals as their flexibility and suppleness at the joint varies. It is possible for the wrist to be laid back nearly 90 degrees, although one rarely sees that much of a bend in the joint. During the forward swing, the angle between the racket handle and the forearm is reduced by varying amounts, depending on the kind of grip used and on the purpose of the shot. Western grippers meet the ball much sooner in terms of body reference points and with much more of a laid-back wrist than do players with different grips. Continental grippers meet the ball later and with a straighter wrist. Eastern grippers are somewhere between. Regardless of the grip used, individual physical characteristics cause differences in these points and, consequently, in the amount of wrist action.

In addition to noting the degree to which the wrist is laid back during the swing, players and teachers should be concerned with the degree to which the wrist is cocked. Although it is not necessary to cock the wrist to the extent that the racket head is markedly above it at contact, neither is it proper to so relax the wrist that the racket head dangles below the hand. The latter position, which can be described as a rounded wrist, does not permit a firm grip. Consequently, the wrist should be straightened from the rounded position at least enough to allow the racket to be held firmly at impact. Whether the racket face is above or below the wrist is not important. For very low balls it may be below the wrist; the hitter should lower his arm at the shoulder and carefully avoid the loose, rounded wrist position.

With the backhand, similar mechanical principles apply even though the hand is placed differently on the handle (the knuckles are more on top, with the hand in more of a palm-down position). When the arm is extended straight out from the shoulder socket, the wrist is in a natural "straight" position. When the wrist is used to move the thumb and fingers toward the rear fence, the wrist is "laid back." As with the forehand, the amount of wrist action during the swing varies among individuals, creating differences in the wrist position at contact. The matter of choosing either the straight wrist position or the laid-back position can be settled by experimenting to see which works best for an individual.

When serving, the hand and wrist are used differently. Here a great deal of wrist action can be used to give speed to the shot. Again, though, the hand and wrist must control the momentum of the racket to place it on the ball properly. Flipping the racket up and over the ball too early or pushing it up from beneath the ball too late results in bad shots. The timing of the wrist action is critical and for most learners

Figure 2–5   The rounded wrist position shown in A is a weak position because it does not permit a firm grip on the racket. The wrist should be cocked as much as is necessary to ensure firmness, as shown in B.

requires a great deal of practice to perfect. Beginners should experiment with attempts to consciously apply more or less wrist action in the swing to correct whatever faults and deficiencies are apparent. Thinking of the wrist as a hinge often helps here. A player uses tighter or looser hinge action to suit his needs and, as we pointed out earlier, the hinge action will be affected by the *grip* pressure he applies during the swing.

The Stance

Several principles derived from study of the body in action govern the placement and use of the feet while stroking.

The most efficient stance for groundstrokes is sideways, with both feet placed along a line parallel to the intended line of flight of the ball. Such a stance lets the hitter swing along the intended line of flight of the ball more naturally than does any other stance, and as we shall point out later, such a swing is likely to result in a more efficient hit. In addition, the sideways stance lets the hitter use the mass of his body to add force to his swing more efficiently than does any other stance.

Stances with the left foot placed markedly away from the line make it slightly more difficult for the hitter to swing along the line, especially on full-speed shots. An extreme open stance, in which the body faces the net, for example, creates a tendency to pull the racket across the line as it moves through the hitting area. In tournament play, however, the speed of the oncoming ball often forces a player to hit from such a stance. As a result, most players develop the ability to make adjustments in the arm action that enable them to guide the racket toward the target (through the hitting area) even while facing head-on to the net.

When accuracy rather than speed is required, a moderately open stance is often the most efficient position. The restricted backswing inherent in such a stance enables the player to maintain a tight sequence of moves in the swing, and the result is often better timing and racket control.

A first-class player must be versatile enough to adapt his stance and swing to meet the needs of each particular situation. Whatever hitting stance he is able to take that does not require unusual adjustments that complicate the swing needlessly is the proper one for that situation.

The Backswing

When working with beginners, many teachers advocate a straight, flat swing in which the racket is carried back at waist height. The forward swing begins after a momentary pause to change direction of the racket. The simplicity of such a swing is regarded as an advantage for teachers and beginning players; it is easy to demonstrate and easy to imitate.

A large majority of ranking players, however, do not pause at the end of the backswing, particularly on the forehand. They prefer to keep the racket in continuous motion and make a smooth continuum of the back and forward swings.

To accomplish this, a kind of *loop* motion is used. Some players raise the racket as the first move of their backswing, then carry it back, down, around, and forward in a circular pattern (the term egg-shaped is often used to describe such a swing). Others carry the racket straight back to start the backswing, then make a small circular motion (loop) at the end to start the forward swing. As with the egg-shaped swing, this swing is continuous.

We recommend the latter method because it is simple and efficient. Moreover, we would like to see continuous motion (rather than a stop-and-go action) successfully combined with the speed and length of the backswing. From the standpoint of mechanics, the characteristics of the backswing should be consistent with the objectives of the hitter. When he wants to hit with a great deal of force, a long, fast swing is advantageous. If his objective is control rather than power, the backswing should be relatively shorter and slower, with the length and velocity carefully tailored to produce only that amount of force needed for his purpose.

Of the three kinds of backswings, the loop is more suitable for hitting balls at various heights. By raising the racket to start the swing, a player can place it in good position for high balls, and by adjusting the depth of the loop at the end of the backswing, he can swing effectively at low balls. The straight, waist-high swing, on the other hand, prepares him only for a waist-high shot and requires an awkward adjustment for high balls. This is not to say that players cannot learn to make that adjustment. Many do and develop effective strokes even though their technique differs from that of the majority of ranking players. We must conclude, therefore, that it is foolish to make dogmatic assertions that one or another kind of backswing is universally best for everyone.

Among players who use the loop backswing on the forehand, we see differences in technique. Some keep the elbow down, thereby maintaining the flat, vertical position of the racket face throughout the swing. Others raise the elbow during the backswing and, by so doing, slant the racket face down. The raised elbow is then forcefully pulled down toward the right hip to whip the racket around to the end of the backswing and down into the loop to start the forward swing. As it whips around, the racket face changes from a markedly slanted-down position to whatever other position the hitter has chosen for contact.

In terms of mechanical principles, the elbow-down, racket-on-edge position is the simplest and most efficient way to swing. However, many players find such a position less comfortable and less natural than the high elbow position. Flexibility of the shoulder joint often influences players' methods here. Some find it almost impossible to keep the elbow down while they carry the racket up during the backswing. Flexibility of the wrist also has a bearing. As the elbow moves down to start the forward swing, the wrist also comes into play and affects the position and speed of the racket. Players with good wrist control can control the varying positions of the racket. Others with less control of the wrist are likely to suffer from inadequate racket placement at contact.

It should be remembered that these statements are only generalizations. Neither method may be wrong, and either approach may be appropriate for any particular individual. The elbow-down, racket-on-edge position is probably best suited for casual players who spend insufficient time on the courts to master the complicated moves and timing of the other method. Serious players, on the other hand, may eventually hit more effectively by using the elbow and wrist to whip the racket around, even if such action leads to occasional mis-timing and poor hitting. Each player should be permitted to work out by trial and error the combinations of methods that provide the most success. His choice of method will depend on the kind of game he

Figure 2–6   The elbow-down, racket-standing-on-edge backswing is shown in *A*. When the elbow is raised, as in *B*, the racket face closes and must be adjusted again during the forward swing.

plays — or would like to play — and on how thoughtfully and studiously he works at his game. The manner of stroking he uses may be a compromise between what is in a mechanical sense less likely to cause a bad shot and what is anatomically most comfortable and natural for him.

The Forward Swing

For consistently accurate hitting, a player should move his racket along the intended line of flight of the ball as his racket passes through his hitting area. With such a swing path and with the laid-back wrist position described earlier, he can lengthen his hitting area and thus not have to time the ball so precisely; he can meet the ball at any of several points along the line and still hit with reasonable accuracy.

If, on the other hand, his racket travels in an arc across the line, it will be in the proper hitting position — square to the line — for only an instant. At each other successive instant it will be angled to either the right or the left of the line. An arc swing requires precise timing for accurate hitting. The racket must meet the ball at only one point — that point in the arc where the racket is perpendicular to the line of flight of the ball.

Although in a geometric sense the swing along the line is the most efficient way to hit, in a mechanical sense it is not the natural way. As the body rotates during the forward swing, it causes the arm and hand to move in an arc. The hitter must consciously extend his arm and move his elbow away from his body and toward the net

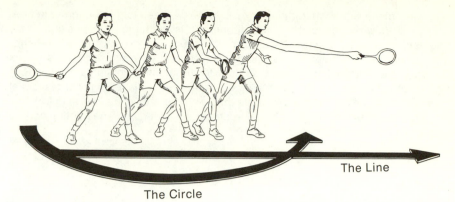

The Circle

The Line

Figure 2–7 To swing along a line through the hitting area the hitter must move his elbow past his right hip and away from his body in the direction of the shot. The concept of a long-armed long hit depicted above helps many learners develop this point of form.

to make the arc more closely approximate a segment of a straight line. A moderate amount of attention to making this adjustment is usually adequate to correct even the most pronounced circular forward swing.

The plane of the forward swing must be adjusted to attain the ball action wanted. For a top spin shot, the swing must be in an upward plane, starting below the contact point and finishing above it. There are several ways this movement can be accomplished. One is to straighten the knees during the forward swing. This action is often used as an addition to a hitter's conscious attempt to swing his arm in

Figure 2–8 The most efficient swing is one in which the racket moves through the hitting area along a line tangent to an arc, as shown at right. Such a swing enables the hitter to maintain the proper hitting position of the racket longer than does a circular swing used by many inexperienced players. The swing along the line creates an elongated hitting area in which precise timing and critical racket adjustments are not always necessary.

an upward plane, although traditionally players have been told to bend their knees and to stay down to the ball. Another technique is to change the position of the shoulders during the swing to make the right shoulder move up (on a forehand) as if the player were rotating his shoulders about a horizontal axis. This action promotes an upward swing. A third method is to straighten the hitting arm while lowering it during the backswing. Such a motion enables the player to lower his racket while still maintaining the proper angle between his racket handle and forearm. From the lower position, any combination of arm, shoulder, and knee action can be used to start the upward swing.

The Sources of Force

Earlier in this discussion we suggested that teachers should provide learners with the opportunity to practice at adjusting the variables in their swing. In addition to the variables that were mentioned — the angle and slant of the racket and the plane and line of the swing — the amount of force applied during the swing must also be adjusted by the hitter. To help the student gauge this variable accurately, teachers should explain and demonstrate the sources of force in a well-coordinated swing.

On the forehand, a player can generate racket speed by (1) swinging his arm at the shoulder, (2) transferring his body weight from the rear foot to the front foot, (3) turning his hips and shoulders clockwise during his backswing and counterclockwise to start his forward swing, and (4) using some wrist action. On the backhand, elbow action can be added to these motions.

The amount and degree to which these "sources of force" are used in a swing depend on the purpose of the shot. If, for example, a player intends to drive a backhand full length and full speed, he should attempt to use all of the sources available to him. When he intends to return a fast serve to the feet of a net-rushing server, however, he may not need all of these sources of power. Instead, perhaps, body rotation or even the weight shift may be eliminated. With arm and elbow action alone he may be able to supply enough force for his intention: a three-quarter length shot of medium speed to the server's feet. Adjusting the force of his swing in this way is one mark of a good player; he tailors his swing to each situation. Permitting and encouraging such adjustments is a mark of a good teacher; he realizes that good form is relative to the task at hand.

Attaining Maximum Force

The sources of force in any swing must be applied in the right sequence. The slower but stronger muscles of the body should go into action first with the successively weaker but lighter (and therefore faster) muscles of the body following. On the forehand, for example, whenever possible, the forward swing should begin with the weight shifting on to the left foot (a common expression to describe this move is "stepping into the shot"). The backswing is made during the step, with the hips and shoulders turning clockwise, as if to be "cocked" or "coiled" for the forward swing. The forward swing begins after the foot is planted, with the hips turning coun-

Figure 2-9 When returning the serve a player can move the racket faster when his elbows are close to his sides, as shown in A. In effect, he shortens the radius of his swing and thus reduces the inertia of his racket. With that shortened radius, less effort is needed to move the racket and consequently more of his muscle force is available for speed. The position shown in B is far less efficient.

terclockwise. The hip action is the result of the force exerted against the ground by the rear leg. Once the hip action is well advanced, the shoulders begin to rotate. When the shoulders and the hips begin to face the net, the arm swing is begun, after which the controlled hand action described earlier is applied. On the backhand, elbow action is added after the arm has started to swing from the shoulder.

On the serve, still additional sources of power are used: the server develops potential for angular momentum as he turns his hips and shoulders clockwise about a vertical axis during the backswing. He applies linear motion by shifting his body weight to the front foot.

Vertical momentum is attained by a combination of several moves. The knees, bent during the backswing, are straightened as the upward swing begins; the right shoulder, down during the toss, is forced upward as if rotated about a horizontal axis. Meanwhile, the muscles of the upper arm are used to force the arm upward. As the racket moves upward (from the "back-scratching" position), the arm is made to straighten, and the forearm is rotated (pronated) to attain a flat hit for added racket speed. Almost simultaneously with elbow extension and forearm rotation, wrist action is applied to gain additional speed. When the actions are well-timed, the arm, elbow, and wrist are fully extended, thereby providing the longest radius possible at contact.

Ideally, serving techniques should be in accord with the mechanical principle that states that for a given angular velocity, the linear velocity of a point about the

Figure 2–10   A close-up of the bent elbow position, by which the hitter shortens the radius and whips the racket through a loop and up into the ball. This "back scratching" position is one of the most common points of form among good servers.

center of rotation varies directly as the length of the radius varies. In serving, the entire arm, forearm, hand and racket are moving as a unit in the same amount of time. But since the arc through which the racket moves is larger than the arcs through which both the elbow and the hand move, it is obvious that the racket is moving faster than the elbow and the hand. Here the underlying principle is basic: the longer the lever, the greater the speed. Since speed is the object when serving, the player should reach for the ball at full stretch.

During the serve, the upper arm (attached at the shoulder) and the lower arm (attached at the elbow) function as levers and should be controlled by the player in accordance with an additional mechanical principle. In rotary motion, the amount of resistance to change depends not only on the mass, but also on the distribution of the mass about the axis — that is, its moment of inertia. Thus, the server bends his arm during his preparatory swing to shorten the radius (to reduce the moment of inertia) of his arm, hand, and racket. With that shortened radius, less effort is needed to move the racket, and consequently more of his muscle force is available for speed. Finally, when speed is attained, he straightens his arm (lengthens the radius) during his hitting action to gain additional speed at contact.

Rotation of the trunk is an important point of form for fast serving. When it is done properly and is combined with a shift of weight, the hitter's right side is made to come around and across the line. The extent to which he can bring his right side around with force determines to a large extent the degree of force in his swing. Here footwork is a matter to consider. Many good servers simply step across the baseline with their right foot as if this were a natural outcome of the swing. But others *jump* across the baseline to land on the right foot, which has been flung across the line during the swing. Their counterclockwise body turn is part pivot, part jump, the effect of which is to drive the right hip and shoulder around with even greater force than can be applied by merely stepping across the line. The combination of upward thrust with body rotation in this technique creates a sort of rising spiral effect not unlike that of a figure skater executing a leaping spin. The angular momentum created by counter rotation during the backswing transfers to the whole body as the thrust of the legs drives the hitter into the air.

Yet another technique is becoming increasingly common among top-flight servers. Many of them jump upward rather than forward and in so doing land on the left foot. The upward thrust appears to contribute a larger share to the total force that is generated than it does in the other kinds of serving motions. The question of which technique is best for a particular player is probably best answered from a practical standpoint: the technique that works best *is* best. Since all three kinds of foot movements appear to be workable, all are worth experimenting with. Whichever gives the best results should be the technique the player selects.

Attention to the position of the tossing arm during the swing may also result in faster serves. Most good servers tuck the arm against the body after making the toss, for good reason. If that arm is extended away from the hitter's body, the effect is to slow down the turn (the amount of inertia of the arm is increased as it is extended from the axis of rotation). Probably equally important is the position of the rear leg. If it is permitted to swing wide of the body, it too will offer resistance to the turn. Hence we see modern servers draw the rear foot up close to the front foot to provide a narrow base around which to pivot. Both of these positions—the arm tucked in and the legs close together—reduce the moment of inertia and enable the server to turn his body at a faster rate than is possible when the arm and leg are extended during the swing.

TIMING

For maximum ball speed when serving, the various parts of the swing must be timed properly so that they are applied in the proper sequence. Here the principle of summation of forces is important. Each phase of the stroke should begin before the preceding one stops, and each should start at the point of greatest velocity of the preceding phase. For example, if a player brings the vertical action of his lower arm in to play *after* he has already straightened his legs, he will have wasted the vertical momentum built up by the leg action. Or if he waits too long before shifting his weight, he will have to hurry each subsequent phase of his swing and may not be able to apply force long enough to attain maximum speed.

One approach a player can use in order to discover his best timing is to experiment to see what sequence provides the best hits. He should be encouraged to shift his weight sooner or later in the toss, to apply upward thrust sooner or later after the toss, and to use his final wrist action and forearm rotation sooner or later in the swing.

It is difficult to determine the proper time interval between various phases of the swing. Perhaps only a guiding principle can be offered as a partial solution to the problem of building the proper sequence of successive moves in both drives and serves: there should be no pause between phases of the swing, yet the time interval between the start of one phase and the start of the next should be long enough to permit each phase to attain maximum speed, and short enough to prevent "slack" from developing between the various parts of the swing.

Chapter Three

PSYCHOLOGICAL ASPECTS OF TEACHING TENNIS

Having presented background information from which teachers can analyze playing and teaching styles, we will now discuss several learning principles around which teaching methods may be developed. Teaching is likely to be more effective when it is done in accordance with these principles. However, knowledge of pedagogic principles alone does not guarantee success. To ensure effective teaching, teachers must understand how students differ in needs, interests, and attitudes. Moreover, instructors must learn to allow for various personalities, temperaments, and physical capabilities among students. Accordingly, in this chapter we will elaborate on such differences and list several implications for teachers as they attempt to deal with these differences.

PLANNING INSTRUCTIONAL PROCEDURES

Researchers and theorists provide the principles of learning; teachers provide the conditions and methods for learning. Among experienced teachers, methods vary. A procedure that is successful for one may not work as well for another. Even for the same teacher, a method may work for one student and not for another. Teachers must consider what each student brings to class in terms of aptitude, intelligence, and experience. Students will differ in the extent to which they possess these qualities; as they differ, likewise their potentials for learning will vary. It is imperative, therefore, that teachers know the kind of raw material with which they are working. Only then can they begin their instruction at the proper place and be headed in the proper direction.

Assessing Potential for Learning

The simplest method of assessing students' potential for learning to play is to observe them in loosely structured play or in rally situations. Many experienced teachers start their courses this way, making notes of mistakes that should be corrected and strong points that should be reinforced. These first decisions should be tempered by other information that may offer reasons for the behavior observed and suggest methods to use with various individuals. One way to attain this additional information is to provide a questionnaire on which students explain their reasons for choosing tennis (in a voluntary program), how much and what kinds of instruction they have had (individual or group), what they expect to get from the course, and what ambitions, if any, they have in the game. As a follow-up to this kind of survey, teachers can engage students in casual conversation before and after class, during which time they may probe for more information that will help them interpret students' remarks.

Classification tests such as those described in Chapter 5 are another means of getting useful information. The tests are easy to administer and are enjoyable for most students. They are also useful as motivating devices for additional practice.

Equally important and useful is close observation of the students' first attempts at whatever drills are prescribed. Here teachers must be alert to recognize separate smaller parts of a skill that affect the quality of the performance of the total act. In our discussion of task analyses later in this chapter, we will elaborate on this point. From the results of observations and classification tests, and from the students' remarks on questionnaires, teachers can determine the point at which to begin instruction and plan appropriate methods for presenting their material.

Allowing for Individual Differences

Some of the important differences that students bring to class result from diverse factors in their backgrounds. As the cultural levels, economic conditions, and social positions of their families vary, so will their attitudes toward such a genteel sport as tennis. One child, for example, may come from a family in the country club set where tennis is played by youngsters *and* adults. Almost certainly his attitude, interest, and enthusiasm for the game will differ from those of a boy whose family is in a lower social set where tennis is not played. The first boy may feel a need to learn to play and consequently will accept instruction eagerly and enthusiastically. The second boy may not care the least bit whether he learns to play. For him, the teacher may have to use all the motivational devices at his command. He should watch the boy carefully to determine what, if anything, about the game appeals to him. Upon finding something appealing, the teacher may have to permit the boy to play at that part of the game (to hold his interest), even if it requires changing the planned teaching sequence. If, for example, the disinterested student appears to like serving (he may have seen someone serve and, imitating him, found that he likes it), it may be wise to permit him to serve, although serving may not yet be called for in the teacher's progression. Another student may like the continued action that backboard rally practice provides and may be bored with the teacher's drills. The best approach to such a student may be to permit and encourage him to work against the board. A third student may prefer the effect created by slicing and cutting his shots to that obtained by driving as the teacher suggests. If it becomes apparent that such a student needs the freedom to play a certain way in order to keep his interest, he should be granted it. True, such a permissive attitude creates some problems for teachers, but in the long run it may lead to better teaching with "difficult" students. Allowing students to wander around within the activity is certainly better than having them wander away from it completely.

The areas of native ability and previous training further compel teachers to be aware of individual differences in students. Some children run faster and throw harder than others. Some are better coordinated; some are endowed with or have developed certain specific psychomotor traits that provide aptitude for tennis. Reaction time and speed of movement are examples of such traits. A student who is quick to react and to move is likely to perform better during volley instruction, for example, than is the student who is slower in these areas. Such differences should be considered as teachers plan their lessons; plans should be flexible enough to accommodate individual students even in a group situation.

Determining Instructional Objectives

An equally important point for teachers to consider as they plan instructional procedures is the performance expected of their students at the end of the lesson or course. Teachers must determine at the start of instruction the skills they hope students will be able to perform at the finish. Only by properly describing the expected final performance will they be able to provide methods that will enable students to reach that goal.

A description of the desired end performance is best made by compiling a list of final objectives, statements describing the tasks the students are to be able to do when demonstrating for the teacher at the end of instruction. Psychologists offer the following guides for making useful objectives: objectives should (1) describe the final performance that is expected, (2) describe the important conditions under which this behavior is to occur, and (3) describe the minimum acceptable performance.

We offer the following statements as examples of suitable objectives: Students are to demonstrate the wrist adjustments necessary for the accurate placement of forehand volleys when hitting against balls aimed accurately at them at speeds appropriate for their level. They must show how to bend the wrist back to hit to the right and how to straighten the wrist to hit to the left. They must place a majority of their shots within five feet of either sideline when hitting from the ideal singles volley location.

The reader will agree that these statements, when considered as objectives for volley instruction, meet the criteria for objectives listed earlier. The fact that several statements were necessary to fully describe the conditions to be met by the student does not detract from their usefulness as objectives. They can serve as a base for determining instructional procedures and for evaluating learning.

One major responsibility teachers face in their planning is to choose objectives that are compatible with the skill level of students. Whatever goals are set must be within their range of accomplishment. Not all students come to class with the same potential for learning, nor do they all expect to achieve the same amount of success. The expectations of the student are determined by his image of himself as a performer, which in turn depends on his perception of the task at hand. Consequently, teachers must show that their drills are such that even the slowest learners can feel capable of performing them—and will indeed do so successfully. By building backlogs of success in this way, teachers will have begun to inspire confidence, to modify the levels of expectation of the students, and to motivate them toward the next higher level of accomplishment.

Making Task Analyses

To determine the most efficient instructional procedures, teachers must know the specific, detailed skills (often called subtasks) that a general tennis skill requires. They must not only describe each skill but must also analyze each separate part of it. Making such a task analysis is one of the most crucial steps in determining methods of instruction. Only in this way can teachers provide the necessary steps of instruction and present material in the proper sequence that leads to skill attainment. When teaching an intermediate class to make a net approach for volleying, for example, the teacher may have to offer instruction on several subtasks. Along with knowing when to go to the net, students must know when to stop running as they advance to the volley location and how to make the ready hop that places them in the conventional ready position. They must also know how to step properly to reach the ball or to get away from it after having made the ready hop. Lastly, of course, they must know the technique of volleying, which itself includes additional subtasks (placing the ball, taking the speed off the ball, putting backspin on the ball and so on). To overlook any of these in the teaching process and to assume students will automatically learn them as they practice the total act of going to the net is likely to result in insufficient instruction. To avoid making that mistake, teachers must develop techniques for teaching these subtasks. Their plans should include as much detail as necessary (thereby providing for those students who need detail), while at the same time they should be comprehensive enough to let faster learners proceed at their own rate.

SELECTING CLASS ACTIVITIES

Up to this point in our discussion of teaching methods, we have stressed the importance of the teacher perceiving and understanding the different needs, interests, and attitudes of students. No two students are alike. Each brings to class his own pattern of readiness—a pattern determined by background, experience, temperament, physique, muscular development, and countless other influences. Teachers must adapt their methods to as many different patterns as possible. In the remainder of this chapter, we will list additional learning principles that teachers should consider as they make these adjustments.

Using the Whole and Part Methods

In the teaching of tennis skills, one of the major decisions the teacher has to make is whether to use the whole method or the drill-on-parts method of teaching, both for the entire game and for particular strokes.

Some teachers use the whole method; they have their beginners playing the full game immediately. They claim that this method will best enable the student to

Figure 3-1 *A.* An effective part method for introducing inept learners to the serve is demonstrated. From the starting position shown, the ball is thrown up and the racket is dipped behind the player's back. It is then quickly flung up and forward to meet the ball. *B.* Although it is seen frequently among teachers, the starting position shown in the second frame is not realistic. When the racket rests on the shoulder or hangs loosely behind the back as shown, the hitter often inadvertently learns to push at the ball rather than to swing at it. Once acquired, this habit is difficult to break.

acquire the necessary automatic habit patterns. Experiments indicate, however, that the efficiency of learning by wholes, as compared with learning by parts, appears to depend on the meaningfulness of the material to be learned, which in turn depends on the intelligence of the learner in each particular learning experience. Learning by the whole method is more efficient only when the material to be learned is easy, unified, and of a definite pattern that unites many single items into a significant whole. One can hardly say this is a description of a tennis game, with its different kinds of strokes and different purposes for shots. Because of the complexity of the pattern of tennis play, the whole method does not seem to be well adapted to early tennis instruction.

A moderate amount of skill in the basic strokes is a prerequisite for tennis play. Instruction and practice designed especially to instill the strokes will most effectively promote basic tennis skills. In private work and in group work, it is probably best for teachers to try always to teach the whole of one stroke (and only one stroke at a time). When working on the forehand, for example, they may demonstrate and explain the entire swing: the turn and backswing, the step and forward swing, the follow-through, and the finish. Students who can comprehend and assimilate all of these elements are permitted and encouraged to try the swing, always making the complete swing. For others, however, the complete swing may be too complicated, and it therefore must be broken into parts. Some students will benefit from starting with the racket back, thus eliminating the backswing. They are then able to concentrate on only the forward swing. Other students should be permitted to hold the racket in the contact position so that the tosser can almost hit the racket for them. By permitting these variations, teachers can accommodate students at various levels of ability. Fast learners are able to move along at their convenient rate, while slow learners move along through the difficult (for them) parts of the swing.

Teaching for Transfer

One simple approach to students at all levels of ability is to make use of the principles of transfer of training. Transfer is the name applied to the process of using past experiences in meeting new situations. It refers to the fact that an individual acquires habits and skills in one activity that can prove useful and helpful in another activity. Certain knowledge and skills carried over from some sports and games can be useful to students in their efforts to learn to play tennis. If a student has played baseball, for example, he may be shown the similarities between the hitting stances in each sport or, perhaps, the resemblance of the service swing in tennis to the overhand throwing motion in baseball. He should then be encouraged to apply the familiar baseball skills to tennis. Relating one set of facts to another in this manner is often an effective method of helping beginners through difficult parts of their early training.

An important point for teachers to remember is that habits or skills that have been learned in one activity may interfere with or retard learning in another activity; a kind of negative transfer may occur. For example, a student may find it difficult to learn to block or punch his forehand volley if he has just finished practicing his forehand groundstroke, which is taught as a long, smooth, follow-through motion. The habit of following through may have a hindering effect on his ability to learn the shorter stroke recommended for volleys. A learning principle that relates to this problem holds that the time interval between practice periods for skills in which there are conflicting movement patterns should be as long as possible, in order to avoid (or at least reduce) the interference of one skill with the other.

The implications of negative transfer give rise to this question: "What is the best method of progression in teaching—from groundstroke to groundstroke, or from groundstroke to volley?" Each teacher, by analyzing his methods and theories of stroking, must decide the answer for himself. If his analysis of his teaching system indicates that there are more similarities and fewer conflicting habits between groundstrokes (that is, between the forehand groundstroke and the backhand groundstroke) than between the groundstrokes and the volley, then the order of progression should be from one groundstroke to the other. It must be remembered, however, that individuals vary in their ability to carry over or to exclude movements between activities.

Varying the Approach to Students

Individuals differ in the manner in which they learn. They have different degrees of receptiveness and responsiveness to whatever approaches are made by the teacher. What works effectively with one student may not work with another. Some students, for example, learn quickly from verbal cues and guides. Others depend more on visual guidance; they profit more from demonstrations or photographs from which they can "get a picture" of the movement or skill. Still others rely more on mechanical guidance; they want the teacher to guide their hands or arms through the proper movement pattern so they can duplicate the feel of it.

When working with groups, the teacher must "reach" all students, regardless of the kind of presentation they prefer. Each lesson, therefore, should begin with a brief explanation followed by a demonstration. Very soon afterward, as students begin to practice the skill being taught, instruction should be individualized, but only after students have been permitted to imitate the demonstration presented by the teacher.

Again, a certain amount of permissiveness is recommended. Students' attention should first be directed to the total picture, so to speak—the gross framework, psychologists call it—and not to the specific details that make up the movement (these can be covered afterward). When teaching the serve, for example, the teacher should first help students get a general impression of the full swing and then encourage them to try to repeat the broad outline of it. Filling in the details should come later when students get the general idea of the swing.

Experienced teachers simplify the instructions that accompany their demonstrations: "Throw the ball up, then 'throw' the racket at the ball" may be all that needs to be said about the serve at the initial stage of instruction. For some students, however, teachers will have to provide check points in the swing that will help the learners trace the proper path of the racket. Learners may be told to guide the racket down and past the knee, up toward the rear fence, forward and down behind the back, then finally upward and forward into the ball. Even while responding to the reference points of "knee–fence–back–ball," each learner will eventually adapt the gross framework to his own individuality. As students differ in strength, suppleness, and fluidity, so too will their strokes differ. Knowledgeable teachers permit and even encourage variations in form that appear to work for the particular student.

Providing Teaching Cues

One of the most often repeated statements in regard to acquiring athletic skill is "practice makes perfect." The experienced teacher or coach, however, knows that this is not true, and that motor learning is not merely a process of repetition until a habit is formed. Instead, it is more a process of constant change or variation. A number of tries are made, errors are noticed, and other tries are made. Such learning is often spoken of as "trial and error" learning, but perhaps this is an inaccurate description of the process, for the learner, in succeeding trials, does not purposely repeat the errors committed in earlier trials. If he did, there would be neither change nor improvement. Instead, the learner makes variations in later trials so that they are more nearly correct than earlier ones. In tennis, for example, the learner may note that the racket was held too loosely or that the racket face was slanted too much.

Figure 3-2 Students with a common fault are separated from the class and given special attention. Here they are being shown how to press their rackets against the net band to get the feeling of how the wrist is to be laid back at contact.

When he repeats the action, he corrects the mistake, changing a part here or there to determine whether or not the change makes any difference in the end result. A series of such modified repetitions made under the watchful eye of the instructor constitutes effective practice. For this reason, the process of skill acquisition might more accurately be termed "successive approximations," wherein the learner successively approximates the correct position or action after each trial that does not produce the desired result.

What does the learner do? What does he respond to? How can he be guided in practice in which he attempts to modify every unsuccessful execution? In the beginning stages of the learning process, a learner needs cues from the teacher to guide his actions. Most experienced teachers have devised a set of "picture words," catchy phrases and colorful expressions that give students a clear idea of what to do. "Stand the racket on edge," for example, can be a valuable guide to a beginner who tends to turn the racket over in contradiction to the teacher's instructions to "finish with the racket face perpendicular to the ground."

If the learner does manage to finish with the racket on edge as the teacher suggests, and if his hitting and his placement begin to improve (and presumably they will, or the teacher would not have selected this as a teaching point), then the learner will want to continue to practice keeping the racket on edge. What seems to follow, then, is a process in which the learner takes over from his teacher the guidance of his performance by learning to "feel" that his racket is in the right or wrong position. He is learning to respond to cues in his muscular "feel," and he makes whatever corrections are necessary in his swing in order to make it feel right. Usually, the ability to feel the stroke comes only after many repetitions of those verbal cues used by the teacher, or even by the learner himself, that have guided the learner to the proper execution of the stroke.

MOTIVATING THE LEARNER

Psychologists hold that telling is not teaching; a person learns by doing, but only if he understands and is interested in what he is doing. Experienced teachers recognize the latter part of this statement as an expression of the ever-present problem of motivation — of energizing and activating students so that they will want to learn. It is the problem of controlling behavior and of structuring learning situations to make students work with increased effort and to keep their attention focused on the task at hand. The amount of effort and energy students expend in a task determines, in part, how well they perform. Consequently, the processes by which teachers regulate, control, and direct students' energy are of prime importance to both teachers and students.

Controlling the Level of Arousal

There are several functions teachers can perform to increase the motivation of students. One is to control the level of arousal, the level of alertness and excitability among students. Psychologists suggest that there is an optimum level at which most individuals perform best. Generally, activation to an intermediate point midway between excitement and boredom leads to best performance.

In assessing students' level of arousal, teachers should consider the demands of the learning task they have structured and the degree of sophistication in physical skills among students. Here, as in all areas of the teacher-learner relationship, teachers should be prepared for a variety of responses to whatever drills or learning situations they provide. Students will differ in the degree of anxiety and stress with which they face a particular situation. For one student, instructions may be clear and meaningful. For another, they may be ambiguous and confusing. The student in the latter case will feel stress and as a result may perform far below his capabilities.

Emotional handicaps may also affect a student's level of arousal. A timid person may be so afraid of embarrassment that he freezes up completely when forced to perform conspicuously. For such a student, teachers must somehow create an environment in which he is not afraid to try, and they must provide tasks that are within his range of accomplishment. The timid individual may be better off if left alone to rally against a backboard, avoiding the embarrassment of participating in a drill in which he is certain to be the poorest performer and to be noticed as such.

Too many instructions and too many details to attend to during a performance may also cause stress. Inexperienced performers are limited in the amount of information they can attend to. Some can focus on only one stimulus, one point of information at a time, as if they have only a "one channel" mind. For these students, the teacher or coach must point out only the most important points of the skill, and these points should be brought out one at a time. In this area inexperienced teachers are often accurately criticized for offering too many instructions, for talking too much.

Our "pattycake" approach to forehand volley instruction is an example of an extreme accommodation made for the purpose of rendering a set of instructions in familiar terms (Fig. 3–3). The concept of volleying comes easily even to beginners who have had not extensive experience in sports when they relate the volley to the childhood game of pattycake. The learner simply raises his or her hand (and racket) to place the racket behind the ball. Since the teacher will practically hit the

Figure 3–3 A young girl is introduced to the forehand volley by relating it to the childhood game of pattycake.

racket for the beginner on the first few tosses, confidence in the ability to make the shot will naturally follow.

In team coaching, the level of arousal of players preparing for competition is extremely important. A player is likely to perform better if he *feels* he is prepared to compete. One way to provide that feeling is to permit players to decide for themselves how best to prepare for a match. One player may want several days of intensive competition with a teammate of equal ability to sharpen his competitive urge. Another may want to play a teammate he can beat fairly easily in order to develop confidence and a winning attitude. A third player may simply want to rally with a steady partner to sharpen his strokes and to gain the confidence that he is hitting well. When a coach provides for the individual preferences of his players in this way, he is indeed helping them get ready to play. Such preparation contributes toward setting each player at his optimum level of arousal for the ensuing competition.

Motivating Through Reinforcement

Another technique for increasing students' motivation is to provide proper reinforcement for their efforts. Reinforcement is the procedure by which a coach or teacher provides rewards for the purpose of shaping, developing, and maintaining behavior. It is based on the premise that in a given situation a player will tend to repeat a response (in tennis, a stroke or a tactic) that is reinforced and to discontinue a response that is not. Reinforcement is an essential condition for most learning. Teachers and coaches should be constantly alert for opportunities to use it effectively.

In tennis, the most obvious and frequent application of reinforcement occurs when a teacher or coach makes favorable comments after a player strokes a ball with acceptable form. The teacher's remarks are satisfying to the student; therefore, the student tries to repeat the stroke pattern that brought that satisfaction.

The uses of reinforcers are of course far more complex than the simple offering of verbal praise. Teachers — and coaches especially — must apply reinforcement not only for the purpose of improving a student's stroke at a particular time but also to motivate players to have a proper attitude toward the entire program. For this reason, they must consider other kinds of reinforcers that are readily available to them.

Several reinforcers that can be used effectively can be grouped under the heading of *social reinforcers.* For some players, merely being accepted as a member of the squad is reinforcement enough to motivate them to respond favorably to the coach's procedures and policies. They are happy to be one of the group, doing whatever the group does, for in this way they attain the esteem of their peers and win social recognition. For them, this is often the most effective reinforcer.

For other students, however, success in competition is a major need. They must see that they are progressing, either from the results of direct competition or from the teacher's and peers' appraisals of their performance. For them, a succession of losses or bad performances can be terribly discouraging and can often lead to listless performance, sometimes even to withdrawal from the activity. The teacher's task in such a case is to provide activities (challenge matches, contests, competitive drills) at a level that makes reinforcement readily available. In Chapter 12 we describe several drills that can be adapted for this purpose.

Various kinds of *material* awards can be made to function as reinforcers, especially with very young children. Badges, ribbons, and medals work well for this purpose. Contests may be devised and winners rewarded with breast patches or arm bands with suitable inscriptions (such as "Best Forehand," or "Backboard Rally Champ"). As children mature and grow older, however, they attach less value to such material awards and respond more noticeably to social reinforcers. Teachers and coaches must consider the level of development of their students as they look for appropriate reinforcers.

One of the important sources of reinforcement is often the nature and conduct of the activity itself. If the practice sessions are pleasant, interesting, challenging, and beneficial, a coach will have little trouble keeping his players interested and motivated. In striving for this goal, the teacher must pay attention to a number of specific details. The class activity or practice session should be conducted in an attractive setting, with adequate space and equipment to prevent minor grievances from magnifying. Pleasantness depends on the kind of social interaction as well as the physical arrangements. The teacher must be sensitive to each player's temperament and personality. He must make each feel that he is getting the amount of attention and instruction he needs, whether it is offered as constructive criticism or as commendation and praise for successful performance. The player must have the feeling of making at least some progress, of achieving some success, measured either against the performance of others or against a previous performance of his own.

One technique by which teachers can provide a record of progress is to give simple tests of skill and form on which students can be scored periodically. Counting the number of balls stroked into a certain court area, or the successful hits made against the wall, or the number of times a ball is made to cross the net in a rally are examples of such tests. Charts and graphs showing the improved scores on these tests can be used to create a desire in students to better their scores. Students should be made to understand, however, that such tests are being used as a device to help them reach their goal of becoming a tennis player and are not ends in themselves.

Students who improve their scores significantly may be permitted to move from one court or from one section of the gymnasium to another, where a more advanced skill is being taught. Alternatively, students may be awarded points, at intervals, for accomplishment on each drill, with the points being totaled at longer intervals to determine standings and placement. When learners are made to feel satisfied with small steps such as these while not losing sight of the ultimate goal of becoming a skilled player, the whole process of training and learning is made easier and more pleasant.

Feedback

One of the most important concepts in skill learning is known as feedback, the process by which information is made available to the student to enable him to compare his performance with some standard. The student uses the information to change or correct his performance, either while he is performing or afterward. The information he uses to guide his movement or to change a movement in a future performance is obtained either from some external source (such as the teacher's remarks) or from his own internal receptor organs. Regardless of its source, feedback is one of the most important variables affecting learning.

There are two main kinds of feedback: intrinsic and artificial. In tennis, a player has a kind of intrinsic feedback in every shot: he sees that his shot is in or out, high or low, good or bad. Such information is often enough to make students want to practice (and to improve) without the aid of a coach or teacher. Such trial-and-error learning is not the most efficient way to learn, however. A player often may not be able to determine what points of form were incorrect and what caused an error. As a result, good form may come only after many long, arduous practice periods, if it comes at all. In contrast, teachers and coaches can facilitate learning by explaining when and how errors occur and by suggesting ways of correcting them.

Another kind of intrinsic feedback arises from the organic sensations that occur during or after a performance. This is often called kinesthetic feedback because it refers to what a hitter feels during a stroke. If the result of a particular swing is satisfactory, he will want to make his next swing feel that way again, hoping thereby to make another satisfactory shot.

Many experienced teachers and coaches use gimmicks and gadgets to help learners develop a feel for a particular stroke or for some small part of a stroke (several gimmicks used for this purpose are described in Chapter 8). Most teachers, however, rely on the spoken word and attempt to describe and demonstrate proper positions of various parts of the body (the elbow, wrist, or shoulders, for example) in order to help the learner look right when stroking. Hopefully, with continued practice he will begin to feel what is right. In this way teachers use artificial feedback — information not usually available in the performance of a task — to lead the learner to the point where he is able to benefit from intrinsic feedback — that is, from his knowledge of the results of a particular stroke and what the stroke *feels* like.

While the value of the verbal feedback offered by the coach cannot be denied, its limitations for class use are obvious. The teacher can attend to only one hitter at a time. Of course, he usually offers mass instruction first, during which he explains and demonstrates for the entire class. Minutes afterward students are dispersed and are permitted to hit balls, presumably with the new form the teacher recommends. The usual result, however, is that they either revert to their old tendencies or they adopt some new technique that seems to work for them. The danger here is that by adopting a "bad" form that provides temporary success, the beginner may hinder the development of more suitable form that will eventually let him play effectively at a higher skill level.

One solution to this problem is to have students work in pairs and to teach them to teach each other. In this plan, ball-tossing drills may be arranged in which half the class tosses while the other half hits. Hitters first swing at balls tossed carefully and accurately so that problems of judgment and timing are minimized. They are therefore able to concentrate on the points of form first described by the teacher and later repeated by a tosser when he considers it necessary or helpful for a particular hitter. In this way a student is not left unattended, so to speak. Instead, he is under constant supervision, always under the watchful eye of either the teacher or another student, both of whom are helping him to develop acceptable form. Only when he begins to display such form is he permitted to rally "on his own."

To make such a so-called buddy system work, it may be necessary for the teacher to demonstrate the most obvious and common faults and the corrections for them. As he does so, he must begin to encourage tossers to actively coach their hitters and must persuade hitters to consider each tosser as a temporary assistant teacher. For each pair, he provides easily recognized cues and easily understood expressions they can use as they work together. In our discussion of group methods in Chapter 5, we explain how best to arrange student pairs for this kind of instruction, and we elaborate on the teaching cues to offer students for use in this plan.

When working with youngsters, similar problems of form often develop. Small children may not have strength enough to serve powerfully or to volley backhands with good form, for example. As a result, they may adopt an unusual form that seems to work for them. The teacher must evaluate this situation carefully before recommending changes in technique. Children may first need to reach a certain physical level of function through the normal process of growth and development before they can be required to play the game with classic form.

There are two possible solutions to this problem. One is to adapt the learning situation to the developmental level of the students. This can be done by having them use paddles or short rackets and by having them play some scaled-down version of tennis (see Chapter 4). The second is to have the learners ignore the results of their shots and simply hit for the purpose of developing acceptable form. This is not easy to do, however, for youngsters want to know if their shots are good or bad, and any successful hits they do make are strong reinforcers.

Shaping the Strokes

Shaping refers to the technique by which teachers use reinforcement procedures to carefully guide learners through a planned program of steps, from easy to more difficult, toward the development of acceptable form or behavior. In the process of shaping tennis strokes, the teacher first reinforces any part of the stroke that even approximates good form. He does not expect instant replication of the form he demonstrates or provides as a model, even from his most apt students. Instead, he anticipates that students will have to be led carefully through several small steps to attain the final step — good form. At each step, learning tasks are simple enough so that reinforcement is within the reach of all students. At each succeeding step, the tasks are more difficult and the teacher is more strict in what he considers worthy of reinforcement. Gradually, through reinforcement at each of the small steps, the learner's performance begins to resemble the final form desired.

When the group procedures described in Chapter 5 are combined with the instructional procedures described in Chapter 6, a suitable sequence for shaping strokes is provided. Slow learners pass slowly through the various steps. Apt learners may even skip steps if the teacher feels their ability warrants it.

In the early steps, the teacher's requirements for good form may be stated as very simple directions: (1) stand sideways, (2) hold the racket firmly, or (3) keep the elbow down and the racket on edge. In later steps students may be required to (1) adjust the swing for high and low balls, (2) adjust the timing when hitting from an open stance, or (3) use controlled hand action for force and placement. By modifying the requirements at each level and by arranging tossed-ball drills in which tossers coach their hitters, learners are provided with practice, instruction, and reinforcement, three elements essential for shaping skill performance.

Figure 3-4 A nine-year-old girl is shown in one of her first attempts to hit a tossed ball. Errors in form to be corrected are a low backswing with its resulting pendulum-like forward swing, and a flat-footed, straight-legged stance. However, she has already learned to hit with a laid-back wrist.

Processing Information

During stroke practice the teacher's role is that of an analyst and a conveyor of information. He observes the stroke, considers the cause and effect relationships at contact, then relates the stroke to the flight of the ball. He concludes what mistakes occurred and what correction is to be made, and he passes this information on to the student in as meaningful a way as possible. He may explain technically, demonstrate, diagram, or mimic; he may even guide the learner's hands and arms. Regardless of the method he uses, he must also help the learner understand the conditions under which the fault occurred and when to expect those conditions to arise again.

The student has a more active role than may be inferred from the preceding paragraphs. One modern learning theory suggests that the student functions as an information processing system. He is continually being fed information about his environment, which in tennis we can call the conditions of play. One kind of information he processes has already been described: the consequence, the result of his stroke *after* having swung. The instructions that are offered to correct that stroke can usually be applied only to a subsequent stroke that occurs under the same conditions. Identical conditions for successive groundstrokes are not likely to occur, however. Instead, the next shot, the next ball a hitter has to play, is likely to be higher or lower, faster or slower, shorter or deeper than the previous one. He therefore must make a judgment that will enable him to set the variables of the stroke (the slant and angle of the racket and the plane, the line, and the force of the swing) properly for that second stroke. This suggests that teachers should not only help students "groove" their swings, but should also help them develop skill at adjusting their swings to the varying conditions of play. This means, of course, that students must learn to recognize how play conditions change. They must be aware that they are farther from the net — or will be — for one shot than for the preceding shot, or that one ball is higher — or will be — than its predecessor. By learning to anticipate the conditions under which they are going to have to hit the oncoming ball, they are more likely to set the variables properly for that particular shot.

It is often helpful to provide specific practice at adjusting the variables. One good way of doing this is by having students aim at the same target (the cans in which balls are packaged serve well for this purpose) on every shot regardless of their location in the court. They soon learn that it takes a higher as well as a stronger shot to hit the target when stroking from some distance behind the baseline than it does when stroking from close to the service line. And to hit higher or lower, the slant of the racket and the plane of the swing must be adjusted. Usually with only a moderate amount of this kind of practice, students learn to make accurate judgments and adjustments even under more realistic conditions of play.

Teachers can direct students' attention to the conditions they must watch for in order to accurately judge the flight of the ball. Many beginners do not know what cues to look for; they must be taught to recognize the force of the opponent's swing, the sound of impact, and the trajectory of the oncoming ball. They can then predict what amount of force and what kind of trajectory are likely to provide a high ball or a low one, a fast or a slow ball. Processing such information before making the stroke is fully as important as working out corrections from the information gathered during or after the stroke.

Chapter Four

PROGRESSION: FROM HAND TO PADDLE TO RACKET

In both club work and school work a question often asked of teachers by parents of young children is, "How old must my child be before starting to play tennis?" Most experienced teachers feel that whenever a child is able to judge and time a ball in flight reasonably well, he is ready to begin. This does not mean, however, that teachers must wait until youngsters *have already acquired* eye and hand coordination. Experienced teachers know it is possible to help pupils develop this essential skill more quickly by providing planned activity for that purpose, rather than by simply letting nature take its course. A few simple ball-tossing and ball-catching drills are usually adequate for setting the stage for formal instruction. They help make youngsters ready to learn.

For children, tennis is not an easy game to learn; the racket is usually too big and too heavy, the ball usually travels too fast and bounces too high, and there is usually too much court space to cover. Because of these difficulties, not many eight- or nine-year-olds take to the game enthusiastically. Furthermore, young children are often taught in groups, and in school situations particularly the groups are at times too large to be handled efficiently in the space provided. Many experienced teachers consider this to be a constant problem and describe it this way: "Too many players, too few courts." This obstacle together with the problem of providing equipment — rackets, balls, and nets — often deters the school teacher from offering tennis in the school program.

The activities described in this chapter are offered as solutions to these problems. An ingenious teacher can conduct them so that as many as 25 to 30 pupils can be accommodated on only one court, or in a space only as large as the usual elementary school gymnasium. If no court or gym is available, the usual playground space can be easily converted to an area suitable for the games we will discuss. The only equipment that will be necessary can be made in a school shop, picked up as discarded material from tennis clubs, or purchased at very little cost.

Improvised versions of the game make it possible for the teacher who is inexperienced and unskilled in tennis to introduce his pupils to the game and yet avoid the embarrassment of having to demonstrate difficult strokes or shots. Most teachers who now feel inadequate for teaching the game, can, because of their general skills in ball catching and throwing, do an adequate job of laying the groundwork for tennis development in their pupils despite lack of playing ability.

For purposes of the following discussion, it may be convenient to list the activities to be described in ladder form, with hand tennis being the lowest rung. The higher rungs are, in ascending order, paddle tennis and starter tennis. The teacher who introduces his pupils to the game at the levels appropriate for their abilities is likely to be free of the problems involved in an advanced and more difficult tennis program. If he prepares carefully and chooses wisely, he will probably engender sufficient interest and enthusiasm to have a successful program. As a result, he will probably be instrumental in encouraging many youngsters to become tennis players at a later age, when they are able to handle the fullest version of the game.

HAND TENNIS

Most teachers who work with little boys and girls know that only an occasional youngster who has had an unusual background of experiences or who is naturally endowed with certain basic athletic abilities is ready to begin full-scale tennis. For other children — for the majority, in fact — it may be necessary first to provide informal activity that will help them develop skills that resemble tennis behavior and that will provide a foundation for the more specific tennis instruction that comes later. A list of several simple ball-tossing and ball-catching drills suitable for this purpose follows. Not everyone in a particular class will need all of this kind of practice. The conscientious teacher assesses the initial capability of his pupils — of each individual pupil — and provides the aid that each needs or will benefit from.

1.   Pupils throw a ball underhand against a wall or backboard and catch it as it rebounds from the wall. They are far enough from the wall to permit the ball to bounce several times. They catch it with two hands on any convenient bounce.

2.   Pupils throw overhand against a wall and move to catch the ball on any convenient bounce. They are told to throw by "scratching their ear" with the ball, by keeping the elbow high, and by stepping with the left foot (left-handers step with the right foot). They are told to catch the ball in one hand: the throwing hand.

3.   Pupils play catch with a partner, tossing underhand and catching with the throwing hand after one bounce. The receiver is shown how to move alongside the ball to catch it in forehand fashion.

4.   Each pupil drops a ball on his right side and hits it against a wall with his throwing hand (if right-handed). He may first use either an underhand or a side-arm swing. As skill increases, however, he uses only a sidearm swing to hit in forehand fashion.

5.   One player of a pair tosses and the other hits the ball back to him after one bounce. The tosser tosses underhand; the hitter hits with a sidearm swing of his throwing hand.

6.   One player of a pair tosses and the other catches the ball "on the fly" with his throwing hand. The catcher bends his elbow to raise his hand to provide a target for the tosser. He reaches forward to catch the ball (he should be able to see the back of his hand after he catches).

In all of these exercises, pupils take turns, alternating between tossing and hitting. For motivational purposes, they may be allowed to compete against each other by counting the longest rallies or the highest number of successive good hits or good catches.

PADDLE TENNIS

After providing practice and instruction in catching, throwing, and hitting with the hand, the teacher's next logical step is to introduce his pupils to tennis equipment. We suggest, however, that there be some intermediate steps before pupils take up full-size equipment.

One of the teacher's main tasks is to help his pupils develop efficient tennis strokes. For many youngsters, this is impossible with a full-sized, regular weight racket. Most youngsters do not have enough strength in their fingers, hands, and forearms to control a large racket. As a result, their early attempts at using the racket result in bad form, wild, uncontrollable shots, and discouragement.

The wise procedure is to provide a smaller, shorter, lighter implement that enables pupils to swing properly and to hit accurately. We suggest a wooden paddle.

Equipment

Paddles can be inexpensively made in most school shops. We recommend an oval shaped head of 1/2 to 3/8 inch thick plywood with a hitting surface of 8 inches by 8 inches across the face. The handle is 7 inches long and 4 3/8 inches in circumference. When made of five-ply birch or fir, such a paddle weighs about 10 ounces. To serve as a grip guide, tape is wrapped around the handle to form a "butt."

Because it is scaled down in size and weight to meet the strength limitations of young students, a paddle is easier to control in the swing than a regular racket. Moreover, because of its solid hitting surface, which is less resilient than gut or nylon string, students can control the ball better.

"Dead" balls, either of sponge or rubber, or regular tennis balls punctured to deaden the bounce are used. The tennis balls need not have nap or fuzz which is required for accurate flight in full length play. Even badly worn balls, discarded by skilled players because they "sail" or "float," are suitable for this version of the game, where long flight is not required.

The Playing Area

When paddle tennis is used as a lead-up to tennis, neither a court nor a net is required. Any play space on which balls will bounce accurately can be converted to a "court." Two chalk lines, "foul" lines 18 feet apart, are drawn and a rope or cord is stretched across the area midway between the lines and parallel to them. The rope is anchored tightly enough to be three feet high across the area. About 15 additional feet behind each line is needed for playing and scoring. If this space is not available, however, play may be modified accordingly. If a regular tennis court is available, the rope is stretched across it midway between the service line and baseline. In such a space (half a court) eight players can be accommodated (with eight

Figure 4-1 A youngster's first attempt in the hand tennis stage. He starts in the hand-back position, steps into the shot, and tries to guide the ball back to his tosser.

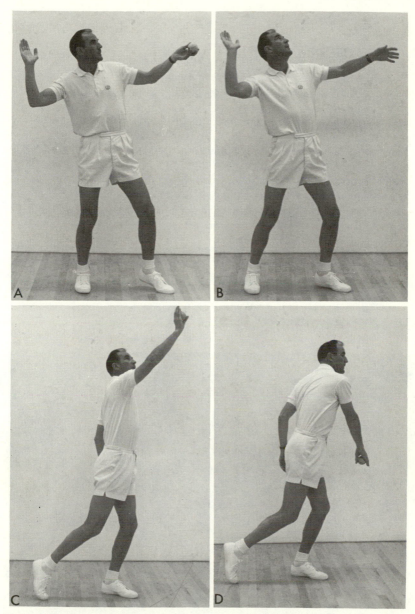

Figure 4-2 Photos show how a beginner may be introduced to the proper serving motion while using only his hands. He first tosses the ball and catches it. After several successful catches he hits to a partner.

more on the other side of the court) if the teacher emphasizes controlled hitting and careful movement.

THE FIRST STEP

Before concentrating on the stroke pattern, the teacher should allow beginners to get the feel of the paddle. They must get familiar with its weight and balance, and they must get an idea of the degree of resiliency between the paddle and the ball if they are to know how much force to put into the swing. For this reason, they should be permitted to rally rather carelessly across the cord while standing only four or five feet from it. They are permitted to play the ball on any bounce (the cord does not stop a low, bad hit), but they try to feed their partner a first bounce, starting each rally with a drop-and-hit. They are not yet told to stand sideways or to make a back swing or a follow-through. Instead, they are permitted to return the ball in any way possible, simply playing "pitty-pat" while using any grip on the paddle handle. When they have developed a "feel" for the paddle and ball, they are ready for formal stroke instruction.

Playing the Game

The objective in our version of paddle tennis is simply for the beginner to learn to rally. Either player starts the rally by making a bounce and hit directly to his

Figure 4–3   A "starter" group of young girls rallies across a string with paddles and soft sponge balls. With the string there are no netted shots; the girls play the ball on any convenient bounce whether or not their partner's shots were over the string. Continual rallies provide more practice than do intermittent hit-and-miss attempts over a net.

partner. This is done in much the same fashion as the drop-and-hit sequence in hand tennis is performed, with the exception that the hitter swings the paddle through the contact point and adjusts his wrist at contact to guide the ball straight ahead. Players attempt to hit above the cord, but the ball may be returned whether it clears the cord or not (the cord does not stop low balls as a net does, and hitters therefore find it easier to maintain a rally). A ball can be played on any bounce, but hitters must stand behind a "foul" line to hit. The objective is to provide the students with practice at hitting *to* each other, not away from each other.

As players improve in accuracy, scoring is introduced, and partners work as a team to try to beat other teams. A point is scored each time a ball stroked from behind the line clears the cord. More points are awarded each time a ball in flight hits the cord (this encourages pupils to aim *at* it rather than to hit high, easy floaters above it), and the count continues in the next rally. On lower balls, the count ends, but the rally may continue with a new count. The pair with the highest number of points for the longest rally of "good" shots is declared the winner.

Youngsters are attracted to this version of paddle tennis because the equipment that is used is more appropriate to their age level and to their ability. The small paddle weighing only 10 ounces is easier to handle than a full-sized racket. The dead ball travels more slowly and does not bounce as high as does a regulation ball. Furthermore, because hitters aim at each other rather than away from each other, they are able to reach and return a large number of shots even in the first stages of play. With proper instruction, young children can acquire a sound background for lawn tennis at an age when the size and weight of the racket and the vastness and speed of the major game are too taxing for them.

Bridging the Gap

Although paddle tennis can and often does serve as a lead-up to tennis, there is no assurance that all paddle players will eventually become tennis players. Many youngsters do not see the connection between the small game played with paddles and the larger games played with rackets. The teacher must point out the relationship between the two and indicate the similarities and the opportunities for carry-over of skills from one to the other. This can be done by arranging an exhibition match at which the group has an opportunity to watch skilled players perform. If the match players are close to the age level of the group, the effect on the group will be more noticeable than if the performers are much older; many youngsters will realize that they already possess many of the abilities and skills required in the big game. Another effective procedure is to arrange for the group to watch the local high school or college team in action. Often, after just such a brief exposure or introduction to tennis, many youngsters will be encouraged to try their hands at the game at the first available opportunity. Other motivational techniques that are normally used by teachers and coaches in other sports can be helpful in tennis; clinics by local, well-known coaches or players, movies demonstrating the game and its techniques, bulletin board displays of action shots of well-known players, and, of course, close personal contact with the more promising players can all be useful.

STARTER TENNIS

Experienced teachers know that the more an introductory game resembles the actual game it leads up to, the more likely are players to make the carry-over from one activity to the other. Clearly, then, there is a disadvantage in limiting lead-up tennis activities to hand and paddle tennis. Teen-agers and grown-ups alike do not always see a close relationship between lead-up games and lawn tennis, and they question the value of first learning to play with a paddle.

To offset this disadvantage, we suggest a third step in the ladder of progression: another small version of tennis known as starter tennis. In this game, play is conducted exactly as it is in regular tennis, with all the equipment reduced in size to make play easier. Short rackets (rather than paddles) are used, a definite court area is marked off (and is much smaller than a regular court), and official tennis scoring procedures are followed. The short rackets are easy to control and therefore are more likely to be swung properly in situations where the heavier and longer standard rackets would be unwieldly. Since play is on a court, with regular scoring, most beginners note the relationship between the game and the larger version that they see experienced individuals playing.

Beginners will soon lose interest in starter tennis if they do not make some early progress. We suggest, therefore, that the progression for teaching be similar to that followed in hand tennis and paddle tennis. Swing drills, bounced-ball drills, and tossed-ball drills—all of these can be helpful and should be used when necessary to build a foundation for actual play.

Equipment

Equipment necessary for starter tennis is easily obtained. Old, deadened, worn tennis balls, ready for discard, can be picked up at any club or tennis center. The balls need not be fuzzy, since they need not be true in flight. If they have retained their pressure and their bounce, they may be punctured for the purpose of deadening them and thus slowing the game down. A net is not necessary (the use of a cord instead has already been described), but where they are available, lightweight volley ball nets will be adequate. With such nets or with a cord, heavy, solid net posts are not required. The cord or net can be tied to the fence at one end and attached to ordinary gym standards (or, in the absence of these, heavy chairs) at the other end.

The problem that most teachers will be concerned with is obtaining rackets for play. Here again, old discards will do; they can easily be modified for use in starter tennis. A regular racket is 26 3/4 inches long. Simply by removing the leather grip and sawing through the handle at a point four to six inches from the butt, one can reduce the racket to a size suitable for most beginners. The shortened version of most rackets of modern design will weigh approximately 12 ounces and will have a handle approximately four inches in circumference. By replacing the leather handle and wrapping several turns of tape around the end to form a new butt, a "new" racket is created that beginners are able to grasp firmly and to swing in a controlled manner.

Many of the "junior" rackets available for purchase at clubs and sporting goods stores can be converted to short rackets in the same manner. Some youngsters will prefer to use converted small rackets for the reason that the head is usually smaller, and thus a short racket with a more even distribution of weight is obtained. Lastly, for teachers and players who want new and solid equipment, some finely made and nicely finished short rackets, made especially for use by youngsters and ladies in the short game, have recently become available for purchase at clubs and stores.

The Playing Area

We have found that a court in which all dimensions except the service areas are reduced to two-thirds of the regular court size is satisfactory for starter tennis. The starter court is thus 52 feet long and 18 feet wide, with three feet added on each side for doubles; the net is 24 inches high. Only the lengths of the service courts deviate from the two-thirds pattern. Experience has shown that it is practical to increase their length to 20 feet. For certain age groups, under certain court conditions, these dimensions may not be suitable. The teacher should be alert to the need for modifying the dimensions to whatever degree is necessary in order to ensure some quick, early success in rallying.

The smaller racket used in starter tennis is one device for making the game easier for small people. The cord and the lowered nets also contribute to this end. In addition, the deadened ball makes it possible for youngsters to avoid having to hit at difficult, high-bouncing balls. Moreover, restricting the size of the playing area so that youngsters are required to cover much less space than in regular tennis makes it possible for them to reach and "have a play on" most balls hit to them. All of these factors combine to make a small, compact form of lawn tennis which most youngsters find appealing, especially if the teacher presents the game to them in an efficient and enthusiastic way.

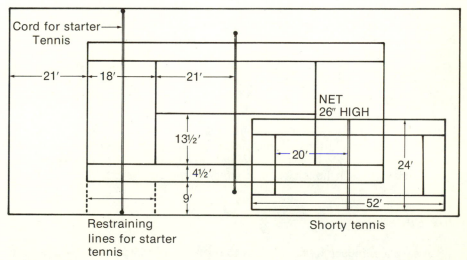

Figure 4–4   Left side of diagram shows placement of restraining lines and cord for starter tennis. Right side of diagram shows manner in which a shorty court can be fitted into a full-sized tennis court.

INSTRUCTION IN THE "LITTLE GAMES"

The Teacher's Methods

When teaching smaller versions of tennis, instruction should be as simple as possible. Beginners want and need simplicity, but they also want and need specific information on what to do. Yet, because their range of comprehension is limited, the teacher must not "talk too much." It is important, therefore, that the teacher reduce his teaching to the simplest terms: short, meaningful words, catchy phrases, tricky gimmicks and gadgets, various markings and checkpoints — all will be more effective than long explanations.

THE GRIPS

One of the most effective approaches to teaching the grips is to draw guide marks on the paddle handles and on the pupil's hands. An "X" is drawn on one of the broad sides of the handle (the back of the handle when the racket is "standing on edge" in the hitting position), and a dot is placed on the diagonal plane of the handle — that is, the plane between the top and the back of the handle.

An "X" is also drawn on the pupil's palms at the base of the first two fingers, and a dot is placed on the back of the hand on the first large knuckle. The "X" on the hand is then merely placed against the "X" on the paddle to get the forehand grip. The dot on the knuckle is placed directly over the dot on the handle for the backhand grip.

In this beginner's stage, the grip for the serve is exactly like that used for the forehand. Later, however, as players get more skillful, the service grip will be changed to make it resemble the backhand grip.

An important point to make here is that these "X"'s and dots are only reference points, and they should not command strict compliance. We permit and even suggest that pupils experiment and adjust their grips to find the positions that feel comfortable and with which they can best relate the position of the palm to the slant of the racket face.

THE STANCE

At the initial level of development, instruction on stance and footwork is minimal. Pupils are told simply to turn sideways and swing. If they have to move for the ball, they are told to adjust the size and the number of their steps so they can make a final step with the left foot for a forehand and the right foot for a backhand.

THE STROKES

A simple approach to the stroke is to break it down into only three parts: the backswing, the forward swing, and the finish position. Hitters are urged to make a straight backswing; the paddle goes straight back from the ready position, then

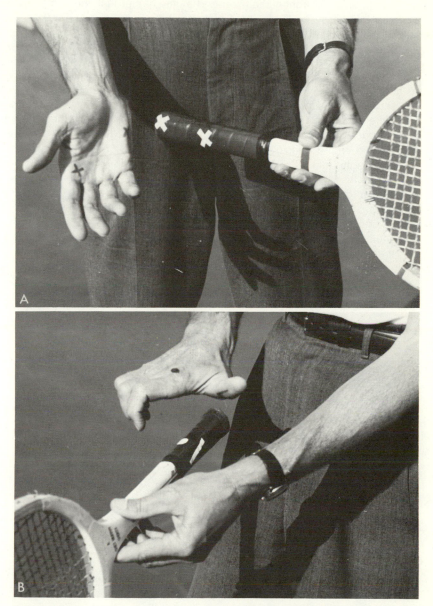

Figure 4-5   A simple way to teach the grips to beginners. Rackets or paddles are marked as shown; similar marks are placed on each pupil's hand. Pupils then simply match the marks, placing X's against X's, and lines against lines to get a proper grip.

moves down, forward, and upward into the ball. Contact occurs at a point approximately opposite the left hip. The paddle is guided through the contact point to the proper finish position, in front of the hitter and a little higher than the contact point.

The backhand may be taught as a simple elbow poke. The player starts his backswing by bending his arm at the elbow to move the paddle up and back across his lower chest. He loops the paddle down and around close to his left hip. He starts his forward swing from that point by swinging his arm from the shoulder while straightening his arm. Contact occurs at a point in advance of his right hip. He guides his paddle through the contact point to a high finish, in front of him.

The serve, too, is simplified. Pupils first trace the path of the paddle. It moves down past the right knee, up toward the top of the rear fence, in toward the body and behind the back, and up toward the ball ("knee–fence–back–ball"). They then practice tossing on the "fence" part of the swing. To make the hit they visualize a face painted on the ball and try to make contact "on the nose." After contact, they reach as far as they can toward the target.

These instructions provide pupils with a broad picture of the strokes that does not focus on a great deal of detail. The teacher does not insist on rigid conformity to his instructions, for within a certain degree of permissiveness, pupils will begin to get the general idea of the strokes and will be on their way toward developing stroke patterns that approximate good tennis form.

Chapter Five

GROUP INSTRUCTION

In school tennis instruction, teachers usually have to handle large numbers of students in limited court space. Only a few fortunate teachers have student assistants and are provided with a sufficient number of courts to conduct what can be considered an ideal learning situation. As a result, many new teachers feel frustrated. "What can we do?" they ask. "How much tennis can we teach with such arrangements? Surely these classes are too large for us to provide enough instruction and practice to maintain students' interest and enthusiasm."

One specific problem created by disproportionate student-teacher and student-court ratios is related to the matter of individual differences. No two students are alike, as teachers well know. Each students brings to class his own pattern of readiness, his own unique personality, temperament, and physique. How then can teachers of large groups make allowances for these differences? And how can they provide the individual attention that students require? In the short time allotted for each class meeting, how can they even observe all of their students in action, let alone offer advice and suggestions to each of them? If the teacher does succeed in devising a variety of methods for approaching students as individuals, he must then provide the play experience that students want and are entitled to after drill and practice. But how can this be arranged when there are far more students than can be accommodated in normal singles or doubles play?

Experienced teachers faced with the dilemma of too many players on too few courts have devised satisfactory solutions. Several formations and procedures used for this purpose will be described in this chapter. They are not offered as the definitive word on group instruction—teaching situations differ too much to permit even the most prestigious teacher to be that dogmatic. After all, the uniqueness of each teacher-learner relationship makes it unlikely that one teacher can arbitrarily adopt another's methods and use them successfully. But what works for one teacher may serve as a guide for another, providing a starting point from which may evolve new, different, and even better methods. The procedures described here are intended for that purpose. They are designed to provide a progression in student activity from the easy to the more difficult, from simple to complex. Definite levels of development are defined, and students are guided carefully through them, always working on skills that are within their levels of accomplishment. At each level, all students are busy in purposeful activity: some are hitting, some are tossing, others are retrieving or coaching. Always the teacher is able to be in at least reasonably close contact with the students.

SKILL CLASSIFICATION TESTS

In class situations, learning may be facilitated if members of the class are divided into small groups of equal or near equal ability. Although members of a class may all be beginners, there will be some difference in their ability to judge the flight of a ball or to time the swing of the racket to the flight of the ball. Differences in strength in the arms and hands of the players will also result in differences in the degree of racket control. Such differences become apparent if simple classification tests are used.

One such test measures the students' ability to rally against a wall or backboard. Each player stands behind a line 20 feet from the wall (handball and squash courts are excellent for this) and hits a ball against the wall as often as possible for one minute. The ball may be hit "on the fly" or after any number of bounces after it comes off the wall. Form is unimportant; the objective is simply to hit against the wall as often as possible in the time allotted.

Another simple classification test can be conducted in a gym or playground as well as on a court. Several students spread out far enough to move freely in all directions for three or four steps. At a starting signal, each tosses a ball up and taps it upward continually with the racket, meeting it in the air at about waist height. The wrist and forearm are turned clockwise for one hit and counterclockwise for the next (the ball is thus alternately hit with each side of the racket face). The number of successive hits is counted. After a miss the player immediately starts another air rally and begins a new count. The highest number of successive hits at the end of one minute is recorded.

Differences in innate ability or in experience and transfer from other activities will be shown by a wide range of scores on these tests. The class can then be divided into small homogeneous groups of two, three, or four players each on the

Figure 5-1 An air-juggle test for skill classification. The player taps the ball alternately with opposite sides of the racket face as many times as he can in one minute.

basis of these scores, and each group may be permitted to work separately from the others during the first few class meetings. Not all students will learn at the same rate, however, and it may be necessary to regroup the class after a few meetings.

PROBLEMS OF FORM

Every tennis teacher who works with groups faces the problems of deciding how much emphasis to place on form in stroking and how much value to attach to effectiveness when it is achieved without good form.

The wise tennis teacher does not overemphasize form in his teaching while ignoring effectiveness in his students' shots. He does not teach form for form's sake. It is hardly his desire to develop strokers with "good" form who are in fact erratic, inaccurate hitters. What he hopes for are players who can perform effectively at whatever level he determines the class objectives to be.

In group situations, differences in strength, in reach, in length of lever arm, in fluidity, in posture, and in other physical factors — and in mental factors as well — will appear. These differences will enable each student to develop his own individual version of the form being taught. We may say that each individual will add his own personal style. But as long as the general principles of stroking are adhered to — the principles the teacher is developing — he need not be alarmed or disturbed as style is added to form. In fact, it would be foolish for a teacher to attempt to make all group members hit exactly alike. Instead, the teacher must be alert to permit and even to encourage variations in style, for any natural tendencies are likely to be a surer and quicker way of getting the effectiveness he is seeking than are forced, stilted procedures. In short, a teacher should teach form for effectiveness while allowing for style.

STROKE INSTRUCTION

Despite some authorities' preference for "instant competition" as a means of introducing new students to the game, most experienced teachers feel that they can facilitate the learning process by offering instruction rather than "free play" as the first step in their methodology. Instruction is usually offered in progressive steps as students are guided through five levels of development: (1) learning the swing, (2) hitting a dropped ball, (3) hitting a tossed ball, (4) moving to hit a tossed ball, and (5) rallying. Students are cautioned to consider each level as only one step in the total plan, and they are made to understand that some degree of skill is required before they will be permitted to move on to the next level.

Building the Swing

When teaching the groundstrokes, most experienced instructors first have their students swing at imaginary balls at waist height conveniently alongside each student. For this activity, members of the group are spread out in the backcourt where they can swing toward the net. Swing practice is more meaningful if it is done in this realistic setting. Students stand 8 to 10 feet away from each other to prevent clashing rackets. They test their spacing by turning around while holding their rackets at arm's length at waist height. If the rackets do not touch, spacing is adequate. Teachers stand at the service line and swing in the same direction as the students. From their positions (backs to the students), they lead the group through practice of the swing. After making several swings to provide a model to follow, they walk among the students checking each one's swing and making appropriate suggestions.

In this primary stage of instruction, teachers must first address the group as a whole. They cannot immediately give individual attention to everyone in the group, nor can they take time to suggest individual variations in form and style. Instruction must be rather general in nature, stressing the broad outline of a stroke rather than a number of specific points. It will be enough if the students at first gain only a general impression of the stroke. Their attention should be directed to only the essential parts of it; work on other details will come later. Teachers must not talk too much. Students have not yet acquired a tennis vocabulary, and their range of comprehen-

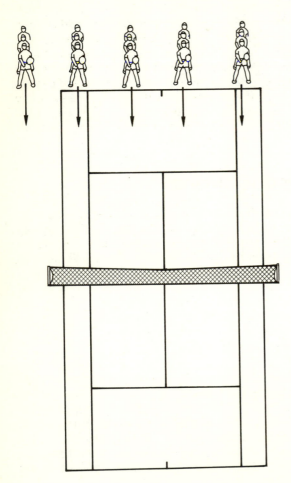

Figure 5-2 For swing practice with a large class and limited space, students are lined up in files of three along the baseline.

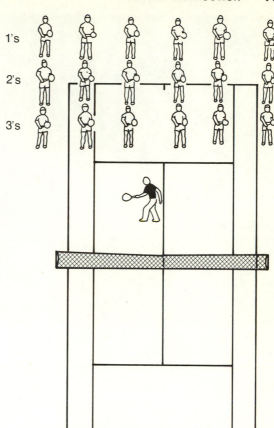

1's

2's

3's

Figure 5-3 Each file counts off from one to three, from the rear to the front. Those in the two front lines then take twice the number of steps forward as their count-off numbers to be in good position.

sion will be limited. Verbal instruction must be reduced to simple terms. Catchy words, distinctive phrases, interesting gimmicks and gadgets—these can be more effective than long explanations. "Swing along the line," "keep the racket on edge," "swing from fence to fence" are examples of the kinds of verbal cues students are likely to respond to.

Hitting a Dropped Ball

After sufficient time has passed for the majority of the group to develop acceptable form while swinging at imaginary balls, experienced teachers move on to the next level of development: hitting a dropped ball. This step is important and necessary because players will need to make a drop-and-hit time and time again in their practice and in their warm-ups for serious play.

A good method of teaching this feeder stroke is to have the class hit against the fence surrounding the court while working in pairs. One player stands about 10 feet

Figure 5-4 A diagram drawn on the court surface helps the teacher explain and demonstrate the proper path of the racket during the forward swing.

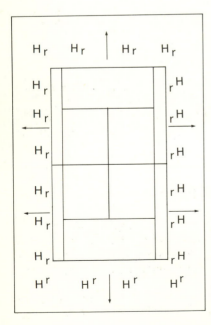

Figure 5-5 Drop-and-hit drill against fence. H = hitter; r = retriever.

away from the fence, drops the ball, and hits toward the fence. The other stands behind the hitter and retrieves the ball as it rebounds from the fence. Students alternate hitting and retrieving while the teacher moves along the line of the hitters to help them build acceptable form even when hitting dropped balls.

Hitting a Tossed Ball

The next step in the development of the stroke—hitting ·a tossed ball—introduces hitters to additional problems in stroking. They must now learn to time the backswing, the steps they take, and the forward swing to the oncoming ball. They must learn to make these moves in the proper sequence and with the rhythm that will permit a smooth, unhurried swing.

As in dropped-ball practice, students work in pairs, one tossing and the other

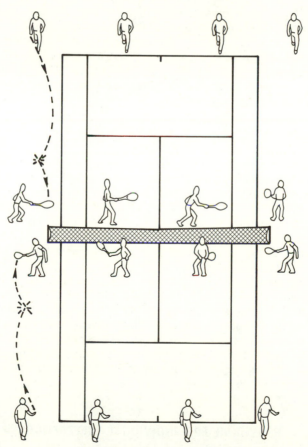

Figure 5–6 In tossed-ball practice, students work in pairs. The tosser stands about 10 feet away from rear fence. The hitter stands about three feet away from same side of net and hits ball back.

hitting. The tosser stands about 10 feet away from the rear fence, with his back toward it. The hitter stands about three feet from the net, on the same side as the tosser, and hits the ball back to his partner (Fig. 5–6). For some groups, it may be necessary to provide the tossers with targets; chalk marks or scuff marks on the court surface, in front of and to the right of each hitter, help him gauge his toss.

With very large classes in a limited space, students may work in groups of three or four. In such a plan, one student hits, one tosses, another retrieves, and, if necessary, still another acts as analyst and coach.

When any two students are able to hit with consistent accuracy, they are ready for instructions on moving to hit a tossed ball.

Moving to Hit a Tossed Ball

Court arrangements for this drill are different from those used in the previous exercise. Here, students will benefit if they are permitted to hit toward the net, for they can then relate their moves to actual play conditions. The tossers stand in a position close to the net in order to make hitters move in the backcourt area. Care must be taken to provide ample room for the hitters' movements. The tossers will make the hitters move forward for short balls and backward for deep ones, to the side for wide balls and away for close ones. Hitters are shown how to move; they are told to adjust the size and number of their steps in order to set themselves into an efficient hitting stance for each swing. Throughout this stage of development, the sequence is "move–stop–step–swing."

Rallying

The final stage in learning the groundstrokes is rallying. If the class is large and only a few courts are available, it will not be possible for the entire class to rally at the same time. With beginners, six players on a court is the maximum number that should be permitted both for safety reasons and for efficient learning. Almost always, therefore, "stations" must be designated at which most students continue to hit at tossed balls on certain courts, while only as many students as can safely do so rally across the net on other courts.

In the early stages of rallying, it may be best to permit students to stand a step or two inside the baseline. Either player may start a rally with a feeder stroke (a bounce-and-hit), and players attempt to rally (not to cause a "miss") by providing easy-to-handle first bounce shots for one another. Balls may be returned after any number of bounces, but the objective is to hit accurately enough to provide a one-bounce hit. When the teacher thinks any two students are ready for advancement, they are encouraged to hit harder and to play from the conventional rally location, one step behind the baseline.

PROVIDING FOR INDIVIDUAL DIFFERENCES

Not all students learn at the same rate. Often, an individual is thwarted by some particular point of form. When teachers notice this, they may provide special prac-

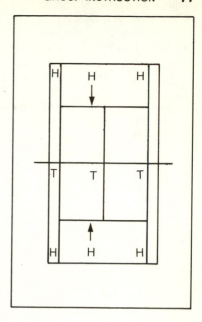

Figure 5-7   Rally across the net. H = hitter, T = tosser.

tice for that individual on that particular point of form. The implication of such special attention is, of course, that teachers must digress from group plans and somehow apply several individual plans instead, each adapted to the needs of individual "problem" learners. Some useful techniques for accomplishing this task are described here.

Using the Whole and Part Methods

Learning theory suggests that many skills are learned best by the whole method and should be broken down into parts only when the whole is too complex for the learner. When conducting a lesson in the groundstrokes, for example, teachers should stress the timing and coordination of the whole swing. They will then be permitting those students who are capable of grasping the move to start their learning at the point most beneficial to them. They will not be holding back fast learners, which would occur if the teachers were to require the students to work on separate points that they were already capable of combining into a whole swing.

Teachers must notice the slow learners, for whom the whole swing is too complicated. The swing must be broken down into parts small enough for them to understand, and they must be given the individual attention they need as soon as it is convenient for the teachers to do so. This is best done by permitting students to work apart from the larger class in small groups on whatever parts of the swing bother them. Some may need to start with their rackets back, fixed in the backswing position, while they stand sideways. Others may need to start with their rackets held out in front while in the sideways stance. Still others may be capable of making the full swing but may need work on judgment or timing. By assigning students to work on specific details at special stations, individuals may work at their own rates and on their own levels, under the watchful eye of the instructor, the assistant, or some class member who has already mastered the particular part of the stroke. As students solve their specific problems they may be permitted to join the total group again.

The Range of Correctness

Differences in form must be expected among students in any group. Differences in physique — in height, strength, reach, and flexibility — are likely to cause strokes to differ. We may say that these differences are permissible if they fall within a certain range, which can be thought of as a "range of correctness." Any variation in a particular point of form that does not cause a marked change in the total pattern of the stroke should be permitted, provided the player can hit effectively that way. If, for example, a player's backswing differs slightly from what the teacher prefers to see (most teachers have a favorite "look"), it may not be wise to suggest a change if the player is still able to bring the racket into the right position at impact. In this way, teachers allow for differences in form resulting from differences in physique and muscular development.

GIVING INDIVIDUAL ATTENTION

The use of stations at which students work on separate parts of the strokes under the supervision of the instructor or assistants has already been described. By moving from station to station or by having players move to the teacher's station, it may be possible to make personal contact with every individual in the class. In the latter method, players move to another station to make room for classmates after the teacher has observed and made comments. If the group is large, however, the amount of individual attention teachers can give personally, even in this way, is limited. They can, however, provide another kind of personalized instruction by using the buddy system.

In the buddy system, students work in pairs and coach each other. This arrangement requires that the students be instructed in and have knowledge of specific checkpoints relating to the mechanics of strokes. This is not usually a difficult matter, for even a 10-year-old boy can recognize whether a racket is standing on edge or not, after he has seen the teacher demonstrate it in his own swing and in the swing of other students. "Racket head up," "elbow bent," "point toward the fence" — these are examples of the kinds of simple expressions often used by group teachers in the buddy system. The system permits teachers to multiply their instruction by the number of buddies coaching at any particular time.

PROVIDING ACTUAL PLAY EXPERIENCE (Figs. 5–8 to 5–17)

After several periods of instruction, teachers must provide the actual play experience students want and should have. But what kind of play can be arranged for a large group? Certainly, the group cannot have full-scale competition. Perhaps the

Text continued on page 82.

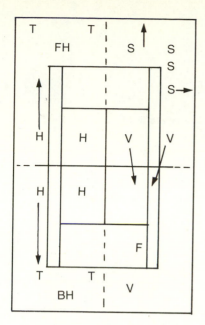

Figure 5-8 Stations on one court: FH = forehand; BH = backhand; S = serves; V = volleys; F = feeder; H = hitter; T = tosser.

Figure 5-9 Drop-and-hit to target man. Tossed balls are hit to tosser. H = hitter; T = target man and tosser.

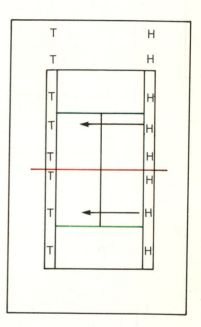

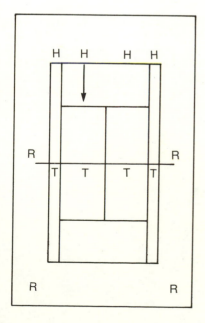

Figure 5-10 Tossed balls are hit across net. H = hitter; T = tosser; R = retriever.

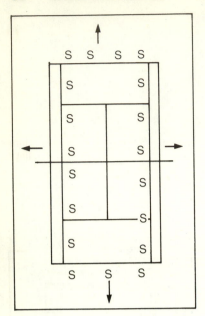

Figure 5–11 Serve against fence.

Figure 5–12 Serve across net. Groups serve on signal and take turns. S = server; R = retriever; X = players waiting turn.

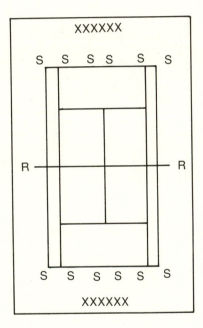

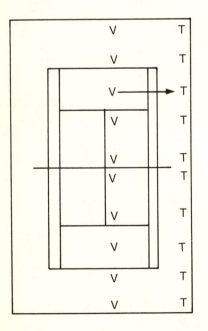

Figure 5–13 Volleying a tossed ball. V = volleyer; T = tosser.

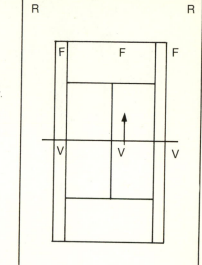

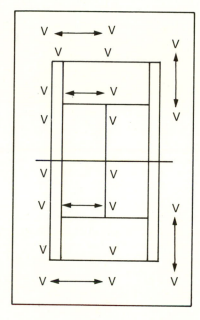

Figure 5-14 Volleying a ball driven by feeder. V = volleyer; F = feeder; R = retriever.

Figure 5-15 Partners volley to each other. V = volleyer.

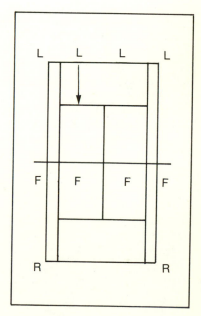

Figure 5-16 Lobbing a ball hit by feeder. L = lobber; F = feeder; R = retriever.

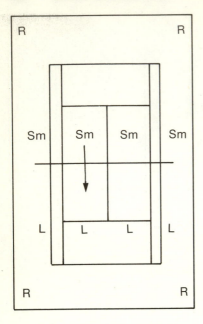

Figure 5-17 Overhead smash; smashing a lobbed ball. Sm = smasher; L = lobber; R = retriever.

best that teachers can do is simply to provide drills that are similar to actual competitive play situations. Again, assigning stations for practice and play enables them to do this.

Segments of a particular court are designated as stations, or if space permits, each court may be designated as a separate station. Several members of the class are assigned to a station to practice on one particular skill, or on one particular shot. One group on a court may be practicing forehand cross-court shots, while another on the same court may be hitting backhand cross-courts. At another station, students may be making and returning serves, while at a fourth station other students may be practicing going to the net and hitting passing shots against a net man. Meanwhile, other members of the class—those ready to play—may be permitted to play on the remaining courts. The small groups are rotated from time to time so that eventually every player is assigned to each of the stations and to the full courts for play. During all of these drills students are working at stations most appropriate to their levels of ability. Meanwhile, teachers move from station to station, dividing their time carefully, so that all hitters get some individual attention.

Chapter Six

STROKE INSTRUCTIONS FOR BEGINNERS

We have already referred to differences in style and form that are seen among top-flight players. No two of them swing exactly alike. All of them differ somewhat on such specific points as the length of the swing, the amount of wrist action, and the extent to which the body is used to apply force. They differ, too, in a general sense, in the degree of fluidity in their stroke patterns. Some have long, fluent strokes; others have short, compact ones. Some appear to be making an effort to hit hard; others seem to be much more relaxed. Noting these differences, inexperienced teachers often become uncertain about the kind of form to teach. If so many different styles work for so many different players, what is best for the students in their groups and classes?

In actuality, instead of complicating teachers' tasks, these differences make their jobs easier. Obviously, teachers should not insist that all the details in swings be made exactly alike by all players. Not everyone has the same degree of flexibility between joints, or the same amount of suppleness and dexterity in body movement, nor even the same degree of strength for racket control. Consequently, even under the strict guidance and control of the most exacting teacher, class members will not (and should not) play with identical styles. To overlook individual variations that make strokes appear to be different would be a serious error on the teacher's part.

Of course, certain questions still remain after teachers have provided and allowed for individual differences in physique, temperament, attitude, interest, and general athletic ability. What *should* they teach? What kind of form should they start with? What is the basic pattern or model around which they should permit and even encourage individual variations?

In answering these questions teachers should consider the mechanics of tennis discussed in Chapter 2. Strokes built around the principles of mechanics are almost certain to be good. If students are first given the general pattern of a swing, they will soon make minor adjustments as they adapt the pattern to their own abilities according to what feels comfortable and seems to work for them. The swing may continue to be mechanically sound; if it permits efficient and economical motion, it must be considered good form.

A TEACHING SYSTEM

The kinds of strokes and the lesson sequence described in this chapter are based on a logical application of mechanics and learning principles. Together they produce a certain kind of form, a certain look, but form is stressed only as a means to effective play and not as an end in itself. Simplicity and efficiency are the key-notes.

Instruction is offered on specific parts of the swing in the following order: (1) the grip; (2) the waiting stance; (3) the turn and backswing; (4) the step and forward swing; and (5) the follow-through and finish. The first two of these are static, fixed starting positions from which the swing is begun. The last three are woven into a fluid swing with smooth, continuous motion.

Students should attempt to imitate the correct form of a swing in massed swing drills (or privately, in individual work) as described in the preceding chapter. After at least a reasonable degree of proper form is developed, the class (or individual) should be guided through the levels of development described in Chapter 5: stroking a dropped ball, stroking a tossed ball, moving to stroke a tossed ball, and lastly, rallying. Such a sequence provides step-by-step advancement from simple to more difficult drills. Conscientious teachers can modify the degree of difficulty at each level so that the learning tasks are within the range of accomplishment of most students.

In elementary instruction, the teacher need be concerned with only the basic strokes of the game: the forehand and backhand drives, the serve, and the forehand and backhand volleys. Lobs and smashes, half-volleys, drop shots, and even slices off the groundstrokes can be considered supplementary shots that players should be introduced to only when they are ready to move into the intermediate level of play.

The Forehand Groundstroke

Stroke instruction must often begin with the teacher distinguishing between certain terms that can be confusing to most beginners. A ball stroked from the hitter's right side is called a forehand; one from the left side, a backhand. A ball stroked after it has bounced is called a groundstroke ("the ball hits the ground, then you stroke it"); a ball stroked before it bounces is called a volley. There are forehand and backhand groundstrokes and forehand and backhand volleys. Experienced teachers begin with the forehand groundstroke because for most students it is the easiest stroke to learn and therefore is the stroke most likely to motivate them to continue their practice exercises.

THE GRIP

Because sizes and shapes of hands vary—as do the sizes and shapes of handles—one must conclude that there is more than one correct way to hold the racket. Teachers cannot expect all pupils to position their hands precisely in the same places on the various planes and edges of the racket handle. Instead, students should be allowed to experiment and to make *slight* adjustments, if necessary, to make their grips feel comfortable and adequate.

Figure 6-1 For class demonstration purposes, the swing is broken down into four parts: (A) the waiting stance, (B) the turn and backswing, (C) the step and forward swing, and (D) the follow-through and finish.

Figure 6-2   The forehand grip is often described as a shake-hands grip. (From Chet Murphy, *Advanced Tennis,* Dubuque, Iowa: Wm. C. Brown Company, 1970, p. 2.)

Students will recognize reference points from which they can make adjustments if they simply shake hands with the handle. If done properly, the large knuckles of the first and second fingers are placed directly behind the handle, not under it nor on top of it. The fingers and the thumb are wrapped around the handle. The first and second fingers are separated and the thumb rests in the space between them. The handle of the racket passes diagonally across the palm of the hand from the base of the first finger to the corner of the palm.

THE WAITING STANCE

The stroke begins from the typical athletic waiting stance, with the body facing the net, the feet spread, and the knees bent for good balance. The left hand supports the racket at its throat, and the right hand is on the handle. The racket slants slightly upward and away from the body, and its face is perpendicular to the ground (standing on edge).

THE TURN AND BACKSWING

The backswing and the turn to the sideways hitting stance are made simultaneously. The turn may be made either by pivoting on the right foot or by stepping around with both feet. To make the backswing, the player releases the racket from his left hand and with his right hand carries it straight back toward the rear fence. He turns his shoulders clockwise as his arm moves back and he keeps his elbow down and fairly close to his side. He bends his wrist back slightly during the backswing, but he keeps his hand and racket face in the edge-down position.

As his racket begins to point toward the rear fence, he makes a *slight* backward, downward, circular motion with his forearm to place the racket slightly below waist height.

THE STEP AND FORWARD SWING

As his racket goes into its circular motion, the player steps toward the net with his left foot and turns his hips and shoulders in a counterclockwise direction. His racket, meanwhile, changes direction; it is made to move forward and upward into an imaginary ball at waist height opposite his left hip.

THE FOLLOW-THROUGH AND FINISH

The player guides his racket through the imaginary contact point by moving his arm upward and forward toward an imaginary target straight ahead (his upper body has now begun to face the net).

The swing ends with his racket in front of him and a bit higher than the imaginary point of contact. Here, too, his racket is in the edge-down position, as it was throughout the swing.

ADDITIONAL TEACHING POINTS

For imaginary low balls, the downward circular motion at the end of the back-swing is exaggerated. In addition, the knees must be bent to prevent the racket face from getting much below the hitting hand. For imaginary high balls, the major adjustment is in the angle of the arm at the shoulder socket, but the elbow may be bent more and the wrist cocked more than for lower balls.

For imaginary wide balls, students take two or three steps toward the right sideline. For close balls, they move toward the left sideline. In each case, the steps should be adjusted so that the swing can begin as the player finally steps with the left foot toward an imaginary net.

Figure 6–3 A hitter is shown practicing a bounce-and-hit against the backstop. Here she is able to gauge her bounce accurately and to adjust her left-foot step for any misdirected bounces. In the fourth frame she is shown holding the finish position, posing on balance. Balance is one of the keys to accurate hitting, and it is seen best in the finish of the stroke. If she is unable to pose on balance, quite probably it is because she did not step properly and had to make adjustments with the arm, wrist, or elbow.

HITTING THE BALL

After having had sufficient time and practice to develop acceptable stroke patterns when swinging at imaginary balls, students should be permitted to move on to the next level of development: bouncing and hitting the ball. For convenience and efficiency, balls should be hit against a fence. While facing the fence in the ready position, the player starts his backswing and then drops a ball slightly in front of and to the right of his location. As the ball bounces he steps with his left foot and completes the stroke.

Teachers must decide when students have made enough progress to warrant their moving on to the next level of development: hitting a ball tossed by a partner. The procedures used at this and the remaining levels of instruction are described in the chapter on group methods (Chapter 5).

In all hitting exercises, students must be reminded to look at the ball. The action at contact may be too fast to permit them to actually see the ball on the racket, but they are likely to hit more solidly if they *try* to see it there.

In the early stages of learning, students must be taught to adjust the speed of their backswings to the speed of the oncoming ball. When hitting at a slow ball, the backswing can be slow. When hitting at a fast ball, it must be faster. In either case, the transition from backswing to forward swing can be made smoothly by using the circular motion described earlier.

Control of direction comes from proper timing. To hit straight ahead, the ball should be met at a point opposite the left hip, or approximately so (the proper point will vary slightly among players as their grips vary). To hit to the left, the ball should be met sooner (closer to the net). To hit to the right, the contact point is farther back from the net. These adjustments in the timing of the swing enable the hitter to have his racket face pointing toward the target at impact. If, in addition, he is able to move the racket along a line toward the target, he is likely to develop a good degree of accuracy.

During the early part of the forward swing, the racket must be adjusted so that it is slanted properly at impact. It may be slanted markedly skyward (opened) for a very low ball, slanted to a lesser degree for a waist-high ball, and possibly slanted downward (closed) for a face-high ball.

Students should be encouraged to do more than simply follow through on their strokes; we urge them to guide their rackets along the intended line of flight of the ball. We demonstrate and explain how this is done: the elbow and the lower arm are made to move past the right hip, past the belt buckle, and away from the body in the direction of the shot.

In the early stages of learning, students should be urged to pose on balance in the finish position for a count of two before recovering to the waiting position. By trying to pose, they learn to hit with good balance; they learn to make the proper adjustments in footwork, especially with the left-foot step as they swing. In other words, they learn to place themselves into a good hitting stance.

The Backhand Groundstroke

Many experienced teachers consider the backhand to be one of the easiest strokes to teach. This is not to say it is one of the easiest shots to make, however. Hit-

Figure 6–4 Balls laid out on the court as shown provide visual reference for a pupil learning to adjust his timing to vary the direction of his shots. To hit cross-court to his left, he makes contact above the first ball (the ball closest to the net). To hit straight ahead, he makes contact later, above the middle ball. To hit to the opposite side, he meets the ball still later, above the last ball.

ting on the left side of the body is an unnatural movement that makes the shot more difficult than the forehand for most beginners. Nonetheless, the shape of the stroke, the look of the swing, can usually be built rather quickly and easily. The learner begins with uncomplicated movements: he brings his hitting hand back and in toward his left hip by bending the hitting arm at the elbow. Then, with a karate-like action, he straightens his arm and swings his hand out and away from the hip as if to strike an object a sharp blow with the leading edge of his hand. This is a simplified version of the backhand, and every learner can immediately make such a swing. For the more sophisticated swing that the teacher hopes to develop, the student must learn to turn the hips and shoulders, to transfer his weight, to lengthen the arm action, and to time his swing to the oncoming ball. After a few minutes practice at the simple backhand swing, most students are ready for more detailed instructions to build the sophisticated version.

THE GRIP

For backhands, the hitting hand should be moved counterclockwise from the forehand grip so that the large knuckle at the base of the first finger lies either on the top plane of the handle or on the bevel, to the right of it. The fingers are wrapped around the handle, and the inner finger is spread slightly from the middle finger. The thumb may be extended diagonally up the back of the handle, or it may be wrapped around the handle. As on the forehand, the grip is firm throughout the entire stroke, and the wrist is cocked just enough to prevent the racket from dangling loosely on low balls.

The critical point about the backhand grip is the position of the wrist at contact. If it is in front of the handle, the hitter can only pull the racket toward the ball. If it is on top of the handle, or nearly so, he will have more of a feeling of pushing the racket through the contact point. This provides more strength and therefore more racket control (resulting in better ball control), along with more force in the swing (when needed). Consequently, students should place their hands near enough to the top of the handle to move the wrist away from the front of it.

THE WAITING STANCE

As with the forehand, the backhand begins from the conventional waiting stance described earlier. The player returns to that stance immediately after finishing each shot in order to be equally ready to turn to the left for backhands or to the right for forehands. The forehand grip is used in the waiting stance by most players because it is the more natural of the two grips.

THE TURN AND BACKSWING

The turn to the hitting stance is made either by pivoting on the left foot or by stepping around with both feet. The left hand supports the racket during the turn,

Figure 6–5   For demonstration the backhand groundstroke is broken down into four parts: (A) the ready position, (B) the turn and backswing, (C) the step and forward swing, and (D) the follow-through and finish.

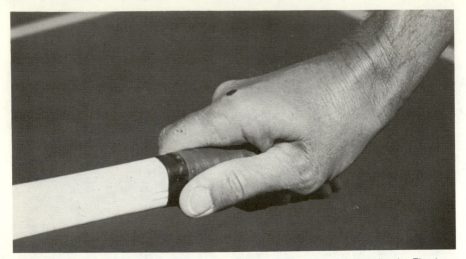

Figure 6-6 The backhand grip may be described as a "palm down" grip. The large knuckle at the base of the first finger is on the top plane of the handle. The thumb is shown here extending along the back plane, but the hitter may wrap it around the handle if he prefers.

allowing the right hand to be moved to the backhand grip.* The hips and shoulders turn in a counterclockwise direction while the racket is carried back toward the rear fence with arm and elbow action (the upper arm moves at the shoulder, the lower arm at the elbow). When the right hand grip is secure the left hand is removed from the racket. During the backswing, there is a natural turn of the forearm, wrist, and hand that causes the racket face to open slightly.

THE STEP AND FORWARD SWING

The forward swing begins with the player stepping toward the net with his right foot. As the step is made, his hitting hand makes a downward circular loop close to the left hip, from which point the racket is swung forward and upward into an imaginary ball at waist height. The arm is swung from the shoulder, the elbow begins to straighten, and the shoulders are turned to the right as the racket comes into the contact zone, an area between the belt buckle and a few inches forward of the right hip.

THE FOLLOW-THROUGH AND FINISH

Here, as on the forehand, the hitter will benefit from finishing with the racket high and in front, for he can then check the line and plane of his swing and the position of the racket. It should have moved along an imaginary line toward the imagi-

---

*A two-handed backswing is necessary because in actual play the left hand is needed to support the racket while the right hand changes from the conventional waiting grip (the forehand) to the backhand.

nary target and in an upward plane as it passed through the contact area. The racket face should be standing on edge (or nearly so).

HITTING THE BALL

As on the forehand, students will benefit from first hitting dropped balls toward a fence. Here the drop is made while facing the fence. The turn and backswing and step and forward swing follow immediately afterward.

When hitting a tossed ball, the player should start the backswing as soon as he determines the direction of the oncoming ball. The player must adjust (1) the speed of the backswing to the speed of the ball, (2) the additional steps needed to move into position to hit wide balls and close balls, and (3) the final right-foot step as the forward swing begins. The hitter tries to pose on balance in the finish position to check the accuracy of the final step.

At impact, the racket is held firmly enough to keep the handle parallel to the ground, or nearly so (except for high balls, where the raised arm makes the racket slant upward). For low balls, the player lowers the racket by bending his knees. For high balls, the racket is raised by changing the angle of the arm at the shoulder socket.

Contact should occur at a point approximately opposite the right shoulder, but students should be allowed to experiment to find the point that is natural and comfortable for them. The swing must be timed so that the elbow straightens at this point, or possibly even a little before contact.

The hand, wrist, and forearm are used to adjust the slant of the racket for balls at various heights. For low balls the racket should be opened slightly; for higher balls it should be standing on edge or closed slightly.

PLACING THE BALL

The hitter directs the ball to either the right or left by changing the timing of his swing from that used for straight-ahead shots. To hit to his right, he meets the ball sooner in terms of the body reference points mentioned earlier; to hit to his left, he hits later in terms of those points.

In addition, the player should move his racket toward the target as it passes through the contact area. He can do so simply by guiding his hitting hand toward the target and by timing his body turn properly. At impact, his upper body should be sideways to the net. It should not begin to face the net until after contact; otherwise, the racket will be pulled across the intended line of flight of the ball, with a less accurate shot as the likely result.

The Serve

For learners with previous throwing experience, serving is often the most natural of all strokes. For this reason, teachers should describe and demonstrate the similarity between the serving motion and an exaggerated overarm throwing motion.

Students should be permitted to use whatever throwing ability they have in the serving action. A convenient expression used in this approach to service instruction is: "Throw the ball up, then 'throw' the racket at the ball."

Not every learner has previous throwing experience to relate to, however. For those who have not, serving is often a complicated action and teachers may have to offer more detailed instruction immediately after the brief demonstration of the similarity between serving and throwing. In keeping with the learning theory discussed in Chapter 3, the "whole" method of instruction should be used first; the part method should be used only with those who need it.

THE GRIP AND STANCE

For beginners we recommend the forehand grip, but we suggest that the grip should be changed toward the Continental when the players reach the intermediate level.

Students will quickly learn the stance if they are directed to place the toes of both feet against an imaginary line drawn through their location toward the target. The front foot should point toward the right net post. The rear foot may point in whatever direction affords most comfort, but it should be spread far enough from the front foot to permit and encourage a shift of weight during the forward swing. The body weight should rest mainly on the rear foot.

THE SWING

The swing starts from the "aiming" position, in which the racket face is at chest height, pressed gently against the ball, standing on edge, and pointing toward the target. The wrist and forearm are adjusted so that the knuckles of the first two fingers are up. From this position the player swings his racket down past the right knee, up toward the rear fence, forward to and behind the back, then up and forward into the ball. For brevity, this swing is described as "knee–fence–back–ball." The ball is tossed on the "fence" part of the swing and the body weight is transferred to the front foot after the toss. The right foot swings across the line *after* the hit to support the body weight on the follow-through. The racket moves through the contact point and finishes in front of or to the left of the left knee.

After students get accustomed to the knee–fence–back–ball routine, they are ready for more detailed instructions. They may be shown how to raise the elbow while raising the racket during the "fence" part of the swing. This movement enables them to keep the hitting hand in the knuckles-up position used at the start of the swing. This is a simpler and more efficient swing than one in which the forearm is turned clockwise to direct the racket face skyward during the early part of the swing. We prefer to see the racket face and the palm of the hitting hand face skyward only during the "back" part of the swing, when the player bends his elbow to lower the racket behind his back.

Figure 6-7 The full-swing serve may be taught by guiding the students through the following check points: knee–fence–back–ball. When they learn to trace this pattern with the racket, they are told to throw the ball up on the "fence" part of the swing, and to "throw" the racket at the ball.

COORDINATING THE TOSS WITH THE SWING

After learning to trace the path of the racket, students must be shown how to co-ordinate the toss with the swing. While in the aiming position, they hold the ball firmly in the fingers and press it gently against the racket strings. The swing starts with the ball and racket moving down together. The left hand (with the ball) is moved toward the left thigh and then, without pausing, is moved vertically upward to make the toss. The ball is released at about face height and is thrown straight up from its release point to a point slightly higher than the server can reach with a fully extended arm.

Meanwhile, the racket is carried through the knee–fence–back–ball positions described earlier. The swing is timed to make the racket meet the ball just as it starts to descend from the peak of its arc. Just before contact the wrist and forearm are adjusted to make the palm face the net. This position lets the player place his racket directly behind the ball, on the nose of an imaginary face. The racket is guided through the contact point toward the target area for as long and as far as the server can comfortably reach. It will then naturally move to his left as his right side comes around, to finish alongside his left leg.

PLACING THE SHOT

An imaginary face on the ball is used to provide reference points for the proper placement of the racket. Hitting on the chin results in a high shot; on the forehead, a low shot. Contact at a point between the head and chin results in a trajectory somewhere between high and low.

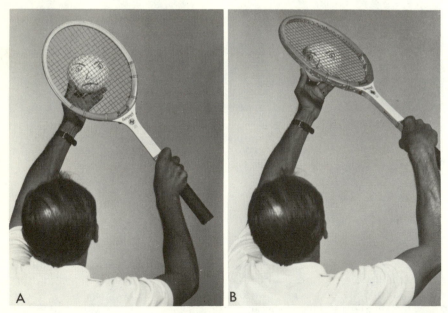

Figure 6–8   Imagining a face on the ball often helps a learner place the racket properly at contact. For a flat serve the racket meets the ball on the nose. For a simple spin serve the racket makes contact either on the nose or on the left eye, and the hitter immediately curls his wrist (as is shown in the second photo) to brush the racket up and over the left eye.

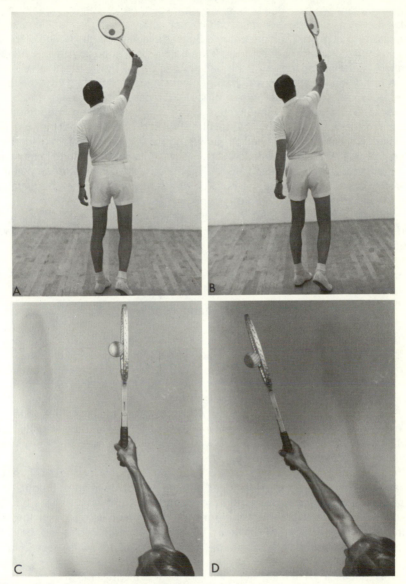

Figure 6–9 Subtle changes in the position of the hitting hand just before contact enable the server to change the direction of his serve. In the first frame the hand faces the net, which enables the server to place the racket directly behind the ball. The result is a flat shot directed straight ahead. In the second frame the edge of the hand is leading. The racket thus makes contact on the right side of the ball. The result is a slice, and the ball veers off to the left. Changes in the placement of the toss enable the hitter to control the height of his shot. In the fourth frame, the ball can be seen farther in front of the player than it is in the third frame — a position that enables him to slant the racket over the ball more adeptly and thus hit it in more of a downward trajectory.

At this point we remind students that not every serve need be a good one; only one out of every two tries must go in. We suggest, therefore, that students learn to use the first try as a guide for the second try, correcting the reason for the miss if the first one does not go in. The correction to be made is either in the timing of the wrist action or in the placement of the toss. If the ball is tossed too far forward, the serve will almost certainly be too low. If the ball is tossed back too far, the shot will be too high. A few practice serves in which students try to toss straight up from the release point are usually sufficient to correct all but the most serious tossing errors.

As we have said, a convenient reference point is "on the nose." Beginners must learn to time the hand action as the racket comes into the ball so that they can place the racket on that point on the ball. If bad timing permits the racket tip to lead at impact, the racket will hit the forehead of the imaginary face. If the hitting hand leads at impact, contact will be on the chin. By being attentive to these reference points and by relating the hand action to the position of the racket at contact, beginners will learn to place the racket on the ball properly.

Hitting on the nose provides a flat serve with little or no spin on it. Such a serve is adequate for less adept beginners. More accomplished beginners, however, should begin to practice a spin serve, in which the racket brushes over the left eye of the imaginary face. The technique for this serve is described in Chapter 7.

The Forehand Volley

In the beginning stages of volley instruction, we permit students to use the normal forehand and backhand grips already learned for groundstrokes. We suggest, however, that players must eventually learn to use the Continental grip, because its position between the forehand and the backhand obviates the need to make a change for forehand and backhand volleys.

Even at the beginner's level, players will not always have time while volleying to turn or to step into a sideways hitting stance. Instead, they will occasionally have to hit while facing the net. For this reason, volley instruction is best begun by placing students in a posture facing the net.

In the waiting position, the racket is held in the regular forehand grip and the left hand supports the racket at the throat, holding its face up to chest height. To start the swing, the left hand releases the racket and the right wrist is bent back and cocked, while a simple arm motion carries the racket face up and back to place it behind the intended point of contact. The backswing is stopped just before the racket points straight back away from the hitter. From that point it is pressed forward into the ball.

When necessary, the hitter steps with his left foot as he starts his forward swing. The left-foot step is made in whatever direction is necessary to reach the ball or to get away from it. There are times, however, when he may not have to step to volley. When the ball is close to him, he can often simply turn his hips and shoulders to his right and hit from that position, with his feet facing the net. The ball should be hit as far in front as the laid-back wrist permits the player to do so comfortably. The forward motion stops immediately after contact, and the racket is brought quickly into the ready position.

The ball is directed toward its target by adjustments made in the hitter's wrist and elbow. A fairly straight wrist at contact and an early contact point will direct the

Figure 6–10 A simplified version of the forehand volley. Note the short backswing and follow-through, with a minimum of body rotation.

ball to the hitter's left. A substantially laid-back wrist will steer the ball to his right. The elbow plays a minor role in left-to-right control of the shot (it is more important in up-and-down control).

For a chest-high ball, the forearm should be nearly perpendicular to the ground. If instead the elbow is raised to cause the forearm to slant diagonally, the ball will be hit downward. For higher balls, of course, this would be appropriate. If the ball is at waist height or lower, however, the elbow should be down.

Figure 6-11 A simplified version of the backhand volley. Note that body rotation is minimal and that the hitting arm provides what little force is needed for this shot.

The Backhand Volley

In elementary volley instruction, we permit the student to use the backhand grip learned earlier for groundstrokes. For his first moments of practice at this level, we let him take that grip even while in the waiting position. Soon, however, we encourage him to wait with the forehand grip and have him practice changing to the backhand as he makes his backswing.

The player begins his backswing by turning his upper body to his left while moving the hitting arm at the shoulder and bending it at the elbow. With this arm, body, and elbow action, he carries the racket back toward his left shoulder, stopping the racket just before it touches his shoulder.

During the swing, his wrist is cocked and laid-back, and his elbow is down, in order to keep his racket head slightly above his wrist. Meanwhile, his left hand supports the racket at the throat to help in making the backswing and to permit him to change grips if necessary. He releases his left hand as he starts his forward swing.

The forward swing begins with a short motion of the arm at the shoulder and elbow to move the racket forward into the ball. The wrist and elbow are adjusted to provide the proper racket angle on the ball at contact, which occurs at a point slightly in advance of the right shoulder. The swing ends immediately after contact, and the racket is returned quickly to the ready position.

If the ball is comfortably and conveniently alongside the player, he merely pivots in place to hit, as described. When it is farther from him, he pivots on the left foot and steps with the right to reach it.

The reader will note that we have stressed stepping with the left foot for forehands and with the right foot for backhands. We do this for two reasons:

1. Although a volleyer often can reach a ball by stepping with either the right or left foot, a crossover step with the foot that is farther from the ball provides maximum reach for wide balls.

2. When an elementary player is permitted to make a choice of either a right- or left-foot step, he usually reacts slowly — more slowly than he would if prepared for only one step. Thus we stress stepping with the foot that is farther from the ball. The hitter steps across his body and toward a sideline for wide balls; he steps in the opposite direction, toward the other sideline, for close balls.

Chapter Seven

STROKE INSTRUCTION FOR INTERMEDIATE AND ADVANCED PLAYERS

In group tennis instruction at the intermediate and advanced levels of play, students come to class with stroke patterns already established. The teacher's job is to build on these patterns, to correct faults in them, and to encourage continued use of them if they are sound and within the range of acceptable form. It is not necessary nor is it advisable to break down every student's stroke and to start building from the ground up. Nor is it advisable to stress specific total form on each stroke; students should not play in total imitation of one form. Instead, each individual should be permitted to use his own strokes; at the same time, he should be advised to make his strokes more efficient by making whatever corrections or additions the teacher considers appropriate.

In stroke analysis teachers should judge what they see in class against what they know to be mechanically sound. They must recognize certain variations that are being used effectively by various individuals. Certain deviations from prescribed form are permissible differences—unless these variations are so different as to preclude the eventual development of good form.

It is difficult in a broad discussion to determine when a particular variation should be permitted and when it should be changed. Each variation should be considered separately and a judgment made as to its effect on the outcome of the shot. In addition, the potential of each particular student for making a change should be assessed. Students who want to play only social tennis and who are not committed to serious practice and training are not likely to want to—nor are they likely to be able to—change certain techniques that now seem to be working for them. For such students teachers must assume more permissive attitudes than they would for players who aspire to bigger things in the game.

THE TEACHING METHOD

Even though most students in classes at the intermediate level have had previous stroke instruction, very likely they have not established completely satisfactory patterns that will be consistently effective at the higher level of play. Consequently, intermediate and advanced instruction should begin with a review of material covered earlier in elementary classes. The logical way to provide review for an entire class is to use mass swing drills similar to those described earlier. These drills can be performed in the first few class meetings. All the basic strokes can be quickly covered, perhaps even as many as three or four on the same day, depending on the length of the class period.

When reviewing the basic strokes, teachers should stress only the common fundamentals—points of form seen in the strokes of most top-flight players. These points are common among good players because they provide an efficient and effective way to hit; in other words, they work for most people. For this reason students should be urged to incorporate these points of form into their stroke patterns if they have not already done so, and to work to develop and refine them if they are already familiar with them.

While teaching common fundamentals, teachers should look for common faults. In a large group it is not unusual to find several students having the same particular problem or committing the same particular error. For these students, a modified group approach is usually necessary. In this approach the teacher determines what point (or points) of form certain individuals need to improve. The students may then be placed into a separate group where they may be offered instruction and practice specific to their needs. This can be done immediately after the review of fundamentals, or it can come after the teacher has seen the student in realistic practice.

Students in intermediate classes are already "players"; they can already rally or at least begin the rally. Consequently, instruction at this level should be offered mainly through rallying practice. Tossed-ball drills (as described in Chapter 5) should be provided when necessary, but they should not be the main item offered to intermediate and advanced players. Rallying for practice and playing for practice are certainly more meaningful and usually more productive and economical of time and effort.

In addition to offering group instruction as described earlier, teachers should provide as much individual instruction as possible. Because players at advanced levels have different needs, the approach to each student should be personalized. One player, for example, may need to work on control, while another may need to develop more power. Certain players may lack the strength required to use a Continental, no-change grip for volleys, while others may feel perfectly comfortable with such a grip. Some players may have developed rigid, formalized strokes that now must be made more flexible; others may be "style" conscious and overlook the basic points of good form.

Tennis teachers must plan the entire tennis unit and develop a sequence and time table that enable them to complete the unit in the amount of class time and the number of class meetings allotted. They must determine how much time to spend on each stroke and shot by listing the number of items to be covered, by noting the amount of time available, and by estimating the amount of time required to cover them adequately. Teachers must be selective and must choose only those aspects of the game that can be covered in the time allotted (and with the facilities provided).

INSTRUCTIONS TO THE STUDENTS

In elementary instruction the tennis teacher tries to help students develop "grooved" strokes that can be repeated time and time again. Little variation is recommended or permitted except for small details that enable hitters to handle balls at various heights. In intermediate instruction, however, teachers should begin to stress flexibility and adaptability in strokes so that students will learn to hit efficiently in a variety of situations. Students must learn to adjust the length and force of their strokes as well as the speed and depth of their shots. They must learn to adopt stances and wrist and elbow positions that can add deceptiveness to their basic strokes and that can enable them to reach wide balls and to handle close ones. They must learn to recognize good plays by their opponents, plays that require defensive shots on their part. They must therefore learn to apply underspin. They must also learn to hit with top spin to play aggressively against a net rusher and to prepare net attacks of their own. In other words, instruction should be geared to both offense and defense, with emphasis on application of strokes and shots in various tactical situations. In short, we can say players must now learn when and where to hit the ball in addition to perfecting the mechanics of how to hit it.

The Groundstrokes

The logical initial approach to groundstroke instruction is to observe the students while they rally from the backcourt. Students may be permitted to rally aimlessly to display their form, to rally for accuracy by aiming at targets, or to hit with power to show their potential for playing aggressive tennis. Only in such exercises can teachers notice differences in form and ability that require different approaches for different students.

THE GRIPS

Teachers with the recommended permissive attitude will allow their students to use whatever grips they are accustomed to, provided the grips are within the range of correctness. The range is determined by those limits within which the hand must be placed (toward the bottom or top plane of the handle) to enable the hitter to develop the other points of form that the teacher wishes to present.

The teacher's attitude should be based on the logical premise that there is more than one correct way to hold the racket. Allowances should be made for variations in hand sizes and in handle shapes and sizes. Students should be permitted to experiment to find the grip that makes them most aware and offers best control of the slant and angle of the racket face.

A common fault found among intermediate players is the tendency to use a loose, relaxed grip during the stroke. A more effective grip is a firm grasp used throughout the entire stroke, especially at the moment of impact. The relationship of grip strength to wrist firmness was discussed in Chapter 2. The speed, position, and direction of the racket are best controlled with a firm grip and a firm wrist. Firmness is, of course, a relative matter; strong hands may grip less tightly than weak hands and still manage to control the racket. And since grip tension affects wrist flexibility, the degree of firmness in the wrist will vary among players as their grip strength varies. Teachers should work with various individuals to help them find their own most effective combination of grip firmness and wrist flexibility to serve the needs of their swing.

THE STANCE

Regardless of the level of play, in tennis the best hitting stance is sideways to the intended line of the shot, just as it is in baseball and golf. Unlike batters and golfers, however, the tennis player does not always have time to set himself nicely into the ideal hitting position. The opponent does not place his shots directly over "home plate," nor is the tennis player permitted to set the ball up for himself at a comfortable distance from his body. Consequently, the hitter has to move into position and once there, he must finally adjust his step with the front foot to swing freely and comfortably. This means that for some wide balls he will be in a closed stance. For many close balls he will have to swing while in an open stance, with his body facing the net. He should choose the position that will permit him to transfer his weight, turn his body, and have good balance as he swings.

Figure 7-1 A well-hit top-spin drive. From the loop backswing seen in the first three frames the racket is lowered (in frames four and five) by extending the arm and straightening it. Note that the upper body is facing the net at impact but the hitter still manages to guide his racket along the line of flight of the ball. (From Chet Murphy. *Advanced Tennis*, Dubuque, Iowa: Wm. C. Brown Company, 1970, p. 6.)

Hitting while in a balanced stance is one of the keys to accurate hitting. Balance, or lack of it, is seen best in the finish of the stroke; in practice, hitters ought to pose for a count of two in the finish position. By trying to pose after each shot, they learn to adjust the left-foot step properly, which helps them acquire a good hitting stance.

The idea of stepping away from a close ball and hitting from an open stance is new to many students coming up from elementary instruction. There, they were told to stand sideways as they swing; now they should be encouraged to swing from an open stance when necessary for good balance and for proper weight transfer. When a ball comes directly at them, they should be encouraged to use the two-step sequence described and illustrated in Figure 7-1. The sequence of a right-foot step followed by a left-foot step results in a swing from an open stance. The backswing is made during the first step, the forward swing during the second step.

The point here is that in fast play when a hitter has to *move* away from a ball, he probably will have to *step* away as he swings; seldom will he have time to step toward the ball and play from a neat sideways stance. Accordingly, he should use the two-step sequence, for the second step will place him in an open stance. Such a position is better than being completely sideways and off-balance.

On the backhand, of course, the sequence of steps for moving away from close balls is reversed; it now becomes left foot-right foot. There is not much need for this movement, however, because most balls can be taken on the forehand instead.

THE BACKSWING

Permissive teachers consider three kinds of backswings to be correct and efficient: a big loop (except when time does not permit), a shallow loop, and a straight swing with a loop at the end of it. Intermediate players should be encouraged to use any one of the three despite having learned a flat swing with a stop-and-go motion in elementary instruction.

In terms of the principles of mechanics, a loop swing is more efficient than other swings because it permits continuous motion as the racket moves from backswing to forward swing. Furthermore, it enables the hitter to adjust the racket to the height of the ball before starting his forward swing. The stop-and-go motion, on the other hand, usually results in a very rigid swing (as the player *resists* the tendency of the racket to flip backward at the end of the backswing) or in a very "wristy" swing (if the hitter cannot *prevent* the backward flip of the racket).

Many players will raise the elbow during their backswing, and as a result the racket face will be closed. Although this kind of swing appears to work well for them, it must be considered more complicated, since the elbow and racket face must be adjusted before the racket is brought forward into the ball. Our students who swing this way and have trouble controlling their shots are urged to learn the elbow-down swing in which the racket head is kept as nearly perpendicular to the ground ("standing on edge") as possible. Most students are better able to control the slant of the racket this way and thus are more likely to bring the racket into the ball properly regardless of the slant required for any particular shot.

The backswing in which the elbow is held high is conducive to power hitting. Many top players purposely swing this way, whipping the elbow down as the racket begins to descend in the loop. The racket then moves with great speed to the bottom of the loop and continues forward and upward into the ball. We sometimes suggest this kind of swing for hitters who are unable to generate sufficient power with the elbow-down swing. Normally, however, we prefer to see the swing designed and executed for control rather than for speed.

On the backhand the arm should bend during the backswing so that it can be made to straighten during the forward swing and thus add force to the swing. We advise our pupils to start the forward swing from close to the hip for balls at waist height or lower. For higher balls, the swing should start from close to the elbow or shoulder. Emphasis should not be on elbow action alone, however. The arm should be swung from the shoulder as the body turns during the shot; the arm straightens at the elbow after the swing from the shoulder has begun.

THE POINT-OF-CONTACT

The proper point-of-contact for straight-ahead shots will vary among players as their grips vary. A player whose grip is close to a Western, with the palm toward the bottom plane of the handle, must meet the ball sooner (closer to the net) than does a player whose grip is Eastern or Continental. As a convenient reference point, we say, "Meet the ball when it is approximately opposite your left hip." We provide considerable practice, however, during which we ask each pupil to concentrate on finding his proper point—the point opposite his body at which the racket can be held comfortably and conveniently to hit straight ahead when the ball has come from that direction.

Except for those who use an extreme Continental grip, players should be encouraged to hit with a "laid-back" wrist. The wrist should be bent back slightly during the backswing and kept in that position through the contact point and through most of the forward swing. Intermediate players have a tendency to use too much wrist action in the swing. Special care should be taken to see that the wrist merely serves the needs of the swing and does not dominate the action.

With advanced players it is another matter, however. They must learn to use what can be called "controlled hand action" to suit their purpose on each swing. The wrist should begin to straighten (from its laid-back position) during the forward swing, and the timing of that action should vary on each shot, depending on the direction desired. Contact will occur sooner or later during the hand action, as the hitter makes adjustments in the position of the wrist (affecting the timing) just prior to contact. In this way the wrist or hand action is used for more power, for better control, and for deception.

All of the movements described so far take place within the total pattern of the swing. As the length of swings varies for all players—and for the individual player on different shots—the internal workings of the swings will likewise vary. The teacher will notice many different kinds of individual wrist action. Whatever wrist action enables a player to swing easily and consistently in the simplest or most natural way is the best for him. His choice will often depend on several factors: his hand strength, the degree of flexibility and suppleness at his wrist joint, his personality and temperament, and, occasionally, his concept of a "good shot," of what "feels good" to him.

Figure 7–2   An excellent illustration of how to get down to the ball for a low backhand. Note that the hitter raises her left heel so that she can bend her left knee. In frame *E* we see that she has maintained her firm wrist and racket angle, although her racket face is lower than her hand.

On the backhand, the point-of-contact is approximately opposite the right hip, the exact spot depending upon variations in grips and wrist positions. The relationship between hand position, wrist position, and the point-of-contact is determined by what feels natural and comfortable to a particular player. These details of the swing are also affected by — and in some cases even determine — the timing of the straightening of the arm during the forward swing. A player who straightens his arm early (before contact) usually prefers to meet the ball later in terms of his body reference points than does one who straightens only at contact. There is not a great deal of ground for dogmatic assertions that one or another of these methods is right or wrong. Here, as in other strokes of the game, the total pattern and the internal workings of the stroke are determined by individual characteristics and variations in physique, temperament, and personality. The teacher at the intermediate level tries to help the student discover, through practice and experimentation, what works best for him.

THE FOLLOW-THROUGH AND FINISH

For consistently accurate hitting a player must not only time his swing properly to meet the ball at the proper contact point, but he must also control the direction in which the racket is moving a split second before and after contact. We prefer to see our students move the racket along the intended line of flight of the ball in the contact area. When this is done with the wrist and hand placed properly, the racket will be in the proper hitting position for longer than just a split second. With such a swing, timing need not be as precise as when the racket is moving across the line of flight of the ball. Consequently, the hitter is likely to be more accurate.

It is not necessary to be dogmatic about the finish position except to say the racket should be high (for drives) and out in front of the player. On a flat shot the elbow should be down and the racket face in the edge-down position. Allowances should be made, however, for hitters who find a slight bend or lift in the elbow more natural. Although the racket should be held firmly in the finish position, a loose, relaxed grip and arm may be permitted, with certain provisions: (1) the personal variation should occur *after* contact, (2) it should not cause the racket to swing off-line, and (3) racket control must remain sufficient to prevent bad shots.

PUTTING TOP SPIN ON THE BALL

Despite the need for long, smooth strokes to produce deep drives, students will also have to develop top-spin drives for use against opposing net men. Instructions for top-spin drives need not differ greatly from those offered for flatter, deeper shots. Grip, stance, backswing, point-of-contact — all of these can be identical to those used earlier. The only major changes in technique for top spin are in the plane of the swing, in the action of the ball on the racket, and, at times, in the slant of the racket face at contact. Players should be instructed to lower the racket at the end of the backswing in order to swing up to the ball. During the forward swing, they should attempt to hit the ball an upward glancing blow with a flat racket face. The players should be permitted enough time to experiment at adjusting the plane of the swing (they will swing more or less upward) and the slant of the racket face (to place it more or less vertically) to vary the speed and spin of their shots.

Many advanced players use different techniques for putting top spin on the ball. Some of them roll the wrist in order to roll the racket face over the ball. Others raise the elbow (on the forehand) as the racket comes into the ball, thereby rolling the top edge over it. Still others use a bit of each method: they roll the wrist and raise the elbow. Ordinarily, these modifications make for a less efficient stroke than that made with a flat racket face and an upward glancing blow; however, if the teacher judges that a player can control his shots better when rolling the racket over the ball, the player should be permitted and encouraged to do so.

THE TOP-SPIN LOB

The teacher presenting this stroke can compare it to a heavily topped, high looping drive. The stroke technique for the two shots is similar. The higher trajectory of the lob is attained by swinging in an exaggerated upward plane and by adjusting the bevel of the racket accordingly. Some players close the racket face more than they do for a drive; others open it more. In either case, the swing is very much in an upward plane, sometimes almost vertical. The teacher and player must work together at finding the best combination of swing plane and racket angle. These elements are often dependent on the kind of grip, the height of the ball at contact, the player's dexterity in making adjustments, and his ability to generate racket speed.

THE GROUNDSTROKE SLICE

The slice is a valuable addition to every advanced player's game. Players should be encouraged to use it as a defensive shot when in trouble and as a "neutral" shot during a rally. It is used most frequently in the latter situation, particularly on the backhand, for many players lack confidence in their ability to sustain rallies with drives.

The backhand slice can be an extremely effective technique for returning high-bouncing serves. The ball can be played as it rises and can be "pulled" down with a slanted racket head moving down and forward through the contact point.

Whenever possible, the grip and stance for a slice should resemble those for the drives. The only significant changes in the swing are in the plane in which the racket travels (it should move from high to low) and in the position of the racket as it moves through the contact area (it may be opened, beveled back from the vertical). The more the racket is beveled — and the more pronounced its downward path — the more spin will be applied to the ball. The bevel and the downward direction are adjusted at will by experienced players to vary the pace and spin of their shots.

The slice is useful as an approach shot on both the forehand and backhand. The player hits softly enough to have time to move up into a good volley position, although not so slowly as to make the ball bounce more vertically than is normal. Instead, the intention is to make the ball skid low on the bounce and thus force the opponent into hitting at a low ball.

Generally, the slice is not used for the purpose of causing the ball to bounce

Figure 7–3 A backhand slice return of serve. From her high backswing, the hitter hits down at the ball. Her hitting arm, bent during the backswing, is straightened at impact. Her upper body is sideways at contact but is turned toward the net during the follow-through. The slanted racket face in the last two frames indicates that a slight amount of backspin was imparted to the ball. (From Chet Murphy, *Advanced Tennis*, Dubuque, Iowa: Wm. C. Brown Company, 1970, p. 52.)

peculiarly. Rather, spin is applied to enable the hitter to maintain control of the ball off his own racket. It is a sophisticated means of taking the speed off a ball while maintaining contact with it long enough to control its direction.

THE RUNNING APPROACH SHOT

One significant change in stroke technique is necessary for players moving into intermediate class play: they must often hit approach shots while on the run rather than from a set hitting stance. The efficient player will hit on the run by stepping toward the ball with the foot closest to it (the right foot for a forehand), making the pivot and backswing as the step is taken. The foot is placed naturally so that the toes point toward the net or the post, thus enabling the hitter to push off in the direction of the net. He then starts his forward swing and at the same time steps toward the net with his left foot. He times these moves so that contact between the racket and ball occurs before the left foot comes into contact with the ground. This enables the hitter to move forward, toward the net, during the swing and to get a fast running start toward the net after the hit. A useful variation for players at an advanced level is a running slice in which the ball has sidespin as well as backspin. On a forehand, for example, the racket may be drawn down *and across* the ball from right to left (from outside its line of flight to inside) to impart clockwise rotation. Such spin causes the ball to curve slightly in flight toward an opponent's backhand and to bounce in that same direction. The backspin and the resulting flat flight trajectory of the ball causes a low, skidding bounce. The combined effects of the sidespin and backspin often result in a shot that is more difficult to return than a conventional drive.

THE LOB

The conventional lob motion is somewhat similar to that of the normal ground-stroke drive. Grip, stance, preparatory swing, and point-of-contact are identical in

Figure 7-4   The running approach shot. The player adjusts his steps as he approaches the ball so that he can hit while on the move and from an open stance with his left foot off the ground. In this way he avoids what would be, in this case, an awkward sideways stance, from which he would have to untangle his feet in order to advance to the volley position.

the two strokes. For the additional lift needed on the lob, however, the forward swing must be in an upward plane and the racket face must usually be slanted back (opened) more than it is for a drive. In addition, the ball must usually be hit far more softly than it is for a drive. Consequently, the swing is less forceful and more controlled, it often resembles a steady push at the ball rather than a true swing. Finally to soften the force of impact, to loft the ball, and to control it on the racket, the hitting hand must often be turned clockwise on the forehand and counterclockwise on the backhand at the moment of impact. As a result of this turning action, the ball will usually have backspin. The spin is simply a by-product of the mechanics of the swing; it is not applied deliberately to affect the flight of the ball, its bounce, or its deflection off the opponent's racket.

The lob techniques described so far apply only when the player has time to move properly to the ball and to use his normal drive motion as preparation for the lob. The player does not always have enough time, of course; the lobber must often make a play on a ball that is coming toward him with such speed that he cannot swing as described. Instead, he must use a shorter, more compact motion. This can be related to the volley motion; it is a short punch, a block, or a push with little or no wrist action. The racket, however, must be moved up to the ball to loft it; often the wrist and forearm must be turned to open the racket face. The latter action often imparts backspin to the ball.

For convenience in discussing and teaching the two kinds of lob motions, the first may be called "a drive lob," and the second a "volley lob." In each case, the most critical factor in the stroke is "feel" and "touch" for making a delicate shot. The techniques for softening the force of impact, for making a "touch" shot, are similar to those used for taking the speed off a drive when volleying. That is, the player can relax his wrist and grip, pull the racket back, or use the racket to slice the ball; in addition, he can use various combinations of these actions. The touch shot is not easy to teach, however, and often, despite countless hours of work on the skill, some players are not able to develop satisfactory touch to permit them to use the lob effectively.

THE DROP SHOT

The drop shot is another delicate touch shot requiring precise timing and deft racket work. The intention is to make the ball barely clear the net while it is dropping nearly vertically — and to hit with such little force that the ball will have very little "carry" on the bounce.

This shot can be built on groundstroke patterns. The grip, stance, and backswing can be identical to those used on drives. The forward swing is slowed just before contact, however, and the wrist is turned sharply to open the racket face. The wrist and grip are relaxed to deaden the force of impact (against a fast ball), and the ball is "nursed" over the net (we use this term a great deal in our teaching — on drop shots, drop volleys, half volleys, and on slow chip shots — because it connotes gentleness and softness). Because of the slower forward swing, there is very little follow-through to the stroke; the racket need continue along the line of the shot only long enough to carry the ball delicately toward the aim point.

Players who cannot seem to develop the deft touch needed to make the shot as described are often able to modify the stroke successfully. For them, a chopping motion in which the racket meets the ball in a downward glancing blow while the racket face is slanted back to put backspin on the ball may do just as well. The glancing blow and the slanted racket face enable many hitters to hit a reasonably soft, lofted shot with enough backspin to cause the ball to bounce vertically, or at least enough to reduce the forward carry after the bounce. The result is often a successful drop shot, although the stroke technique differs considerably from the more sophisticated version seen among highly accomplished players.

RETURNING THE SERVE

Consistency in returning serves is one measure of playing ability. A common quality among players who return serves effectively is quickness: they are quick to see the ball, quick to move their rackets, and quick to start in motion. Return-of-serve practice ought to be done specifically for improvement in these areas.

A player's ability to move quickly depends in part on how well he prepares to move. Most top players make themselves feel light, bouncy, and springy while in the ready position. Most of them make a ready-hop just as the opponent's racket meets the ball. As a learning device, students may be instructed to jump up as they see the server's racket move up to meet the ball. They land at the moment of impact, then spring into action as they determine the direction of the serve. Students should be told to watch the ball as they make the ready-hop and to look to see it at impact. Looking at the total figure of the server and then waiting for the ball to come out of that background is a mistake many inexperienced players make.

As the player springs into motion after the ready-hop, he should start the backswing with a quick turn of the hips and shoulders. Here a straight backswing is recommended (even for players who normally use a loop) because it requires less time than does a circular backswing. If there is not enough time to reverse the shoulder action to start the forward swing, a short forward motion of the arm enables the hitter to "block" the return. He keeps a firm grip and wrist to resist the force of the oncoming ball and to maintain control of the racket as he changes from backswing to forward swing.

As a final point, players should be told to hold the elbows in at the sides while in the waiting stance — to shorten the radius of their swing. They will then need less force (or strength) to start the racket in motion and as a result more force is available for racket speed.

The Serve

One measure which distinguishes top-flight players from middle-level players is the effectiveness of their second serves. Tournament players do more than merely put the ball in play; they attack on second serves by placing the ball to an opponent's backhand whenever necessary, even on crucial points, with enough spin to permit speed *and* consistency. To develop such play, we begin service instruction with intermediate and advanced students by limiting our remarks to second serves. Later, we introduce teaching points for the first serve.

Most good servers use the conventional Continental grip, with the knuckles toward the top of the handle. This grip encourages spin action of the ball while also permitting maximum wrist action in the swing. Occasionally, one sees a player who serves with adequate spin and speed while using the Eastern forehand grip. It may be best to permit such a player to retain his serve despite the strong preference for the Continental grip among leading players.

Generally, we prefer to see the racket held more in the fingers than in the hand. As a player moves into the truly advanced level of play, we encourage him to use a quick finger action just before contact to add to the arm and wrist snap of the upward swing. At times, if a player impresses us as being adaptable and flexible, we suggest that he try the long butt-in-the-hand grip. This, too, usually adds to racket speed. If control rather than speed is the objective for a particular learner, however, he will be best advised to hold his racket in the conventional manner, with the handle butt extending beyond his hand.

For an effective and consistent second serve, the ball must have overspin, which makes it curve downward as it clears the net. It is impossible to impart pure overspin alone, however; almost always spin serves are a combination of overspin and sidespin. The ball is struck a glancing blow while the racket is moving up and across the intended line of flight of the ball from left to right. When working with intermediate players, for whom the spin serve is a new experience, we suggest that the racket make contact on the nose of an imaginary face while it is moving toward

Figure 7–5 A loose, free-swinging serve motion showing several points of good form. Note the simple tossing action and the high release. The hitting arm is almost straight to the rear before the arm bends at the elbow to start the characteristic loop hitting motion. During the backswing the knuckles and elbow are up. The palm begins to face skyward only as the racket is brought into the "back-scratching" position. At impact the player is at full stretch. (From Chet Murphy, *Advanced Tennis,* Dubuque, Iowa: Wm. C. Brown Company, 1970, pp. 20–21.)

the left eye. As a convenient guide for the toss, we recommend that the ball be thrown straight up from in front of the player in such a fashion that if it were permitted to fall to the ground, it would land on a line that extends through the server's feet to the direction (the aim point) in which he is hitting.

The American Twist serve may be considered as merely an exaggeration of the spin serve. Intermediate players should be encouraged to learn it, but only after they have learned to control the simpler spin serve. For the Twist, the ball is tossed farther to the left than on any other serve — so far to the left that the hitter must arch his back to reach the ball. He bends his wrist to the left and reaches back and over the ball to make contact on the *left* side of it. As he swings up, from the back-scratching position, he straightens his back and his arm to generate speed as he moves his racket across the intended line of flight of the ball from left to right (see Fig. 7–6).

Figure 7-6 In the American Twist serve, the player throws the ball to his left, arches his back to reach the ball, then swings up and across the ball to impart a combination of top spin and sidespin.

In order to impart overspin to the ball, the racket must carry the ball upward as it moves across the line of flight from left to right. This means that contact between racket and ball occurs before the player has reached the limit of his full extension upward; his racket continues in an upward direction after contact. The hitter thus acts to "brush up on the back top side of the ball" or "carry the ball up on the strings."

In addition to developing an effective spin serve, intermediate players should also develop a hard, flat serve. For such a serve the ball is tossed straight ahead. As a result, the player is more erect as he meets the ball; he is stretching upward and forward to get maximum reach at contact. The swing is timed so that the racket meets the ball when the arm and the wrist are fully extended. At the point-of-contact they form almost a straight line; the arm is extended vertically from the shoulder socket and is slightly forward, with the racket almost a direct extension of the arm.

During the upward swing, the hand and forearm are turned (pronated) to make the palm face the net. This also turns the racket head and makes *it* face the net, enabling the hitter to place the racket squarely on the nose of the imaginary face. The turning action of the forearm helps increase racket speed, and since flat serves are usually intended to be fast serves, most good servers use this action to supplement arm extension and wrist flexion. In order to minimize the amount of spin, the racket is swung straight into the ball along the intended line of flight, rather than across the line as in spin serves.

Players at the intermediate level should experiment with various techniques of footwork while serving to see which works best for them. During the swing, the right foot may simply move around and across the baseline as part of the forward lean during the swing. Alternatively, the player may *jump* across the line to land on the right foot after the hit. Such a jump permits more vigorous body action; the right side is brought around with more force than occurs when the server merely steps across the line. A third method may be even more effective: the hitter may make an *upward* jump, after which he lands on his left foot only slightly inside the court. Such a movement enables the hitter to apply a great deal of force in an upward direction. The additional power provided by the upward jump may be more effective than that gained in the other moves, even though the right side may not be brought around as much.

As players gain control of their serves and begin to work for power, we modify the swing and the toss slightly. We suggest more body turn during the downswing (the shoulders are turned clockwise) in order to twist and "coil" the body. During the upward and forward swing, the body uncoils and the rotary motion thus developed is used to add speed to the swing. This body action does complicate the toss somewhat. As the hips and shoulders turn clockwise during the downswing, the tossing arm naturally tends to move in that direction also. Consequently, the ball must be thrown *forward and upward* (instead of vertically). The arm must also move in this direction if the ball is to be placed accurately in the contact point. The hand moves as if to trace a large letter "J" in the air.

Advanced players should be able to control the placement of their serves. They should be able to hit wide to the receiver's right, wide to his left, and straight at him when necessary. In addition, they must be able to vary the kinds of spin on the ball to accompany each of the different placements. A slice, with sidespin, is best used to serve wide to the receiver's right. Overspin (top spin) combined with sidespin, as in the American Twist serve, can be used effectively when aiming to the receiver's left. Flat serves can be used effectively for any of the three placements.

As indicated earlier, many intermediate players must change the placement of their toss for each different kind of serve. Advanced players, however, should learn to toss consistently to one spot and to make subtle changes in the position of the wrist (and, therefore, the position of the racket on the ball) just before contact. For a flat hit, the racket faces the net and hits the ball "on the nose." For a sidespin shot (a slice), the racket hits the ball between the left eye and the left ear. For the basic spin, serve contact is made on the nose, and the wrist curls at contact to brush the racket across the left eye. A good amount of time and effort is usually necessary to learn to vary the placement of the serve without altering the toss, but the increased effectiveness of the serve makes the extra practice worthwhile.

The Volleys: Forehands and Backhands

Intermediate players should begin to experiment with the Continental "no-change" grip for volleys. Many, however, will find this grip too awkward for effective use. The awkwardness commonly results from some weakness in the grip or from a lack of flexibility in the wrist and elbow. Although the Continental grip does not require a grip change, the volleyer must change the position of his wrist and elbow as he hits first a forehand and then a backhand. Many inexperienced players find this difficult. Those who do should be permitted to use their regular forehand and backhand grips, until they develop more dexterity and flexibility in controlling the racket.

In elementary instruction volleyers are told to punch at the ball and to simply block it back. Such instruction is adequate for the soft, high balls that are played in beginner's tennis. In more advanced play, however, volleyers must learn to handle low balls from below the height of the net and to take the speed off fast drives. These shots require different techniques than those used in elementary instruction.

One method is to drag the racket down and across the ball on both the forehand and backhand (we call it a "drag volley"). The wrist is laid back during the backswing as much as the grip comfortably permits. Within the limits of the grip and the flexibility of the wrist, the ball is met in front of the body. The wrist is almost always laid back at contact; it straightens somewhat only for sharply angled cross-court placements. The racket moves down, into, and slightly across the ball, and the face is slanted whatever extent is needed to lift the ball over the net and provide the depth desired. The downward motion of the racket and the upward slant of its face enable the hitter to put backspin on the ball; we consider this beneficial to control on all except very high and very soft shots.

At times, the wrist is firm for a crisp hit. In other instances, it is allowed to "give" slightly, in order to deaden the force of impact. Occasionally, the swing is a short one, while at other times, it is a long "fence to fence" swing. The hitter is told to adjust the length of his swing, the degree of slant in the racket, and the range of looseness in the grip and wrist to each particular tactical situation. When he wants a soft, delicate shot, he swings easily, uses a short action, and relaxes his grip and wrist. When he is hitting at a low ball from close to the net, he slants the racket more sharply than he does when hitting from farther back.

When the player must hit from behind his service line or go for high, soft shots, the normal short block volley or even the longer drag volley may not be adequate to

Figure 7-7 Advanced players often have to leap to intercept an opponent's passing shot. Here the volleyer can be seen drawing his right foot back slightly, and he appears to fall to his right. He then pushes off with his right foot as he steps with his left to gain maximum reach.

place the ball deep and hard through an opening. A player often must use a drive volley instead. For such a stroke, we encourage more body action than is used on normal volleys. Greater body action results in a longer swing, both in the backswing and the forward swing. We warn against permitting "slack" to develop in the stroke, however. We consider the major difference between a well-played drive volley and a drive groundstroke to be the reduced flexibility at the wrist, elbow, and shoulder joints in the volley. This firmness during the swing generally provides more control than does a looser swing.

When working on control and placement, we stress wrist and elbow adjustments. On the forehand, the ball is directed to the left or right mainly by adjusting the wrist position, which in turn affects the position of the racket on the ball. On the backhand, the adjustment is made in the position of the elbow. These adjustments permit the hitter to make early contact (close to the net) or late contact (far from the net). In fast play most volleyers make the appropriate adjustments as described here.

The various techniques for volleying require a certain amount of dexterity at the wrist and elbow which some players have in greater degree than others. Dexterity is one of the qualities essential for excellence in net play; together with quickness in movement and reaction time, it distinguishes great volleyers from good ones. However, even among players not gifted with exceptional dexterity, control, accuracy, and effectiveness can be developed by providing practice at the drag volley and the drive motions and by directing the players' attention to wrist and elbow adjustments to be made during the swing.

Figure 7-8   Not having time to move his feet, the volleyer simply turns his upper body side-ways and shifts his weight to his right foot. In fast play the volleyer often must hit from such a facing-the-net stance while turning the hips and shoulders during the backswing.

THE DROP VOLLEY

The drop volley is appropriately named; it is a volley that drops softly over the net with little or no momentum after the bounce. Most of the mechanics of the swing are identical to those used for crisp volleys. The major difference that enables the hitter to make a soft, delicate shot is in the grip and wrist. They are relaxed slightly at impact to soften the force of the shot and to take the speed off the oncoming ball. The wrist is turned clockwise on the forehand and counterclockwise on the back-hand to enable the player to hit under the ball a bit to give it backspin. The spin helps make the ball bounce vertically or at least reduces the forward carry after the bounce.

The Half-Volley

The term "half-volley," which is applied to the pick-up shot made when the ball is hit "on the short hop," is really a misnomer; the shot is not a volley at all but a groundstroke (the ball first hits the ground before the player strokes it). The tech-nique for playing it, therefore, resembles that for a groundstroke, and that is the approach we use in our instruction for this stroke.

We stress a reduced backswing and a limited follow-through (both shorter than those seen on a full-length drive), although the actual length of the stroke must vary depending on the hitter's distance from the net and on his aim point. The bevel, or slant, of the racket must also be adjusted accordingly. If the hitter is close to the net, he may have to open the racket face more than he would if he were hitting from farther back. From up close, he may have to "nurse" the ball over gently, while from farther back he may stroke it with more force.

As to the mechanics of this stroke, we prefer to see a firm wrist and very little elbow action (very little "slack," as on the drive volley). The racket should be lowered by bending the knees rather than by changing appreciably the angle be-tween the forearm and racket handle.

The plane of the swing is usually upward, but it must be adjusted according to the strategic situation. When being played from as deep as the service line, the ball may be topped by hitting it with a closed racket face and a relatively flat swing. When hitting from very close to the net and aiming short, it may be hit flat or with backspin; the face may have to be open and the racket swung upward to give the

Figure 7–9   When volleying, experienced players defend themselves and protect their bodies by playing close balls with a backhand as shown here. The elbow is moved out to the side to enable the player to place the racket in front of the body. At the same time, the player glides or jumps in an attempt to get the body out of the way of the racket.

ball the necessary lift. These adjustments in the angle of the racket face are best made with the wrist and forearm on the forehand, and with the wrist, forearm, and elbow on the backhand. The hitter must consider the angle of deflection of the rising ball off his racket as he makes these adjustments during the swing.

The Overhead Smash

The smash can best be compared to the flat serve; it is similar in grip, stance, and hitting motion (as distinguished from the preparatory motion). The swings seen in most good smashes, however, show one major difference between the smash and serve: the backswing is usually more direct and is shorter. Good players do not let the racket flow down past their shoe tops to start the swing; rather, they carry it back higher, either at waist height or sometimes even at shoulder height. This shorter, more direct backswing gives a more controlled look than is usually seen in a good serve motion. For maximum control of the swing, the hitter must not permit "slack" between the movements of his hips, shoulders, arm, elbow, and wrist. In other words, the swing should resemble a hard push rather than a loose throw.

We teach our students to make the short backswing as they move to get to the proper location for hitting. If the lob is short and contact can be made in front of the hitter's waiting location, he turns sideways to his right while moving his left foot forward. He then moves toward the ball with the left foot always closer to the net. To reach a deep lob, he turns to his right by drawing his right foot back, then moves toward the baseline by keeping the right foot closer to the line. In this way he is always in a hitting stance, and as a result he is more likely to be ready to hit. We like to see our students moving to the ball or waiting for it with the racket "cocked" behind them, pointing up and to their left. The hitting motion begins from that position; the racket is dipped quickly behind the back and is then brought up and pushed forcefully into the ball.

A net man will not always be able to move back and set himself in position under the ball to smash it. Instead, he will sometimes have to jump toward the baseline to reach a ball that would otherwise sail clear over him and land in the court. The jump smash requires slight adjustments in weight distribution and timing. The hitter must jump up and slightly backward from his right foot while swinging his left foot back so that he can land on it. He times his moves, his swing, and his jump so that contact occurs while he is in the air, before he lands on his left foot. Often two or three skip steps precede the jump; the hitter must then adjust his steps so that he will be able to jump at the right time, when the ball is in a suitable location to be hit.

Very high lobs are often difficult to judge. Usually they are easier to play after the bounce. Since a very high lob is dropping nearly vertically, it will bounce nearly vertically. The hitter, therefore, will not have to back up much past the point where the lob can be taken "on the fly." The advantage he gains in more accurate judgment and timing will offset the disadvantage of giving up a few feet of court position. With his additional time, the hitter may even use a longer swing, identical to his serve (if he prefers, he may again swing as he does to hit a lob that is in flight).

Footwork

There is some difference of opinion among teachers about the best way to move to reach a ball. Some excellent players always start moving with the foot that is closest to the ball (the right foot on the forehand, for example). Others start with a crossover step of the foot that is farthest from the ball. Still others skip sideways rather than run for close balls; they run only for wide ones.

In our opinion, the first style offers an advantage over the others if speed alone is considered. It permits a player to "push off" with his left foot (on a forehand) and this, we feel, permits a faster start than does crossing that foot over.

Many players, however, have already learned to pivot and cross the left foot over through their early training, in which they hit balls aimed comfortably alongside them. As a result, many players naturally start to move with the crossover for wider balls. With advanced players, we try to teach the distinction between slow balls that permit time for a crossover start and faster balls that require the quicker start. We teach both kinds of starts to pupils at all levels, and we permit whichever is appropriate.

We also teach a third method—the skip start—and suggest that if players prefer this over the other two *for close balls* they should use it. Here again a distinction must be made between easy-to-reach balls and balls that require considerable scrambling. Skipping is much slower than running and thus should be used only when time permits.

For maximum speed in sideward movement, we recommend a technique that can best be described as the "gravity method." As shown in Figure 7–10, the player moves his right foot to his left as he pivots on his left foot. In effect, he is removing a base of support while in the ready position, and as a result he "falls" to his right; he then quickly steps with his left foot to continue to move in that direction. Experiments we have conducted have shown us that these actions are more effective in teaching students to move laterally than are the previously described steps (stepping with the left foot, pushing off with the left foot, or skipping).

Precise and methodical footwork practice is only part of the training method that must be followed to make good movers out of ordinary athletes. A great deal of practice at making sudden changes of direction and body positions and at lunging and stretching should supplement specific "by the numbers" drills, especially with upper intermediate and advanced players. We have devised two drills for this purpose. We believe that regular practice at these drills makes most players more adept at the kind of moves required in match play.

Figure 7-10 An instructor helps a player learn the gravity method of moving. The instructor pushes against the player's shoulder to permit him to raise his right foot. As the instructor releases his hand from the shoulder the player falls to his right. He quickly plants his right foot and steps with his left.

We call one of our movement drills "Touch and Go." Two players (let us call them "A" and "B") face each other in the conventional ready stance, standing about five feet away from each other and midway between the center service line and a sideline. Racket covers are placed on their rackets and they hold the rackets in their regular volley grips. Player A is designated leader; B is the follower. At a signal, players will race each other, attempting to be the first to touch either of the sidelines. Player A starts the action. He moves in either direction (left or right) in any way he chooses (running, skipping, or crossing over) as quickly as he can to "beat" his opponent to either sideline. As he approaches the line, he simply reaches down to touch it with his racket. He may use fakes and feints and quick changes of pace and direction to confuse player B about his intended direction. Player B tries to follow his moves and to anticipate them—and he may even try to outguess player A, if possible, in order to beat him to the line. Action is continuous. After touching a line, the leader must take two steps away from it before he can return to it to touch it again.

It is not necessary to score in this drill. Normally, the challenge of trying to keep up with an opponent or to beat him to a line is sufficient alone to motivate players. As players develop more endurance and stamina, the "playing area" may be widened to include the entire width of the court. Players then start at the center service line and move to touch the sidelines.

A second drill, "Match Your Man," is similar to the preceding yet different enough to make it interesting. Two players face each other standing five feet apart. One player makes several moves left or right to swing at imaginary volleys. The other seeks to match his moves; he tries not to lag behind as he imitates the leader. The designated leader starts the action by making any combination of crossover steps in either direction. He may fake or feint or move deceptively in any way to confuse his opponent, but the action is limited to crossover steps and imaginary volleys only. Scoring is not necessary; with serious players the challenge of trying to keep up with the pace is enough to keep them interested.

We often use both of these drills as "fun conditioners" after daily practice sessions. The better movers are urged to "take on all comers" and to compete against one another. Almost always, the players recognized as good movers in actual play perform well in these drills. Other poorer movers are made aware of their deficiencies by their poor performance here. At the same time, regular repetition of these drills helps all sorts of players and develops an appreciation for agility and mobility in tennis.

Chapter Eight

CORRECTIVE TECHNIQUES FOR COMMON FAULTS

A well-planned system that provides for the sequential development of all the strokes in the game is essential for effective teaching. All the same, a system provides only the starting point from which skillful teaching begins. After initial instruction, several common faults will become apparent among students as they try to apply their strokes to rally or play. Experienced teachers use various methods to correct these faults. Some teachers simply coin a few instructive phrases for the students to remember. Others devise new routines or sequences, or they may even invent and use unusual gimmicks and gadgets. In this chapter we list several such corrective techniques, with the suggestion that they are best used in individual instruction or with small groups of students who need such special attention.

The reader must be cautioned, however, that not all tricks, ideas, or gadgets work adequately with all students. A certain approach may be ineffective and may not bring about the desired change in behavior in one student, while another student may find the same method or material to be exactly what is needed to correct the fault. We offer our suggestions in this chapter with the attitude that if they work for only a few students of each of our readers, they are appropriate in this discussion.

THE GROUNDSTROKES

Most of the corrective techniques described in this chapter can be applied to both the forehand and backhand groundstrokes. The reader need only imagine his student in either of the proper hitting positions to make our instructions applicable to either of the two strokes.

Correcting a Loose Grip

One of the most common of all faults is a loose, relaxed grip during the stroke. For maximum efficiency, the racket should be held firmly throughout the entire stroke, especially at the moment of impact. A firm grip ensures maximum racket control; a loose grip often results in bad timing (the ball is hit either too early or too late), misplacement (the ball does not meet the center of the strings), and misdirected force (the racket is not guided into the ball accurately). A proper grip must be mastered if a player hopes to develop *consistently* effective groundstrokes.

By stressing a firm grip at the finish, the teacher can help the player acquire a firm grip at impact. The development of the firm finish is shown in Figure 8–1. The student stands with her back against a wall or fence and swings as if she were hitting an imaginary ball *parallel* to the fence. She tries to stop her racket during the follow-through to prevent it from banging into the fence on each swing. She soon realizes that she must hold the racket firmly to stop it short of the fence. With repeated swings of this kind she learns to hold it firmly during the swing. This technique works on both the forehand and the backhand; the hitter pretends she is hitting parallel to the fence and to her left on the forehand, and parallel and to her right on the backhand.

Correcting Improper Wrist Position

One corrective technique used to teach the laid-back wrist position described earlier lets the learner see and feel the proper position. The player stands in a hitting position alongside the net and presses his racket into the net band, bending his wrist back as he does so to keep his racket handle parallel to the net. He is told that his wrist should look and feel this way at impact, and that he should try to keep it that way as long as he can in the contact area. He is told that when hitting a ball, the force of the swing and the arm and body action toward the net will make the racket face move progressively ahead of the hitting hand after contact. Except on certain

Figure 8–1   With her back to the fence, a pupil makes a full-length forehand swing. She holds the racket firmly enough to stop the follow-through before the racket bangs into the fence.

Figure 8–2 One method for moving away from a close ball. Inexperienced players must be cautioned to move quickly enough to be able to take two steps as shown. Many of them mistakenly step back with the right foot and wait for the ball while in that position. We prefer the three-step move described in the text for the reason that it almost always ensures that the hitter will not get caught too close to the ball. We stress that she should first get away from the ball (with the left-foot step) and not turn sideways until she has done so. For another example of moving away from a close ball, see Figure 7–9.

shots, he will not have to add force to the swing with wrist action. Instead, he should hold the wrist firm in its laid-back position in order to keep the racket face toward the target as it passes through the hitting area (see Fig. 3–2).

Correcting an Inefficient Hitting Stance

Although the ideal hitting stance is sideways to the net, there are times even in beginners' play when the hitter will not have time to move into this position and still be able to shift his weight toward the net with the swing. Such difficulties often occur on close forehands, where many beginners mistakenly move the right foot back (to get sideways) and then are forced to swing while their body weight is still on the right foot. A more efficient move is to step away from the ball with the left foot and, if necessary, to swing as that step is made. The hit is then made from a slightly open stance, but this at least permits the hitter to shift his weight to his left foot as he swings.

At times it may be necessary for the hitter to move farther away from the ball than one step permits. For this we teach the two-step sequence shown in Figure 8–2. The hitter steps back and away from the oncoming ball with her right foot, then steps with the left foot as she swings. The second step may be toward the net or toward the left sideline, depending on how far from the ball she must move to swing comfortably. The backswing begins on the first step; the forward swing is made during the last step.

Correcting a Jerky Backswing

Many inexperienced players lower the racket as they start their backswing. As a result, the racket is often too far below the intended point-of-contact as the forward swing begins and a bad shot is made.

One way to correct such a swing is to have the student stand at the net as if he is preparing to hit away from, not toward, the net. In this location he practices a backswing at least high enough to let the racket head clear the net. He soon learns to hold the racket firmly and to lift it during the backswing either by raising his arm from the shoulder or by bending his elbow. The instructor then tosses balls for the player to hit. The toss comes from the baseline and should be high enough to give the hitter, who is standing on the same side of the net, a high bounce at which to swing. If he swings properly — above the net — he is able to complete the stroke; if he lowers the racket as he takes it back, he swings it into the net and is unable to finish the stroke. Once he learns the high backswing for high balls, he has an easy time adjusting to low balls by making a downward circular motion with the racket at the end of the backswing.

Correcting an Improper Elbow Position

Many experienced players raise the elbow of the hitting arm and move it away from their body as they start their backswing. As the elbow moves, the racket face begins to close slightly; it slants downward as it moves up and back with the elbow. With such a start, the elbow must then be brought down to complete the backswing and to open the racket face for the proper position at contact. Although such a swing works effectively for many excellent players, it is not the easiest and most efficient way to hit. Students who have difficulty with the swing can benefit from a swing in which the elbow is held down close to the body during the backswing. This swing is simpler and more efficient because the hitter has fewer variables to contend with; he does not have to adjust his wrist and elbow after starting his swing to bring the racket face to the edge-down hitting position.

An effective technique for teaching the correct elbow position is illustrated in Figure 8–3. The player places a ball can under her upper arm and swings at several imaginary balls. As she swings, she keeps her elbow close enough to her body to keep the can in place. Holding the elbow in and down virtually ensures a vertical racket face. After several practice swings, she hits at tossed balls. She then removes the can and is told to make her arm "feel that way" — that is, down and in close to the body.

The can under the arm can also be used to correct a player's tendency to raise the elbow at contact. When working on this or the preceding point of form, though, the hitter should be told to move the elbow away from the body during the follow-through. When this is done properly, the can falls out of its place under the armpit after contact.

Correcting a Circular Swing Path

Equally important as maintaining the proper racket and wrist position is swinging in the proper direction. The proper direction is along the intended line of flight of

Figure 8-3 *A.* When the elbow is moved away from the body and raised toward the top of the rear fence (as shown in the first photo), the racket face is slanted down. The hitter must then adjust the position of his elbow, wrist, and racket head as he completes his backswing and swings the racket forward and into the ball. *B.* A simpler and, for most players, more efficient swing is shown in the second photo. The elbow is kept down during the backswing, thus enabling the hitter to keep the racket face in a nearly vertical position during most of the swing. Such a swing requires fewer adjustments and enables most players to hit more accurately. The can tucked under the arm is used as a training device for this kind of swing. The hitter keeps his elbow down to keep the can in place until after contact. He soon develops the feel of the more efficient kind of swing, with the elbow down and racket "standing on edge."

the ball. In a correct swing, the racket does not travel in an arc through the hitting area. Instead, it comes into the area along an arc and then moves along a line tangent to the arc (the hitter "flattens the arc"). When the racket has moved along the line as far as the hitter can comfortably reach, it again moves in an arc to the finish.

When the racket is moving in a circular path through the hitting area, it will be in the proper hitting position for only a split second. At all other points in the swing, it will be facing in a direction different from that sought by the hitter. The timing of the swing is therefore critical. The ball must be met at only that single instant when the racket happens to be correctly set. The swing along the line, on the other hand, permits the hitter to meet the ball at any of several different points in the hitting area and still hit to the direction he intends. It enables him to keep the racket in the proper hitting position longer and usually results in better accuracy than does the circular swing.

In drill practice for the swing along the line, four balls are placed on the court in front and to the left of the student. The ball closest to the player is placed carefully at the point-of-contact. The other three are placed alongside it, in a line toward the net. The student in Figure 8-4 is instructed to guide her racket along the line of the balls as she swings at imaginary balls considered to be stationary above the balls on the ground. She is told to pretend she is hitting not one ball but all four balls successively. We point out how to do this; she must move her elbow past her right hip and away from her body in the direction of the shot. Most learners need only a small amount of this kind of practice to correct the fault of swinging in a circle.

Figure 8–4 Balls laid out along the intended line of flight of the shot provide visual reference for a pupil learning to swing along the line.

Correcting Faulty Timing

When working with beginners, most experienced teachers start their instruction by building stroke patterns through demonstration, explanation, and imitation. The student tries to imitate the teacher while making "dummy" swings at an imaginary ball. Only when he can make a satisfactory pattern is he permitted to swing at "live" balls, and these are usually tossed gently to him by the teacher. For many beginners, this second step — applying the stroke pattern to a moving ball — is one of the most difficult parts of their early training. They know what to do but do not quite understand *when* to do it. They are often heard to say, for example, "I know I'm supposed to step into the shot, turn my hips and shoulders, and swing my arm from the shoulder, but when should I do these things? In what order should I make these moves, and how closely should they follow one another?" Questions like these point out the need for specific training on a very important element of stroking: timing the swing to the oncoming ball. One approach used to guide beginners through this difficult stage is explained below. Although many beginners acquire a sense of timing through their own efforts and experiments, the procedure shown develops the sense more rapidly.

The student is shown how to relate the shift of weight (the step into the shot) to the bounce of the ball. He is told to start his step *when the ball bounces* and to start his forward swing as soon as he plants his foot. The sequence of moves is "bounce–step–swing," with a slightly longer pause between "bounce" and "step" than between "step" and "swing." When teaching this sequence, we direct the student to start his swing from the "racket back" position while standing sideways to the net.

This eliminates the backswing and leaves the player free to concentrate solely on the forward swing. To make it easier still, we first toss balls from 8 or 10 yards distance before leading up to half-court and full-court play.

Once the student masters the sequence with the forward swing alone, he is permitted to start his swing from the conventional ready position, facing the net. Now we show him how to time his backswing to put it in rhythm with the speed of the oncoming ball. He starts his racket back as soon as he sees the ball coming. He makes a fast backswing for a fast ball, a slower one for a slow ball. In addition, he adjusts the speed to permit continuous motion as he changes from backswing to forward swing.

As the student progresses and moves along into the intermediate level of play, the step and the beginning of the forward swing must be made before the ball bounces. This transition is not difficult to achieve, however. The sense of timing that the student has developed while working on the bounce–step–swing sequence, progressing gradually from tossed balls to half-court and full-court rallies, enables him to adjust easily to the faster balls he faces at higher levels of play.

Correcting Inaccurate Distance Judgment

Beginners often have trouble judging their distance from the ball, and as a result many poor shots are made, with the ball hitting off-center toward either the tip or the handle of the racket. Students attempting to correct this fault should be made to understand that the major adjustment in lateral distance from the ball should be made with the *left-foot* step (on a forehand). A secondary adjustment may also have to be made; the hitter may have to adjust his reach by extending his hitting arm or by bending it to place his racket on the ball properly. Ideally, however, the arm should be comfortably extended for every shot. Thus the student must gauge his distance from the ball accurately, and he must then step properly — with his left foot — as he swings.

We provide practice at judging lateral distance and at adjusting the left-foot step by placing three balls spaced about a foot apart along a line in front of the student, as shown in Figure 8–5. The student then makes several practice swings at imaginary balls assumed to be fixed in place over each of the balls on the ground. As she swings, she sees the need for adjusting her step to place the racket on the ball properly. We then toss balls for her to hit, aiming our tosses carefully to provide a mixture of wide balls and close balls. In this phase, the balls on the ground, at which we aim our tosses, provide visual reference for the amount of adjustment needed.

Correcting a Pushing Motion

While practicing backhands, many beginners develop the habit of pushing the racket at the ball. They mistakenly use a short elbow motion rather than the long swing from the shoulders used by experienced players.

The push usually results from shifting the weight too soon. When the body weight moves to the right foot too soon, the hitter usually hits too early. With such

Figure 8–5 The player learns to adjust her step by swinging at points above the balls on the ground. When she recognizes the adjustments that are necessary to place the racket on the ball correctly, she practices hitting at tossed balls.

timing he must move his elbow out toward the net to make contact. Often, the elbow is so far forward even during the backswing that a proper, adequate wind-up is impossible. Instead, the hitting hand goes back only as far as the belt buckle. When the forward swing starts from this position, only a short, jerky motion is possible.

In most cases, practice and instruction in adjusting the timing start the hitter on the way toward building a better stroke. For instance, learning to meet the ball back farther so that it is opposite the right shoulder at contact often corrects the faulty elbow position and movement. Sometimes, however, a hitter needs to learn a completely different concept of the swing in order to break the pushing habit. He must learn to think of the swing as a *pull* rather than a push.

One effective device for teaching the new concept provides practice at actually pulling the racket. As the hitter holds the racket back at the end of the backswing, the coach or an assistant grasps the racket and holds it firmly at the tip. The hitter attempts to start his forward swing by first shifting his weight and then pivoting at the hips and shoulders. He tries to pull the racket out of the coach's grasp. After several attempts the coach releases the racket as the hitter starts a pull, and the hitter completes his swing. In this way, the hitter is able to keep his body ahead of the hitting hand, and he is able to pull the racket from in front until contact is made.

Repeated practice at this pulling procedure often enables a beginner to correct his faulty push and to develop a smoothly coordinated swing.

THE SERVE

Most beginners have difficulty serving accurately even after they have developed satisfactory swing patterns. Synchronizing the toss with the swing, tossing accurately, and controlling the hand and wrist action at impact are their major problems. When analyzing beginners' serves, teachers should refer to the result of the hit — the flight of the ball — and relate what they see there to what occurs at contact, just as they do when analyzing groundstrokes. Although faulty body positions or poor timing may lead to an ineffective hit, the position of the racket on the ball and the speed and direction in which the racket is moving determine the flight characteristics of the ball — that is, its spin, speed, and direction.

Correcting Up-and-Down Errors

During service practice it is often helpful, although it may seem unnecessary to state such an obvious point, to remind the student that he has two tries to get one serve in play. He may then be told to note the result of his first try, and if it is a fault, to do something different, to make a correction on his second try. He must somehow change the angle at which his racket meets the ball in order to correct a first-serve fault. This can be done in either of two ways: by changing the placement of the toss or by changing the timing of the wrist action.

A fault in the first serve can often be used as a guide from which the server can learn what to do differently on his next serve. To correct a fault that was hit into the net, the ball may have to be tossed back farther. To correct a fault that landed beyond the service court, the ball may have to be tossed farther forward. Such changes in the toss enable the server to change the angle at which his racket meets the ball, enabling him to hit either more on top of the ball or more toward its bottom.

Often, however, the ball may land either too long or too short despite a proper toss. In such cases, improper timing of the wrist action must be corrected. Flipping the racket over on top of the ball too much (hitting the imaginary face on the forehead) will cause the ball to go into the net; not flipping it over soon enough (hitting on the chin) will cause the ball to go too long. Constant practice with emphasis on timing of the wrist action and on proper placement of the toss is needed to correct these kinds of faults.

Correcting Side-to-Side Errors

Errors in direction to either the left or the right are usually easier to control than are errors in length. Most commonly, a faulty serve goes to the left, especially when the beginner tries to put spin on the serve. Referring to the basics of ball control again, one can determine that the ball goes to the left because (1) the player is swinging in that direction (his racket is moving in an arc toward his left as it goes through the contact area), (2) he is placing his racket too far toward the right side of the ball (he may be hitting on the left ear of the imaginary face), (3) he is combining these errors, or (4) he may be facing too far toward his left in his serving stance.

The faulty stance is the easiest aspect to correct and should be the instructor's first order of business. He may simply draw a line from the proper location toward the target area and then have the server place both feet close to the line as he takes his serving stance. The player uses the line as a reference point and experiments with various placements of his feet to find the location that best lets him control the direction of his serve. The line extends for five feet into the court and is used as a visual guide to the proper path of the swing. If, in the contact area, the racket is moving in an arc from right to left across the line, the ball will probably be deflected to the left. By changing the path of the swing to make the racket move either straight along the line or across it from left to right, the direction of the ball will be altered.

Some corrections require reference to the imaginary face on the ball. If the hitter brings his racket into the ball with the right edge of the frame leading, he will almost surely slice the ball too much. As a result, the ball will squirt off to the left. To correct this slice, he may be told to adjust his wrist, hand, and forearm to make his palm face the net at impact. As a result, he can meet the ball squarely "on the nose."

Attending to two reference points — the path of the swing as it relates to the line drawn on the court, and the placement of the racket on the ball in terms of the imaginary face on the ball — usually enables most beginners to start correcting their errors in direction.

Correcting Inaccurate Service Tosses

The toss is one of the critical parts of the serve, and for many learners it is one of the most difficult parts to master. Often the difficulty stems from an inability to control the action of the tossing arm. Although players are told to move the arm straight down and up and to extend it as they toss, many inexperienced players inadvertently move the arm to the left or right or even bend it during the upward motion. As a result, the toss is inaccurate, and the swing must be adjusted accordingly. We say, then, that they are swinging at the toss rather than tossing to the swing. The latter is preferred, of course, for it is most likely to lead to a consistent serve, but it requires a consistently accurate toss.

Many players learn to toss accurately if they are told to look at the tossing hand and to follow the ball with their eyes as they make the toss. Very likely they have been looking up and away from the ball before releasing it. By watching the toss instead, many of them will develop better control of the arm action and will place the ball more accurately. Occasionally, however, a student will continue to have toss problems even after practicing this way. In such a case, a second step is recommended.

The student stands a foot away from the fence directly in front of one of the vertical fence posts, as if he were serving toward the post. He places his racket and ball together in front of him at chest height, in the conventional starting position, with his racket barely touching the fence and pointing at the post. He starts his swing and looks not only at his hand but also at the vertical fence post (he can see it in the periphery of his vision; the post is in the background as he looks at his hand). He uses the post as a guide as he moves his hand (and the ball) down and up to make the toss. He stops his swing halfway through the backswing, of course, but he can still synchronize the toss with the start of his swing, just as he does when actually serving.

Watching the ball during the toss as we have described is different from what top-flight players do. Most of them look up before the ball is released; they then toss into their field of vision. Many of them also move the tossing arm back and to the right as they turn their body to the right to start the backswing. They then toss the ball upward and forward (toward the net) to place it in front of them for the hit. This is more complicated than the straight down-and-up toss and compounds the problems of inexperienced players. Many of them will benefit from the kind of practice recommended here, in which they look at the ball and toss up along the post.

THE VOLLEYS

When teaching the volleys, we try first to build the stroke pattern and then to help the learner develop control of his shots. The corrective techniques we describe here apply to one or the other of these areas.

Correcting a Long Swing

Many beginners have trouble learning the short "block" or "punch" motion for the volley, probably because they have first learned to hit with a long backswing and follow-through for groundstrokes. We find the technique demonstrated in Figure 8–6 to be effective in teaching the shorter swing.

To correct a long backswing, the student stands tight against a fence with his

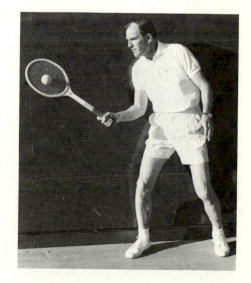

Figure 8–6 To correct a tendency to make too long a backswing when volleying, a player hits with his back close against a wall, as shown. As he takes his racket back, it strikes the wall. He soon learns to restrict the length of his backswing.

back to it and volleys balls tossed or hit carefully to his right side. With his back close to the fence he cannot take the racket back farther than his near shoulder. If he does, his racket rams into the fence and his swing is broken. After only a few tries he learns to shorten his backswing.

The player who needs to shorten his forward swing may be told to pretend that he is hammering a ball into the fence as if he were hammering a nail into a wall. The fence stops his racket at impact. He may then be told to use a similar short swing at live balls on the court. Presumably, he will stop his racket at impact, just as the fence stopped it when he hammered the ball into it.

If a learner persists in following through longer than is advisable, we often correct the problem by tossing several balls quickly in succession. He soon learns to stop the racket quickly after impact to prepare for the next ball, which follows almost immediately.

Learning to Meet the Ball "Early"

We prefer to see the wrist laid back and the ball met forward of the front hip on the volley. To correct a beginner who consistently meets the ball too late (alongside his body), we toss balls from across the net while he stands a half step away from it. We instruct him to move toward the net to meet the ball *on our side of the net.* We explain, of course, that in actual play he is not allowed to reach beyond the net to meet a ball that is in flight. When practicing to correct the fault of meeting the ball too late, however, he is permitted — even encouraged — to do so.

Correcting Faulty Elbow Action

For maximum control of volleys, most experienced players put backspin on the ball. They slice the ball with a downward motion of the racket while the racket face is slanted skyward a bit. This enables them to take some of the speed off the oncoming

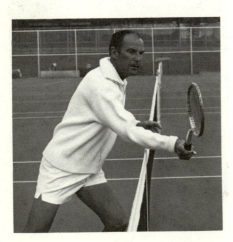

Figure 8-7 A practice drill for learning to meet the ball out in front with a laid-back wrist. The player reaches across the net to make contact on the tosser's side of the net.

Figure 8–8   Pressing a ball can against the body keeps the elbow down. The swing shown in the second frame could be modified to an elbow-down position after only brief practice.

ball and to keep the ball on the racket strings longer. As a result, the ball is usually hit a little less crisply and is controlled better than a flat shot.

Inexperienced players run into trouble when trying to apply backspin to their backhand volleys. When hitting with the downward slicing motion, they often mistakenly raise the elbow. Raising the elbow does enable them to put backspin on the ball, but it also usually causes them to contact the underside of the ball. As a result, they usually hit a high ball—sometimes even a "pop-up"—rather than the downward ball they want.

Learning to hit with the elbow down often corrects the tendency to hit pop-ups on volleys. With the elbow down, the hitter is less likely to contact the ball on its bottom side. Instead, he is likely to meet the ball on its back side. This point-of-contact, together with the downward motion of the racket, enables the hitter to pull the ball down and thus avoid the pop-up.

Two simple practice drills for learning to keep the elbow down are shown in Figure 8–8. Each drill is best followed with the player hitting against balls thrown accurately at the racket. In this way the hitter need not be concerned with matters of form or feel other than the position of the elbow. In one drill the player uses the left hand to keep the hitting elbow down. In the other the player presses a ball can against the body with the elbow while hitting. Usually only a few minutes practice at either procedure enables the hitter to get the feel of the proper elbow position.

Developing Control of Direction

On volleys, we stress that control of direction is attained by making adjustments in the wrist and elbow. These adjustments enable the hitter to place the racket on the ball properly to attain the proper deflection of the ball off the racket. To hit a forehand straight ahead, for example, the ball should be met forward of the front hip while the wrist is bent back. Contact then occurs on the back side of the ball, the side farthest from the net. To volley to his left, the hitter must straighten his wrist slightly to place the racket off-center toward the far side of the ball. To volley to his right, he bends the wrist back even farther than he does for straight-ahead shots, positioning the racket off-center toward the near side of the ball. These slight adjustments enable the hitter to change the point-of-contact slightly; he meets the ball sooner or later in terms of his body reference points. On the forehand volley, such changes are best made by adjusting the position of the *wrist*; adjusting the timing is done on groundstrokes.

On the backhand volley, the major adjustment for placement is in the position of the elbow. The ball is met at a point in advance of the front hip. For straight-ahead shots, the elbow should be adjusted so that the hitter can place the racket directly behind the ball. To hit to his left, the player moves his elbow forward (away from his body and toward the net) while letting his hand and racket lag behind. The elbow moves forward to whatever degree is necessary to enable the hitter to make contact slightly off-center toward the near side of the ball. To hit to his right, the player holds his elbow in closer to his body so that he can make contact slightly off-center toward the far side of the ball.

The simplest procedure that we recommend for teaching these points of placement is to toss balls softly for the hitter to volley. We first place balls only to his forehand. We ask him first to hit directly to us. Then we tell him to hit to our left (he bends his wrist back), and finally to our right. Usually after only a few of each of these kinds of hits he develops the feeling for making wrist adjustments for placements.

We proceed similarly on the backhand. The player first hits directly to us, then sticks his elbow out to steer the ball to our right, and, finally, holds the elbow in closer to hit to our left.

Chapter Nine

SINGLES TACTICS AND STRATEGY

Strokes can be regarded as the tools and weapons a player uses to control the ball. Through constant practice, most serious-minded players can learn eventually to place their shots reasonably well and to add speed to their shots. However, strokes alone are not sufficient to win consistently. A player must not only hit the ball well; he must know where to hit it. He must also know where to stand and how to move. Above all, he must know how to think — how to analyze his opponent's game to discover weaknesses that will enable the player to use his own strength against those weaknesses. Accordingly, the discussion that follows is centered on two very important elements of match play: strategy (a player's game plan), and tactics (the ways in which strokes are used to implement the game plan).

TACTICS FOR BEGINNERS

In elementary tennis, players should be permitted to play — to serve, return, and rally to win — as soon as they have developed a reasonable amount of control of their shots. The teacher's criterion for control at this level, however, should be much lower than that set for play at more advanced levels. Beginners are not yet *players*; they are only *rallyers*. They may not yet have been introduced to net play or to hitting with spin. They may not even be able to place their shots except to hit them "easy, over, and in" and possibly, in one or the other half of the opponent's court. This is about all that beginners should be expected to do, given their limited command of the game. Gradually, as they enlarge their capabilities and learn to do more and better things with their strokes, they can be shown how to do more and better things tactically, also. For the time being, though, simplicity is the key word — simplicity in their strokes, in their tactics, and in their overall plan for winning.

The simplest plan that can be devised is to merely try to "outsteady" an opponent while stroking from the backcourt. This is exactly what beginning tennis should be — steady tennis (as contrasted with pressure tennis and power tennis, both of which come later). Both players play from the backcourt, possibly two or three steps behind the baseline, and rally back and forth hoping to draw an error. Since at this level of play the backhand is usually the weaker of the groundstrokes, most balls should be aimed to an opponent's left side. Here we see the beginning of what will later become the basic shot for baseline play at even higher levels of skill: the backhand cross-court. Beginners are not yet able to stroke hard and steadily, however; their shots are—and should be—high, lazy floaters, three and four feet above the net. Consequently, we see players adjusting their positions in order to avoid balls aimed to backhands; they try to make the play on the favored forehand side instead.

Such maneuvering points out the need for control of direction even at the elementary level of play. Beginners must be able to hit continually to the backhand but must also be able to surprise an opponent with an occasional shot to his forehand. If control of depth is possible, a mixture of short and deep shots should be used along with the basic shot to the backhand. Above all, though, beginners should stress steady baseline play in which they patrol their baseline while trying to outrally the opponent. Steady tennis should be the objective and is the winning way at this level.

TACTICS IN INTERMEDIATE AND ADVANCED PLAY

Generally, there are three basic plans for play in a match. One is to serve and rush to the net to win points by volleying from that position. This style of play is known as "the big game" and is currently the vogue among top-ranking male players. A second plan is to remain in the vicinity of the baseline and to outstroke the opponent from the backcourt. As we said earlier, beginners should play this way because of their limited abilities. A third plan is a combination of the two: hard, accurate groundstrokes are followed to the net, and weak returns from the opponent are volleyed away for winners. Most experienced tournament players have built their games on this pattern, although many of them appear now to depend on the serve as the principal attacking shot.

Intermediate-level players should work toward combining parts of each of these plans. Serves should be used as attack shots to draw weak returns. Groundstrokes after the serve should be used to maneuver the opponent or to continue the attack. Volleys should be used as finishing shots made after a safe net approach. Such an "all-around game" is the best foundation on which to build for future development. Later, after gaining experience, players can learn to use whatever special abilities or qualities they have for more advanced play.

Sustaining the Rally

The all-around game recommended here requires that a player have the ability to sustain rallies. When the player is able to keep the ball in play from the backcourt long enough to match an opponent's rallying ability, he can wait for and obtain a safe opportunity to attack. Generally, the basic rally shot should be hit deep to the opponent's backhand, because at all except the top levels of play this is the weaker stroke. Since the opponent also plays to the weaker stroke, backhand cross-court shots are predominant in good baseline play.

Hitting deeply and consistently to an opponent's backhand may seem like a large order for an average school player. It is not as difficult as it may at first appear, however, for shots to the backhand need not have much speed on them. All that is required is depth enough and accuracy enough to make the opponent hit from behind his baseline. Suggestions for the control of depth are made later in this chapter. As for the degree of accuracy required, most conscientious players of average ability can develop it with a moderate amount of practice. It is not necessary to hit within inches of a sideline. A ball landing six or eight feet from an opponent's left sideline will still have to be stroked with a backhand (assuming, of course, that he is a right-handed player). If he succeeds in running around his backhand to use his stronger forehand, his weakness in position will offset any advantage he has gained by the move.

Among tactically inclined players, the backhand cross-court is not usually intended to be a winner. Instead, it is used to keep the opponent at bay, behind his baseline and hitting with his weak stroke. When two players are able to use this shot in a rally, they are in a sense sparring with each other, each trying to create an opening for a knockout blow.

Controlling the Rally

Although the ability to keep the ball in play is essential, it alone is not sufficient in intermediate and advanced play. To win consistently at these levels, a player must be able to stroke accurately and forcefully enough to move his opponent for the purposes of creating openings and drawing weak shots and errors. To the extent that a player is able to make his strokes work for him he will be in control of the rally and is likely to draw weak shots or even errors from his opponent.

To control the rally, a baseliner must be able to control the depth of his shots. Depth control comes from controlling the height at which the ball clears the net. At times, in order to get more depth, a player must hit higher as well as harder. He must select a certain height above the net for each shot, and the height may vary depending on the speed and the purpose of the shot. Rally shots should clear the net by at least a foot, and possibly even by as much as three feet, to provide a margin of safety while also providing the depth necessary to keep the opponent behind his baseline. If they are hit into this height with only a medium amount of speed, they are likely to land deep in the opponent's court, causing him to hit from behind his baseline. This will keep him in the backcourt. If he insists on going to the net from there, he will be making a hazardous approach.

A judicious mixture of deep drives and sharply angled slices may force an opponent into bad position (or even draw an error) more quickly than will drives of consistent depth. Many players find it extremely difficult to defend from the baseline when they are forced to run diagonally forward and then diagonally backward on successive shots.

Hitting on the Rise

A player's ability to control the rally is often related to the amount of time he allows his opponent to return to good position between shots. If, for example, a server has moved his opponent out of court but he plays the receiver's return

Figure 9–1   A vertical guide-board at the net post helps youngsters visualize the proper height of net clearance for various shots. "One" shots are within a foot or so of the net (passing shots, hard serves, drop shots, other extremely hard shots); "2" shots are in the next highest level, extending to three feet above the net (most rally shots); "3" shots are in the next level and extend to six feet above the net (time-savers needed to recover to the proper position); "4" shots are high enough to be out of the net man's reach (lobs, either defensive or offensive).

after a long bounce from a position deep behind the baseline, he will be giving the receiver time to recover. The server would be wiser to hit the ball earlier, from closer to his baseline—if possible, even from inside it. Usually, it is greatly to a baseliner's advantage to hit the ball while it is rising. The sooner he hits it, the sooner it will be on its way to the opponent, and the less time the opponent will have to recover his position and chase the ball down.

Hitting on the rise is not difficult to learn. All that is required is that some attention be paid to changing the slant of the racket at contact. Since the rising ball is coming to the racket in an upward plane, it will deflect upward off the racket face (the angle of incidence equals the angle of reflection). Consequently, a hitter must turn his wrist a bit to adjust the racket face at contact. A moderate amount of practice at hitting a rising ball will enable most good strokers to make this adjustment when necessary.

Choosing the Right Shot

In order to control the rally, a player must be able to apply pressure to his opponent either by serving well enough to draw a weak return or by returning his opponent's serve well enough to minimize the effectiveness of the shot. If he succeeds in either case, he is likely to have a choice of shots to make early in the rally, and if he chooses wisely, he is likely to be in command of the situation. We may say that he must choose the right shot at the right time.

Figure 9–2 *A.* A player hitting from wide in his court must often play for position so that he can recover for his opponent's return. If he hits cross-court or to the center he has to return only to #1 or #2 to be in good position for the opponent's return. His cross-court shot also ensures that he will not have to chase any wider than his left sideline, as he might have had to do if he had hit down the line. When in trouble, the wise player plays for strength in his position; cross-courts get him out of trouble and keep him in the rally. *B.* Player in the foreground is shown in the proper ready position on the line that bisects the angle of the opponent's possible returns. Line #1 is clearly shown to be to the right of the center mark — that is, the player is off-center to the right. Note that if he were at the net, proper positioning — on the line that bisects — would place him off-center to the left.

The matter of selecting the right shot at the right time can be simplified by listing the possibilities. Every shot is made for one of the following reasons: (1) to spar with the opponent while waiting for an opening or for a weak shot; (2) to secure good position when the opponent has attacked; (3) to move the opponent as preparation for an attack; or (4) to attack—to make a "kill," a put-away.

Smart players who make their shots for either of the first two reasons keep in mind the basic principle of position play: as your opponent makes his shot, be ready and waiting on the line that bisects the angle of his possible returns.

In applying this principle, an experienced baseliner stands directly behind his center mark *only* when his opponent is hitting from close to his own center mark. When the opponent is hitting from near the corners of his court, the baseliner is a step or two away from the mark in the opposite direction from which his opponent has moved. The baseliner is purposely off-center, in order to be on the bisecting line (which may be called the line of good position).

The problem of maintaining good position by being on the bisecting line is closely related to the matter of choosing the right shot at the right time. When a player has been forced wide to hit and he is fearful of not being able to get back to good position, his best shot is either down the middle or cross-court, depending on how wide he is. The down-the-line shot should be used only if the opponent has a stroke weakness there or if he, too, is out of position.* If the opponent is in good position and has good strokes on both sides, a smart baseliner plays for strength in his own position. He does this by making his opponent hit from the center or from close to the farthest corner. In this way he creates a situation in which his own line of good position is brought closer to him than it would be had he hit parallel to the sidelines. Consequently, he will have less distance to travel to reach the line of good position, and when he does reach it, he will be positioned correctly for his opponent's return.

When an opponent has made an effective approach shot and has advanced to the net behind it, the baseliner's best plan may be to lob. The smart baseliner considers the quality of his opponent's volleying and smashing ability, and assesses his own potential for passing or lobbing accurately. If his strength is in passing shots or if the opponent is weak at volleying, he may wisely decide to drive. But if he feels he may not be able to pass or prevent a winning volley, the better play may be to lob. The intention in such a case would be to draw a weak return which may then be hit aggressively for a winner or to draw an error. Continuous use of the lob mixed with drives in this manner will often take the sting out of the opponent's net attacks although he is not noticeably weak at either volleying or smashing.

Playing Power Tennis

Despite the emphasis here on steadiness and accuracy, players who are able to hit forcefully should be encouraged to do so. Those who serve hard enough to draw weak returns and those whose groundstrokes and volleys are crisp enough to

---

*By avoiding the down-the-line shot when wide in the court, the player ensures that he will not have to run any farther than the far sideline for the opponent's shot. The opponent is lured into hitting parallel to that sideline as he aims to the apparent opening. The bounce of his shot, therefore, does not carry outside the sideline, as it would have had he been permitted to hit a cross-court to the same apparent opening.

Figure 9–3 A server is shown advancing to a volley position. After his medium-speed serve, the server has time for four or five steps before having to "check" in the volley position. He pauses momentarily and prepares to move to reach for or to get away from the oncoming ball. After making a volley from the location shown in the last frame he will move up to a better location for his next shot.

put pressure on the opponent should be encouraged to move into the volley position at every safe opportunity.

To play effectively from the forecourt, a player must understand good position play and must develop a kind of "court sense" which he can use to guide him in his selection of shots. The ideal volley position with respect to the net is midway between the net and the service line. A player cannot always reach that position for his first volley, however. As he moves in to volley after either a serve or a groundstroke, he has to stop to change direction in order to reach the opponent's return. Usually, this stop occurs at a spot closer to the service line than to the ideal volley position. Experienced players adjust their steps so they can hop to the ready position just as the opponent's racket meets the ball, regardless of their location in the court (terms often used to describe this hop to the ready position are "check" and "split stop"; the net rusher pauses momentarily to check on what his opponent intends to do). From the check position they can move in any direction to make a play on the opponent's return. After hitting the first volley, they move up to the ideal volley position for the second hit.

After a hard first serve, a server has time for only two or three steps before his opponent makes his hit. Consequently, he often gets caught in "no man's land," but this is a calculated risk he takes; volleying from there may not be very dangerous after a hard first serve. After a softer second serve, the server has more running time, often enough time for four or five steps. This permits him to run as far as the service line before having to make his check. From there it takes only a short hop to reach the ideal position for his second volley.

A player rushing to the net after a groundstroke faces certain position problems. For instance, if he tries to go to the net after hitting from three or four feet behind his baseline, he will not reach a good volley position for his first volley. This is the main reason for the fact that even power hitters must select only safe opportunities to go to the net.

The net man's position with respect to the center service line should vary as his opponent's position varies. If the opposing baseliner is hitting from close to his center mark, the volleyer should be on the center line. If, however, the baseliner is hitting from close to a sideline, the volleyer should be off-center a bit toward his opponent. He should move right or left to place himself on the line that bisects the angle of his opponent's possible returns. Throughout the point he should be trying to move in as close to the net as possible to reduce the width of that angle, at the same time maintaining an alertness for a possible lob over his head.

The placement and purpose of volleys should vary depending on the volleyer's position (and of course on the opponent's as well). When the player is volleying from behind the service line, the ball may have to be *stroked* to give it the necessary pace. When he is volleying from closer to the net, however, the conventional punch or block volley is usually adequate. High balls often can be angled away for winners or hit forcefully enough to draw errors or weak returns. Low balls, on the other hand, may often have to be played carefully. They seldom can be put away for winners unless the opponent has first been maneuvered into leaving an opening.

SPECIFIC PLAY SITUATIONS

Having presented an overall picture of strategy and having indicated some effective tactics for various levels of play, we now present additional teaching points that apply to the five basic play situations: serving, returning the serve, rallying from the backcourt, going to the net, and playing against a man at the net. At any time during a match, a player is likely to find himself in one or another of these situations. Awareness of the points presented here, when accompanied by a degree of skill appropriate to the level of play, is likely to make his play more effective.

Serving

1. If the server does not intend to follow his serve into the volley position, he ought to experiment a bit to find the most effective location along the baseline from which to serve. In the deuce court, standing close to the center mark and aiming down the line to the backhand is usually the most effective procedure. Occasionally, however, serving from close to the sideline and angling the ball at the receiver will be the most effective approach. From the ad court, experienced players usually stand midway between the center mark and the sideline. This gives them a good angle to the backhand without placing them too far out of position to reach a return along the line. An exception is noted when the receiver can return well enough to take advantage of the open court to the server's right. In such a case, the server stands closer to the mark.

2. Most serves should be aimed to the receiver's backhand, because at all but the most advanced levels of play the backhand is the weaker stroke. Placements should be varied enough, however, to prevent the receiver from moving around a ball hit to his backhand. Occasionally, the serve should be hit straight at the receiver (either a fast first serve or a tricky, spinning serve) to prevent him from moving in confidently.

3. The effectiveness of the second serve is the measure of a player's serving ability. If the receiver is attacking second serves effectively, first serves should be hit easier to ensure getting more of them in, even if it means giving up chances for "acing" the receiver on the first serve.

4. Depth on the serve is as important as it is on groundstrokes. The server

should be prepared to adjust and change his toss and wrist position (to change the position of the racket on the ball) to improve the depth of his serves.

5.   After a serve wide to the receiver's alley, the server recovers to a ready position on the line that bisects the possible angles of the receiver's returns.

6.   When a player intends to run to the net after a serve, the best location for serving is close to the center mark in both courts; this gives him the shortest distance to run to reach a good volley position.

7.   The first serve usually provides a much safer opportunity to volley than does an easy second serve. It may therefore be necessary to hit first serves at three-quarter speed to ensure getting more of them in and to avoid serving an easier second ball.

8.   If the receiver handles the server's best serves well enough to draw weak volleys, it may be best for the server to stay back and wait for a safer groundstroke approach shot.

9.   If the service returns are continually low and bothersome to a net-rushing server, he should purposely vary the length of his run before making his check. He may occasionally stop short of the serving line to let low balls bounce up nicely for a groundstroke. At other times he may move in all the way, hoping to intercept returns intended to be deep to his former position.

10.   When the server runs to the net to volley the return, he should run to a location that places him off-center toward the receiver. In that position, he faces the receiver as he makes his check. He reaches for sharply angled cross-court returns by moving on a line perpendicular to the line of the oncoming ball.

Returning the Serve

1.   The receiver's location should vary, depending on the speed of the serve and on whether or not the server is running in to volley. Against a fast serve, the receiver may have to stand a step or two behind the baseline. Against easier serves, he may stand on the line or even inside of it. Standing behind the line allows him more time to move and to swing, but it also gives him a large angle to cover. Standing inside the line, on the other hand, reduces the angle he has to cover but requires quicker movements on his part. In match play, the receiver ought to experiment to find his best location in each match.

2.   Regardless of his location relative to the baseline, the receiver stands on an imaginary line that bisects the possible angles of the server. He may, however, "cheat" a bit and move toward his weaker stroke to leave less of an opening there.

3.   High-bouncing spin serves that the server follows to the net should be taken on the rise and high on the bounce to permit the server less running time before making his check. The return should be aimed at the service line to cause the server to hit at a low ball. When the server is hitting a half-volley, the receiver should anticipate a weak, short return and move up inside the baseline step to await the return.

4.   If the server does not follow his serve to the net, the return usually should be aimed deep to his backhand to make the server hit from behind the baseline. Occasionally, however, a cross-court to the forehand may be necessary to ensure getting back to good position. This occurs when the serve is sharply angled and the receiver is hitting from wide of his sideline.

5. The style of play in "percentage tennis" implicity requires the receiver to use his most consistent shot much more often than a risky one—and almost always on a crucial point. Players should experiment in practice to determine their best shot (forehand or backhand? cross-court or down the line? drive or slice?). It is often helpful to count and tabulate good and bad shots during practice to convince each player of the logic of this approach and to instill confidence in this philosophy.

6. Cross-court returns should be aimed to the short corner; a deep cross-court is more likely to be within reach of the net man. Down-the-line returns may be either short or deep.

7. To reach wide-angled serves, the receiver moves perpendicularly to the lines of flight of the oncoming ball. For these serves he should skip sideways if time permits, in order to avoid making a wide crossover step. If possible, he should get close enough to the ball to hit with an open stance; this permits better balance and allows a quicker recovery to position than does an extreme sideways stance.

8. If the receiver intends to follow his service return in, in order to intercept the server's first volley with a volley of his own, his percentage return is along the sideline. If the server is forced to volley from close to that line, the receiver will have less distance to move to reach a line of good position for his next shot.

9. When a player is going to the net on the return of serve, the open stance while hitting on the move (described in Chapter 7) is the most effective way to proceed. It allows a running start from a location closer to the net than does a closed stance in which the receiver waits for the ball to come to him.

10. Generally, it is easier to return the ball to the direction from which it came, i.e., along the same line of flight, because the receiver does not have to make allowances for the ball's deflection off his racket (he does not have to make allowances for the angle of incidence and the angle of reflection as he would when hitting to any other direction).

11. If the server usually angles his first volley accurately and effectively, it may be best to hit low to the center of his court—at his feet—when returning the serve. This will reduce the angles available to him when he makes his first volleys.

Rallying from the Backcourt

1. At all levels of play except top-flight competition, most players have a "built-in" weakness on the backhand. Most rally shots should be aimed there, most attack shots should be played into that weakness, and many defensive shots should be hit there, despite the disadvantage of hitting along the line.

2. Depth on drives comes from hitting higher as well as harder. Players must learn (a) to control the height of their shots and (b) to adjust the height to the speed at which they hit and to their position (distance from the net) when hitting.

3. In order to attack confidently on short shots from the opponent, players must learn to move in quickly to play such shots high on the bounce, if possible, in order to hit down, and hard, with safety.

4. A smart baseliner plays to an opponent's forehand (his strong stroke) often enough to prevent him from covering his weak backhand. He often makes a preliminary attack to the forehand in order to follow with a stronger attack to the backhand.

5. Percentage tennis play implies that a player should hit to those of his opponent's strokes that provide the most errors. This may sometimes be true of a sup-

posedly strong forehand – it may be a more aggressive stroke but also a less reliable one.

6.   A player's position relative to his baseline (his distance from the net) should determine, to some extent, the kind of shot he should try. If he is hitting from inside his baseline with his strong stroke, he may attack. If, on the other hand, he is hitting from deep behind his baseline, he may have to play defensively.

7.   In windy conditions a player must make allowances for gusts, and play accordingly. When hitting with a strong wind, his drives must be low; lobs are difficult to control, and drop shots are risky. When hitting against a wind, his drives should be high to provide depth; lobs are often effective defensive shots, and drop shots are much easier to place accurately.

8.   Factors to be considered in the effective use of drop shots are: (a) the hitter's position from the net, (b) the opponent's distance from the net, (c) the opponent's speed, (d) the player's ability to disguise his shot, (e) court surface conditions and their effect on a player's footing and on his ability to start quickly or to change direction, and (f) wind conditions.

9.   Spin on the ball will affect the bounce of the ball. Players must learn to recognize what the opponent is doing to the ball. In this way, they can then anticipate the kind of bounce. A bounce may often bother them; it should never take them by surprise. The most bothersome bounces are those that occur after a slice or chop. A slice motion that imparts a fast, low trajectory to the ball will cause the ball to skid low on the bounce. A slice with a lofted trajectory, on the other hand, will cause the ball to bounce more vertically (the bounce is slower). When the racket is dragged across the line of flight of the ball, the ball will bounce in the direction opposite that in which the racket is moving.

Going to the Net

1.   In percentage tennis the safest time to go to the net is when hitting a strong stroke from inside the baseline, with the shot placed deep to an opponent's weak stroke. Occasionally, however, the ball may be safely played to an opponent's strong stroke. This can be done when the opponent has been moved out of position and leaves an opening on one side. This may be called "being weak in position," and players must learn to choose wisely between hitting to an opponent's weak stroke or to where he is weak in position.

2.   Although approach shots should be played aggressively, they should also be played carefully enough to ensure getting a very high percentage of them in. Players should be cautioned against defeating themselves by missing too many approaches. They should be told to make the opponent show how well he can pass. This helps a net rusher determine how aggressively he must play his approaches – how much risk he must take on them.

3.   Because the opponent is not likely to have a weak backhand in advanced play, the best approach shot often may be down-the-line, either to the forehand or to the backhand. Such a shot usually allows a net rusher to reach the line of good position, off-center toward the opponent, more conveniently than does a cross-court approach shot. In this sense, the net rusher plays for strength in his own position rather than to a weakness in stroke.

4.   On his way to the net after his approach shot, the net rusher hops to a ready

Figure 9-4   Generally a player should go to the net only when hitting a strong stroke from a location on or inside the baseline. With inexperienced players it may be necessary to mark the court surface as shown to indicate the locations from which to advance to the net. On the increasingly popular red and green colored courts, an effective approach is to use the "traffic light" approach: "Green is Go" (go to the net). "Red is Stop" (stay back).

position and pauses momentarily just as the opponent's racket meets the ball. He pauses only long enough to determine the opponent's intentions and to read the direction of his shot. He then moves appropriately to reach the return.

5. As he runs to the net, the attacker selects the shortest route to the best volley location; he moves in as far as he can to be on an imaginary line that bisects the angles of the opponent's possible returns (the line of good position). Thus he is placed slightly off-center when his opponent is hitting from close to a sideline (a volleyer is off-center toward his opponent; a baseliner, in the opposite direction). (See Figure 9–2(b).)

6. If the volleyer makes his first check behind his service line, he moves in to make a play on any easy balls within his reach. If he manages to play a ball that is high in flight, above the net, he can hit away aggressively for winners. If he is forced to hit at low returns, he plays them carefully and then moves up to a better volley location for his second volley.

7. After each check, a volleyer must be prepared to move sideways with a crossover step to have maximum reach for wide balls. To reach a sharply angled passing shot, the move should be on a line perpendicular to the line of flight of the ball.

8. If the opponent's return is slow enough, the volleyer may have time for two or three steps — after his momentary pause — to move to the ball. Whenever possible he should continue to move forward after his pause to meet the ball closer to the net.

9. An opponent's chop with a great deal of backspin will deflect downward off the volleyer's racket. A heavily topped drive (overspin) will deflect upward. The volleyer must be attentive to these variations and make allowances for the angle of rebound as he aims his volleys.*

Playing Against a Net Man

1. A backcourt player's intentions and choice of shots against a net man should be determined in part by his position relative to his baseline. If he is hitting from behind the line, his safest play will probably be to the volleyer's feet, for the purpose of getting another and safer chance to pass. If he is hitting from the line or from inside it, he may be able to pass outright with a one-shot winner. There are other points to consider, however, to determine the choice in directions. To play by the percentages, a baseliner chooses his most consistent shot (cross-court or down-the-line) and his most effective stroke (drive, chop, slice, or chip) much more often than an uncertain shot or stroke, and again, almost always on the critical points. He does not make what he considers to be a risky try on his part; instead, he makes the play he has the most confidence in.

2. Cross-court shots against a net man usually provide a better opportunity for getting out of trouble than do down-the-line shots. They prevent the volleyer from angling the ball sharply toward the far sideline.

3. Cross-court passing shots must be aimed low to a short corner; deep cross-courts are likely to be within reach of the net man. Down-the-line shots, however, can

---

*The angle at which the ball approaches the racket also affects the angle of rebound. For example, a heavily topped ball that is dropping sharply at impact may deflect downward off the racket. The angle of approach may be dominant over the effect of spin.

be aimed either short or deep, especially if the hitter is in his alley (or wider) as he strokes.

4.   Low shots that the volleyer is forced to play with a half-volley are likely to draw weak, short returns. Baseliners must learn to anticipate these weak shots and move up inside the line immediately after making a low shot to the volleyer's feet.

5.   On any short ball offered by the net man, a baseliner should move in as quickly as possible to make the play as high on the bounce as possible; he should try to avoid hitting up to a net man.

6.   When the groundstroker is forced to hit at a low ball, his best play is often a medium-paced shot to one of the short corners. If he is capable of driving with considerable top spin, he may score winners with such a shot. Usually, however, the percentage play is a moderate shot placed low in an attempt to draw a weak return.

7.   Players should attempt to discover early in a match how well the opponent can smash. This determines how often the lob will be used. Advanced players often use the lob for more than just defensive play, however; they sometimes lob to win outright or to draw errors. For this purpose they lob on the second shot against a net man, after he has closed in for his second volley; he is more vulnerable then for an offensive lob than he will be from the position of his first check.

Chapter Ten

DOUBLES: TACTICS, STRATEGY, AND POSITIONS

Every knowledgeable teacher and coach has had the experience of seeing two good singles players look completely out of place when playing together as a doubles team. Often, either of these players could beat either of the opponents in a singles match. Yet they are out-maneuvered and out-pointed in the game for pairs. Sometimes this is because their shots are not adapted to the doubles game. Usually, however, it is because they do not understand the principles of doubles play and consequently do not work together as a team. Instead of playing *with* their partner, some players seem to join their opponents in playing *against* him.

We feel that most serious players can learn to enjoy doubles and to understand the basic principles of play after only a moderate amount of systematic instruction. With this knowledge, improvement will come quickly as students practice and develop the strokes and shots needed for its application. We do not mean to suggest that *excellence* comes quickly. Mastery of the shots, the moves, and the many other details that make for championship play takes years to develop. Of course, mastery does not come about simply as a by-product of endless hours of doubles play. Instead, it comes only after careful study and analysis of both the simple and the intricate tactics and maneuvers that win at various levels of play.

In this chapter, we will discuss several principles of doubles tennis that determine the patterns of play of winning teams. We will first describe and discuss doubles as it is played at the championship level. We will then describe what we call "middle-level" doubles and will offer suggestions for improving play. To teachers of elementary classes we suggest that much of our material on middle-level play applies to their work also. They may have to make a few modifications in positions and tactics to make them compatible with students' abilities, but for the most part these need not be substantially changed. Finally, we will list several additional principles that are applicable to all levels of play. Teachers and coaches may select and teach any that are appropriate for their classes and teams.

TOP-LEVEL DOUBLES

Doubles is essentially a team game in which individual skill is usually not as effective as teamwork and cooperation. Experienced players realize this and willingly sacrifice individual brilliance for the sake of playing as a partner. They seldom try to win a point single-handedly. Instead, they work *with* their partner, protecting him and helping him out of difficult situations when necessary, and maneuvering with him to attack together when possible.

Experienced players assume that two worthy opponents can cover the court adequately from the basic starting positions. Consequently, it is necessary to move them to create openings and to draw errors or weak shots before trying to win with a placement. It is difficult to win with placements from the backcourt, however. The strategy, therefore, is for both players to move into a good volleying position as soon as possible in each point, sometimes even behind weak or "risky" returns. With all four players at the net, points are decided quickly; the average rally lasts for only four or five shots. This strategy requires a variety of shots; effective serves, consistent returns, crisp volleys, and soft, delicate volleys as well must all be in players' repertoires.

Positions and Tactics

Net play is so essential and can be so effective in top-level play that both teams place a player in the volleying position at the beginning of every point. Both the server's partner and the receiver's partner are in the forecourt and the server and the receiver almost always run forward to join them immediately after serving and returning serve.

THE SERVER

The server stands at the baseline in the middle of his half of the court, a location that gives him the shortest route to reach a good volley position. From there, he is able to run in on a line perpendicular to the service line. He runs until just before the receiver makes contact with the ball at which time he comes to a momentary pause (the check or split stop) and prepares to move to reach the return. The pause permits him to set himself into the conventional ready position, from which he can move quickly to his left or right, or even retreat to smash a lob.

The server's objective is to serve well enough to draw a weak return that can be volleyed aggressively either by the server or by his partner. If the serve is deep and is well placed, the receiver is usually forced into making a defensive play on the return. As a result, the serving team, which is safely at the net, is usually able to continue to attack with volleys.

A spin serve (a combination of overspin and sidespin) hit at three-quarter speed is used much more often than a flat serve, even when serving the first ball in a point, because it gives the server more time to advance to the volley position. Normally, after a three-quarter-speed serve, the server has time for four or five steps before having to make his pause. He therefore can (at the least) reach the service

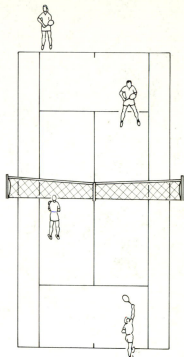

Figure 10-1 The respective starting positions of all four players are shown. Note that each player is in the center of his half of the court with respect to the sidelines and the center line. Note also that the receiver's partner is only one step inside the service line. From this position he can move forward to play aggressively if his partner's return of serve permits him to do so safely, or he can retreat, if necessary, after a weak return.

line for his first volley. From there he can play aggressively on a larger percentage of shots than if he were trapped back farther from the net. Furthermore, since a spin serve usually can be controlled better than a flat serve, the server will manage to get a good number of first tries in. This is important for two reasons: the receiver is less likely to move in and attack aggressively, and the server's partner is more likely to be able to poach successfully on first serves than he is on second serves.

A harder flat serve is used occasionally, however, to change the pace and to prevent the receiver from moving in confidently on all returns. After such a serve, the server usually has time for only two or three steps before pausing to change direction. This places him in "no man's land," usually a dangerous location, but he takes his chances on volleying from that weaker position behind his strongest serve.

In either case, whether volleying from the service line or from no man's land, the server usually moves up toward the ideal volley position (halfway between the net and service line) for his second shot. Most serves are placed to the receiver's backhand—particularly when play is to the right court, because the return is more difficult to make from that location; the receiver's angles are reduced. When serving to the left court, most players place their serves wide to move the receiver out of court. When serving to either court, the server hits to the forehand often enough to prevent the receiver from running around every backhand and to prevent him from moving in confidently on every return. At times the server aims directly at the receiver to keep him off-balance.

The aim point for the server's first volley depends on whether he is hitting at a high or low ball and on the position of the opponents. If the return of serve is high, he may be able to hit down aggressively, aiming to the feet of the opposing net man, into his alley, between the opponents, to an opening toward the far sideline, deep to the receiver, or at the receiver's feet. If the receiver's return of serve is low, forcing the server to hit up on his first volley, he aims either deep or short, depending on the receiver's moves and position after making the return. If the receiver moves forward to midcourt, the server's first volley is hit softly and low to his feet. If the receiver stays back, the first volley is aimed deep to force him to hit from behind his baseline. On these volleys the server tries to keep the ball away from the opposing net man, who may have moved forward aggressively and may even have "poached," hoping to intercept.

THE SERVER'S PARTNER

The server's partner stands six to eight feet from the net and in the middle of his half of the court. The exact position varies among players as they vary in height, reach, and quickness in moving sideward and backward. They select positions that enable them to protect their alley and to intercept balls placed too close to the center. Occasionally, a partner will dash across the center line to intercept returns. "Poaching" in this way is sometimes a spur-of-the-moment decision by the net man. Other times it is a planned move, made after partners first exchange signals indicating their intentions.

To move quickly and to defend effectively, a net man must be alert and ready. Most good net players try to confuse the receiver about their intentions. They make several fake moves by shifting their weight and by shuffling or swaying, hoping in this way to draw a weak or badly placed return. While they are faking and getting set, they try to anticipate the receiver's intentions. They look for cues in his stance or position or swing—cues that indicate the kind of shot he intends to make and the direction in which he intends to hit.

Despite all these moves and preparations for offensive play, however, good net men are always alert for a surprise lob in their direction. In top-flight doubles, lobs are handled by the player who is in the best position to play the ball. Normally, this is the player to whose side of the court the ball is aimed. When lobs are hit toward the server's partner, he is expected to make a play on them; he does not, therefore, ignore the possibility of having to retreat to smash.

The net man plays aggressively on all high balls within his reach. He aims at an opening between the opponents, at an opening to the nearest sideline, or at the feet of the opposing net man. If he is hitting at a low ball, however, he often has to play more safely, in which case he volleys either deep to the receiver (if the receiver has not moved in to volley) or to midcourt, to the receiver's feet (if the receiver has moved in).

THE RECEIVER

In advanced play, the receiver usually stands within a step of the baseline on a line bisecting the server's widest possible placements. He is inside the baseline to take the ball early if he can handle the serve from there; he is behind the line if the serve is too difficult to handle from up closer.

Figure 10-2 Sequence shows a good poach by the server's partner. Note that he has stepped out toward the center line to intercept the return. If necessary, he could have reversed direction from his position (in frame C) to reach back toward his sideline to intercept a return made in that direction. The receiver's partner is caught rather close to the opposing net man. For better defensive play he should stand back farther, sometimes as far back as the service line. From that location he has more time to react to the poach and can also move up to play aggressively when his partner makes a good return to the server's feet.

The receiver usually follows his return in to the volley position. He gambles on being able to return well enough (low enough) to reach the net position safely. To do this, he plays the ball early, on the rise, and high on the bounce. His intention is to hit at the feet of the server (who has run up to volley) to prevent him from making an offensive volley. Lobs are used when the receiver has difficulty handling the serve and when the net man is poaching. The large majority of service returns are aimed cross-court to the feet of the onrushing server.

In playing the ball early from a position inside the baseline and returning low to the server's feet, the receiver makes only a three-quarter-length shot. He therefore does not utilize a full, forceful swing. Nor does he employ a full-speed drive, for he needs sufficient time to move up into a good volley position after his return. For these reasons, most good doubles players play their service returns carefully; they use a short backswing and a short, controlled forward swing. They often chop or slice the ball and hit half-speed or three-quarter-speed returns, especially on the backhand. They feel that such shots can offer better control and permit more running time to the volley position than do fast drives.

Occasionally, however, full-speed drives are used when returning the serve, especially if the receiver is able to hit with a good deal of top spin. Obviously, the best procedure is to return with a variety of shots to keep the server off-balance and to prevent him from anticipating and establishing a rhythm. It is not unusual, therefore, to see good receivers run around serves placed to their backhand; they hope in this way to vary the kind of ball the server gets to hit on his first volley.

After making his return, the receiver usually moves in quickly, hoping to reach a safe volleying position. He pauses momentarily, regardless of his position, as the opponents make their play. After his team's first volley, he either moves in closer to play aggressively or holds his ground to play defensively, depending on the effectiveness of the volley.

THE RECEIVER'S PARTNER

The receiver's partner usually stands in the vicinity of the service line, midway between the sideline and center line. If he feels his partner can consistently return low to the server's feet, he stands in the ideal volley position (halfway between the net and the service line). If he is fearful of the opponents getting high returns to play, he stands back farther, closer to the service line. He holds this position and prepares to volley defensively if a bad service return by his partner permits the opponents to volley offensively. If his partner's return forces the opponents into a defensive shot, he moves forward a step or two, hoping to volley aggressively. He may even poach at times by moving across the center line to intercept the server's volley.

Players who consider defense an important part of doubles have the receiver's partner stand at the baseline, where he can defend against aggressive volleys by the opposing net man. This strategy is being seen more frequently, even in world-class play, because modern servers make it difficult for receivers to return well enough to permit their partners to play at the net. In a variation of this strategy, the receiver's partner stands at the baseline during the first serve and at the service line for the second. The assumption here is that the receiver will be able to handle the easier second serve well enough to protect his partner at the net. In either of the strategies for placing the receiver's partner, the overriding consideration is the ability of the receiver to make his return. Usually, therefore, it is he who directs his team's strategy when the opponents are serving.

MIDDLE-LEVEL DOUBLES

Although aggressive net play is essential for successful top-level play, it is not always possible, nor is it always the winning way, in lower levels of play. Middle-level players often lack one or more of the qualities and skills needed to attack constantly. For example, some cannot serve or volley well enough to move in safely on every serve. This does not mean they cannot win in doubles at their level of play. When teamed properly with a partner who has compensating skills, and when they devise tactics that permit them to make the best use of each other's abilities, they can, indeed, play very effectively. In this section of our discussion of doubles, we suggest variations from the advanced techniques described earlier, variations that often permit a weak server, a slow mover, or even a poor volleyer to enjoy doubles and to win a good percentage of the time when playing within his class. Middle-level doubles partners *should* devise tactics that permit them to play within their capabilities, regardless of how these tactics differ from those of top-flight, all-around players.

The One Up, One Back Formation

The most obvious variation we recommend from top-flight doubles is in the total plan of play — the strategy. Rather than attempting to win by moving into the volley position immediately, a team may often be more successful using the one up, one back formation. They can then use the special individual qualities and talents of each player, while at the same time they can avoid having to use many of their weak strokes and shots. The intention with this formation is to allow the good driver to play from the backcourt (to use his drives) while the good volleyer plays from the net (to use his volleys).

THE BACKCOURT PLAYER

If one player on a doubles team dislikes being at the net and does not play well there but can rally steadily and accurately from the backcourt, then the backcourt should be his base of operations. After serving, he remains at the baseline, where he can play from a position of strength. He also stays back after his return-of-serve. He moves forward to the volley position only when drawn in by a short shot, or when he feels that his attacking drive makes the forward movement safe. Since accuracy usually develops along with steadiness, a good baseliner can usually manage to keep his drives out of the net man's reach. When the opponents make a very good attack shot, he may have to lob. Most good baseliners are good lobbers because this ability also seems to develop along with steadiness and accuracy from the backcourt. Consequently, the baseliner may find that lobbing even the return of serve is an effective tactic at the middle level of play.

When teaching the one up, one back formation, we stress that the baseliner's chief function is to *protect his partner,* who is at the net. He protects him in several ways, depending on the position of the opponents: (1) If they, too, are in the one up, one back formation, he drives deep to the other baseliner; (2) if both of the opponents are at the net, he drives low to the man farther back (if they are equidistant from the net, he drives low over the center strap or to the weaker player); (3) if the opponents have made a very good attack shot, he lobs, sometimes on the return of serve, othertimes during a rally.

These shots used to protect a net man will often draw weak returns, from which the net man can make winning shots. In a sense, then, a baseliner sets his partner up for "kill" shots while he plays to protect him.

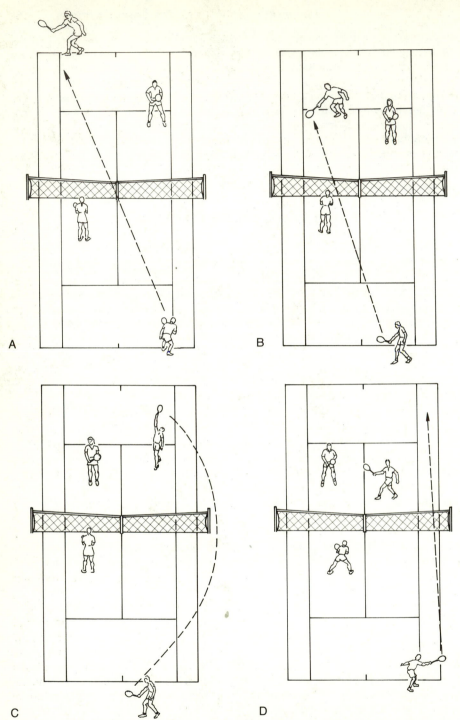

Figure 10-3 To protect his net-playing partner, a baseliner returns deep to an opposing baseliner (*A*). He returns to the feet of a deep net man (*B*). He lobs over a net man (*C*), or drives into the vacant alley of a poacher (*D*).

The baseliner's second function is to advance to the net at the first safe opportunity (unless, of course, he feels hopelessly inadequate at net play). His opportunity will come just as it does in singles play: when he is hitting his strong stroke from inside the baseline, he is in a position to attack and move in. He aims either deep to the opposing baseliner or to the feet of the deeper volleyer when both opponents are at the net. He may even deliberately hit at the net man when the opponent is caught so close to the play that he cannot defend himself.

We stress frequent use of the lob in our doubles instruction, especially in middle-level play. In our opinion, the overhead smash is the weakest shot among players in this class. The logical shot, therefore, for getting out of even the least bit of trouble against opposing net men is a lob. When one of the opponents poaches effectively, we stress lobbing over him. We advise that "the more he bothers you, the more you must play at him, with drives down his alley and lobs over him." Although the lob may not draw an error on his smash nor travel completely over him, it may still restrict his poaching moves a bit and thus leave more room for cross-court drives.

Lobbing the return of serve is one of the most effective plays in middle-level doubles, especially when the lob is made from the right court. Coincidentally, this is usually the side on which the weaker receiver is stationed, and the opposing net man will be especially eager to poach as a result. If the receiver is unable to control his drives or his slices well enough, he may have to resort to the lob as his most frequent return—if for no other reason than as a defensive play. A lob that clears the net man on his half of the court completely disrupts the attacking team. Even more effective in the long run are lobs to the other half of the court, to the baseliner. The purpose is to keep the ball as far away from the poacher as possible. Frequent use of this play tempts many net men to try to reach balls that they are not able to play effectively. They often become impatient waiting for a set-up and roam out of their territory. When this occurs, they soon begin missing more smashes than they make. Then, as their team falls behind in the score, they try even harder to dominate play, and thereby compound the fault.

THE NET MAN

When playing in the one up, one back formation, the net man may at times play only four or five feet away from the net. If his partner can always hit deep and accurately, or low when necessary, this close-in position may be the most effective location for play. Often, however, the opponents' attack shots put a baseliner in trouble, in which case the net man should prepare to defend himself because the opponents are likely to close in and attack him. Accordingly, the most effective position for the net man is usually 12 to 15 feet from the net.

Regardless of his starting position, the net man must be constantly on the move during the point. He moves toward his alley when an opponent is hitting from close to that sideline, and toward the center to intercept when an opponent is hitting from there. He moves forward to play aggressively—it is called "closing"—when he senses the opponents are in trouble (when one of them is forced back deep to hit or is hitting at a half-volley from midcourt), and he moves back to defend himself when they are attacking. He may even have to retreat to the baseline to play defense when his partner lobs short.

THE SERVER

Most middle-level players cannot serve and volley well enough to attack consistently. The server's usual plan, therefore, is simply to put the ball in play and to then defend his half of the court from the baseline. When serving from the right of the center mark, he stands midway between the mark and the sideline, in order to be in position to defend properly. When serving from the left of the mark, he stands closer to his alley than to the mark. From this location he has a diagonal shot to the receiver's backhand, while at the same time he is in good position to defend his half of the court (and still avoid having to hit many backhands). When a receiver can lob well enough to clear the net man, or when he is a left-handed player, the server may benefit from standing closer to the mark.

A variation of these serving formations can often be used effectively when the server is unable to avoid having to play returns on his backhand. This is most often seen in strong-weak doubles play when the weak player serves from the left court, but it works well in all competition. To prevent the left court receiver (who is usually the stronger player) from driving to the server's backhand, the server stands close to the mark as he serves. His partner, meanwhile, stations himself on the same side of the center line, at the net, and faces the receiver. The purpose here is to force the receiver to return along the right sideline. The receiver hits away from the net man, to the server's forehand. The server meanwhile has moved over quickly to be in position to play the return. The rally continues, then, with the server in good position to play only forehands; balls aimed to his backhand are likely to be within reach of his partner, who can play them with his strong forehand volley.

Still another variation of the one up, one back formation can be used to take advantage of the respective strong points of doubles players' games. The stronger player of a team, who presumably serves well enough to attack, dashes to the net on every one of his serves and on his returns. His partner, meanwhile, starts in the backcourt and remains there throughout the point. When serving to the deuce court, the net rusher stands close to the center mark and runs forward to volley from the middle of his team's left court. When serving to the ad court, he stands midway between the mark and the sideline and runs forward to the conventional volley location. In either case, his partner stands to the right of him, at the baseline, and stays there to defend the right side of their court. From that location he is able to use his stronger forehand on almost all balls hit in his direction.

TACTICS FOR ALL LEVELS

Although we have classified certain tactics as suitable for either advanced or middle-level play, the discerning reader will note that many of the moves and formations can be used interchangeably at all levels of play. Teachers and coaches have the option of deciding which tactics are appropriate for their players. As in the matter of form on strokes, there is not only one best way to play for all levels. What works is best, and what works at one level may not work at another. Experienced coaches are quick to adjust the tactics and strategy of their teams; they choose whatever style of play is compatible with the capabilities of their players and the quality of the competition. While doing so, however, they do not ignore basic principles of position play and movement—principles which make even special variations more effective. Some of these we have already discussed. We now close this discussion of doubles play by listing several additional principles that should be considered when teaching, regardless of the level of play.

Choosing Sides

One of the first problems coaches and players face when forming doubles combinations is deciding which player is to play from the left court and which from the right. Some coaches consider serving and returning serves the most essential skills for winning. Accordingly, they place their players in their best receiving positions. Often, then, a great deal of practice and play for practice is arranged, during which service returns are analyzed to determine accurately the players' abilities to return from each court.

Other coaches consider the volleys that follow the serve and return to be most important. They place their players where they can best use their stronger volleys (a good backhand volleyer in the right court, a good forehand volleyer in the left court). The assumption here is that the strong volleyers will be able to capitalize on the tendency in doubles for most shots to be hit to the center. In our opinion this is sound strategy, because in all except top-level play, as pressure mounts late in a match, players do tend to hit to the center, not daring to risk sharply angled or down-the-line shots. For this reason, too, we feel that a left-handed player should play from the right court, so that all centered shots can be played on his partner's forehand.

In strong-weak play, the logical place to put the weaker player is in the right court. There are two reasons for this: (1) he is less likely to have to return the serve with his backhand because most servers have greater difficulty serving to the backhand of a player in the right court than in the left court; (2) after the serve is in play, most balls aimed to his backhand can be played by his partner with his forehand.

There is also another plan that sometimes works to protect the weaker player—a plan that can be used when he can volley at least reasonably well with his forehand. Whenever possible, he takes a position at the net on the left side, closer to the sideline and closer to the net than a regular net man should be. From there he makes a play on only those balls he can reach comfortably with a forehand volley. He leaves so little room on his backhand side that the opponents do not risk hitting to such a small target. Moreover, from his close-in position, practically on top of the net, he is no longer a weak volleyer. Consequently, the opponents soon learn to keep the ball away from him. This, of course, is the reason for using this formation; the stronger player covers more than his share of the court and plays more than his share of the shots, hitting for winners whenever he is able to or protecting his partner when necessary. This requires a great deal of agility and stamina on his part, but in competition where winning is more important than playing politely, such effort is often the effective way to victory.

Playing Parallel

We have already described top-flight tactics in which players start in the one up, one back formation and then move forward immediately after the serve and re-

turn of serve. We have suggested that the continued use of the one up, one back formation is often suitable for middle-level play. A third strategic plan is known as
"playing parallel." It is used a great deal in middle-level play, and one sees it fairly
often in top-level play as well. Parallel play is adopted when the receiving team
feels that they cannot return serve well enough to attack on their returns. It works
equally well whether the opponents play together at the net or in the backcourt, or
whether they play in the one up, one back formation.

Partners who use the parallel formation are always equidistant from the net (or
nearly so); a line drawn from one of them to the other would be *parallel to the net*.
This is true whether they are playing from the backcourt or from the volley positions.
If they decide to change locations at some point in the rally and they move from the
backcourt to the front court, they do so together, thus staying parallel. Normally, the
parallel formation in the backcourt is used only by the receiving team. It can often
be used effectively by the serving team in middle-level play, however, when a
player cannot serve well enough to move in and volley the return of serve. Admittedly, this is not the way doubles *should* be played, but it may sometimes be the
best way, considering the equipment and abilities of the players involved.

MIXING DEFENSE WITH ATTACK

When the opponents move up to volley together, the team playing parallel at the
baseline usually has a twofold plan: they play from the backcourt, hoping to draw
errors with a mixture of drives, slices, and lobs, and they advance to the net together
when given the opportunity on a short shot from the opponents. When the opponents
are both back, they hit to the weaker stroke (usually the backhand) of the weaker
player. When the opponents are one up and one back, they hit deeply to the backcourt man except when the net man is not able to defend himself.

A few words of warning to teachers and coaches who are not familiar with this
style of play may be appropriate here. It is not unusual to see inexperienced players
become confused about tactics when they are playing parallel. Often, the hitter
strokes and remains in the backcourt on the assumption that he is not able to make
an effective approach shot, while his partner moves in to attack. This, of course,
takes the players out of the parallel formation and puts them in the untenable position of playing half offense and half defense in the one up, one back formation
behind a weak approach shot. Unless their defense is good, they present their opponents with an opening between them behind the net man.

To prevent this from happening among our players, we set up a definite rule to
guide a team's action: the player making the play on the ball decides whether his
team is to attack (and move up to volley) or is to continue to rally from the backcourt.
His partner watches him closely while he hits, looking for an indication of his intentions, and then acts accordingly. If the hitter decides to stay back, his partner stays
back with him. If the hitter moves forward after he hits, his partner moves up with him
because presumably the hitter feels he is able to make an attack shot.

PARALLEL FOR DEFENSE

The parallel formation can be used for strict defensive doubles—the kind of
play that often wins although neither partner can volley well. We encourage some of

our young teams to play this way until they reach a point in their development when they can attack.

To play good defense, good lobbing is essential. Our feeling is that players develop lobbing skill more quickly than they do skill at hitting overhead smashes. Moreover, for every one of our lobs the opponents are required to hit a smash, and thus we feel that our players are more likely to be using a relatively safer shot than are the opponents. Lobs are not aimed indiscriminately, however; each is aimed in a definite direction for a specific purpose. If one of the opponents is standing too close to the net, the lob goes in his direction. If one player is shorter than the other, he is easier to lob over. If one player is obviously weaker at smashing, he gets most of the play. A slightly more sophisticated plan is to lob continually to the player most likely to "crack" under pressure.

Defensive players may sometimes wisely choose to lob cross-court simply to have the long diagonal dimension of the court along which to hit. This can be especially effective when the lobber is hitting from the alley or from outside the lines. A lob crossing the net diagonally from such locations often causes confusion in the opponents; each player believes the ball is within his own reach *and* that of his partner. Indecision about who is to make the play often leads to a weak play — sometimes an error, other times no play at all.

A final choice defensive lobbers may consider is a *low* lob to the backhand of the weaker opponent. Such a shot need not even be a true lob; it may even be a soft high drive. Only ranking players can hit high backhands aggressively. A semi-defensive shot placed there will draw many errors among average players and should be used frequently as a change from low drives and high lobs.

Decisions about where to aim lobs usually must be made on the court after the pattern of play has been established. Frequently, however, a coach or team may decide to follow one or another of the plans we have mentioned before play begins, basing their decisions on what they already know about the opponents.

The "Off-center" Position

In doubles as in singles, experienced players move to be in position to bisect the angle of returns when an opponent is hitting from a sideline or an alley; they move to be "off-center" slightly, either to the left or to the right of the center line, depending on whether they are at the net or in the backcourt.

PLAYING AT THE NET

When in the volley positions, partners should move left or right, up or back, depending on the position of the opponents and the kind of shots expected from them. When an opponent is hitting from close to the center mark, their primary concern should be to protect the center of their court. Most of the opponents' shots will be aimed there; it is important, therefore, that this area be well covered.

When an opponent is hitting from close to a sideline, however, both net men should shift toward that sideline sufficiently to protect against both a shot into the alley and a shot toward the center. The man closest to the sideline protects the alley; his partner protects the middle.

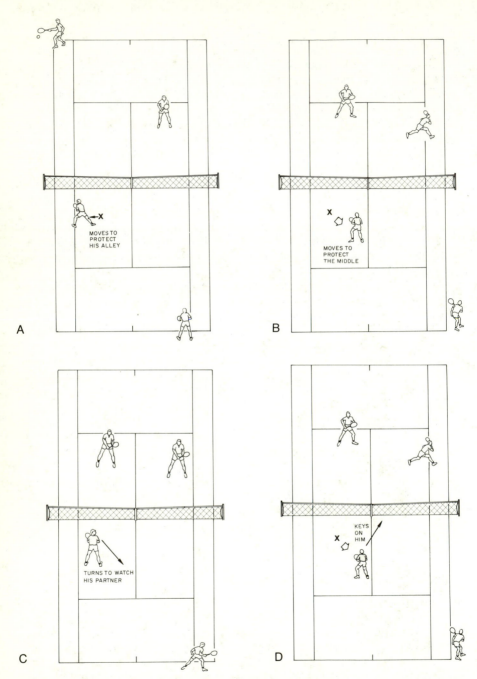

Figure 10-4 A net man moves to protect his alley (*A*), moves to protect his middle (*B*), turns to watch his partner (*C*), or keys on the opposing net man (*D*).

When an opponent is hitting from a *short*, wide angle, the net men must cover both a shot along the line and a sharply angled cross-court shot. To do so, the player farther from the hitter must move forward and toward the center line (to intercept or at least discourage the angle shot), while his partner must move to protect the alley. We find it necessary to constantly remind our players to protect against a sharply angled return.

A net man whose partner is forced wide into the alley moves in that direction also, in order to cover the hole left between himself and his teammate. He moves toward his partner and, in a sense, is flanked by two smaller holes, either of which he can cover better than the larger hole. To prepare for these moves he may either "key" on the opposing net man and prepare to respond to any moves the net man makes, or he may turn to watch his own partner. Players differ in their preferences in this matter. By using the first plan, the net man can prepare quickly to defend against the possibility of his opponent poaching to intercept the return. By turning to watch his own partner to notice his location and intentions, the net man gets an even earlier indication of his own responsibilities. He watches his partner only long enough to determine what he intends to do; the net man then looks toward the opponents, ahead of the ball, to prepare to defend or to close in and attack. We suggest that players experiment to discover which method best enables them to move forward, backward, or to either side to cover any holes created by the opponents' shots and to attack when possible.

PLAYING FROM THE BACKCOURT

When playing from the backcourt, players must work as a team to protect the center of their court and to protect against wide-angled returns from the opponents. Making the opponents hit from the center, whether they are at the net or in the backcourt, reduces the angles for their returns and often lures them into hitting to the center. Protecting the center then is an easy matter; partners move toward the middle (often called "packing the center") and let the stronger player make most of the plays.

Occasionally, however, a baseliner's shot must be angled sharply (when keeping the ball away from an opposing net man, for example). Consequently, an opponent will be hitting from close to a sideline. When this occurs, both backcourt players must move to protect against a wide-angled shot; they must be "off-center" in the opposite direction to which the hitter has moved.

This move is especially effective when an opponent is smashing a lob from close to a sideline. Smart defensive players move away from that sideline a bit to cover the center and the area diagonally across the court from the smasher. This puts them in a position to cover the smasher's strong shot; in addition, the smasher is often lured into aiming to his smallest opening, which adds an element of risk to his shot.

RETREATING TO DEFEND

If the smasher is getting set to hit aggressively, baseliners may have to retreat as far back as the rear fence to take up good defensive positions. The farther back they go, the more time they will have to make a play on the ball, but they will also be required to cover a wider angle. It may sometimes be best, therefore, to stand in a compromise position, halfway between the baseline and the fence, to reduce the angle offered to the smasher while still providing sufficient time to move to reach his smash. Again, the players should be "off-center" enough to protect against the wide angled-shot and a shot along the long diagonal dimension of the court.

Relating Position, Trajectory, and Speed

One of the most misunderstood yet easily taught principles of doubles play is that position and the height of the ball being played determine the proper trajectory and speed of the shot. Ideally, in a fast net exchange, players want to volley through an opening in their opponent's court, or to volley hard enough and quickly enough to cause them to miss. Often, however, the opponents' positions and shots prevent that. In such a case, the intention should be to hit low to the feet of one of the opponents, causing him to hit up. To do this, a player must gauge his speed and trajectory by considering three factors: (1) his distance from the net and from the opponents, (2) their position in relation to the net, and (3) the height at which he is stroking the ball. If he is hitting at a high ball, he may be able to hit it hard along a straight line to their feet. If, on the other hand, he is hitting at a low ball, he will have to hit it easily enough to permit gravity to bring it down after it clears the net; he must use a low, curved trajectory.

Imparting a low, curved trajectory from a low volley often requires the player to hit the ball back with a speed much reduced from that at which the ball came to him. We say he must "take the speed off the ball." The technique for this is described in our discussion of stroke instruction for intermediate and advanced players (Chapter 7).

Teamwork at the Net

A few simple rules agreed on beforehand enable partners to play smoothly together when at the net in an attacking position. All balls hit straight along the center line should be handled by the player in the left court, because his forehand is toward the center. When the opponents hit successive shots to the center within reach of both net men, the player who hit the last ball should take the next one. Most players establish a rhythm when they hit successively this way. Conversely, players left out of a rally for two or three shots often time their next shot inaccurately because they have not been able to follow the ball closely. An exception occurs, of course, if one player is markedly stronger than the other. In such a case the stronger player should make the play.

We also set up rules to follow when opponents lob to our attacking net men. Naturally, all short lobs are hit aggressively in an attempt to win or to draw an error. Smashers are warned, however, not to aim to a small opening (or a short angle) if there is a larger hole (or a longer angle). If the lob is too deep to be played aggressively, the smasher aims *to the backhand of the weaker opponent,* or to the feet of either opponent trapped in midcourt. On lobs between the two net men, the man with the stronger overhead should be allowed to make the play. Even on short lobs to his partner's side, the strong player is expected to play all he can reach and handle, provided he calls out his intention in time to avoid confusion. He calls, "mine" or "I have it" and moves in confidently to play, knowing that his partner is moving to get out of his way. Partners will have agreed that a voice call is never rescinded, and that when each of them makes a call, the first one made is in effect. They never ignore a call, and never overrule one call with another. To do so can often be disastrous.

Most very high lobs are usually difficult to judge and time properly. For this reason we urge our players to let such lobs bounce and to make an overhead play after the bounce. A high lob is usually dropping vertically (or nearly so) and therefore usually bounces vertically (or nearly so). Consequently, the smasher does not have to retreat much to make his play after the bounce. Here we encourage our smashers to "hit a winner" if they have a safe angle or an opening. If not, they aim deep *to the backhand of the weaker opponent*. The smasher's partner, knowing this, moves up to the net position to poach on the opponents' return after the smash. Usually, the weaker opponent is in the right court (the deuce court). The smash, then, hit to his backhand, is hit to the center. This permits the poacher to practically ignore his alley, regardless of which side of the court he is on; he moves toward the center line to intercept. If the smasher chooses to hit toward an alley (because he feels he has a good angle or an opening there), the poacher may have to stay in place to protect that alley.

When one of the net men is forced back to smash a deep lob, players often become confused and fail to act as a team. Many times the player making the smash returns to the net position, only to discover that his partner has retreated. At other times, the smasher retreats while his partner mistakenly waits at the net, assuming the smasher will return to join him. Plainly, neither is a desirable situation.

In order to prevent such misunderstandings, we set up the following rule: the man making the smash decides whether he may best retreat to the backcourt or return to the net position after his hit; his partner watches him as he hits for an indication of what he intends to do, and then acts accordingly. He either retreats to the baseline with the smasher and takes up a defensive position, or he stays at the net, knowing his partner will join him there. The smasher's intentions as he smashes should be determined, in large measure, by his position and depth in the court. If he feels he has been forced back too deep to be able to return to the volley position, or if he feels the lob is too good to permit him to smash aggressively, he retreats and calls his partner back with him. If, on the other hand, he feels confident about making a good smash, he returns to the net position.

Smart net men move to be in good position for all shots, including lobs. When they anticipate a lob, they back away from the net a bit, intending in that way to be able to reach the ball and smash aggressively. Inevitably, however, the opponents surprise a net man and succeed in lobbing completely over him. This occurs often in "strong-and-weak" doubles, where the weaker player stands exceptionally close to the net to compensate for lack of volleying ability. If a lob clears the net man while his partner is in the backcourt, the backcourt player simply crosses over to make the play. The net man, meanwhile, crosses over to the other side so that together they can cover both sides of their court. If both players are at the net and a lob clears one of them, retrieving is a more difficult matter. Normally, the man to whose side the ball is hit is responsible for all balls hit in his direction. However, if he has moved in too closely to the net (which is probably why the lob got over him), his partner may be in a better position to make the retrieve, even though his run diagonally across the court is longer than his partner's run parallel to the sidelines. He may have an easier play on the bounced lob when running sideways (and half facing the net) than would his partner in full retreat with his back turned completely to the net. Again, the net players simply exchange sides; the net player either moves over to be in position to volley from the side left vacant by his partner, or he retreats to the baseline to play defense. His moves are determined by the kind of shot the retriever is making. If the retriever can protect his partner with a low shot to the opponents' feet, or with a deep shot to a backcourt player, his team may choose to play in the one up, one back formation. If the retriever is in trouble, however, it may be necessary to give up the net position.

Poaching

Earlier in this discussion of doubles play, we described the manner in which advanced net men often poach to intercept returns at the net. Poaching at the top level of play is used both offensively and defensively. For offense, the net man moves across the center line to intercept a shot that would normally be his partner's. He poaches because he is in better position, or because he can use his stronger stroke, or because he has a better angle on his shot. For defense, the net man moves to cover obvious openings in his court caused by his team's bad positioning or by their misplaced shots.

The art of poaching lies in being deceptive. A good poacher conceals his intentions, sometimes by standing perfectly still before making his move, other times by constantly shifting, swaying, and shuffling in place to confuse the opponent. In the first instance, the poacher often surprises the hitter by sneaking across to intercept a normally good return. In the second, he often distracts the opponent and causes a bad shot; he sometimes lures the opponent into hitting straight at him as he holds his ground after making a fake or two.

Two additional "tricks" are often used to attract specific shots from an opponent. At times a net man makes an obvious, conspicuous move toward his alley as if to protect it at all costs. His opponent, seeing this, hits cross-court rather than down the line. Knowing this, the net man waits until the last possible split second, whereupon he dashes across the court to intercept the return.

In an alternate plan, the net man appears to be letting his alley open by failing to move in that direction when the opponent is hitting from the corresponding sideline. Then, as the shot is made to the apparent opening — the vacant alley — the net man moves in that direction to intercept.

Moves such as these are used most frequently against the return of serve. Sometimes they are a spur-of-the-moment decision by the net man. Other times they are planned beforehand, and the server serves accurately to make it effective. He aims to the center of the opponents' court to make it possible for his partner to leave his alley vacant without too much danger of being passed there (on a wide serve, the net man has to hold his position to protect the alley). Most top teams have signals to indicate the net man's intentions. Probably the most frequently used signals are a closed fist and an open palm. The server's partner may, for example, place his left hand behind his back to show the server a closed fist. This signifies that he intends to sneak across the center line to intercept the return. The server, therefore, starts up to the net in the normal manner, but changes direction after a step or two and dashes over to protect the side of the court left vacant by the poacher. The open hand signal, in contrast, means the net man intends to hold his starting position. He usually fakes a poach, however, to confuse the receiver. When using this plan, the server stands close to the mark in order to reach a good volley position in the other half of the court when necessary.

Top-level teams poach during rallies as well as on return-of-serves. The technique here is similar; the poacher waits until the last split second, until the hitter has committed himself, then moves across to intercept. Again, the poaching is often preceded by fake moves intending to rattle and confuse the opponent; at times the fakes lure him into hitting directly to the net man, who holds his ground after a fake.

In top-level play, poaching is often carried out successfully when the server's partner stands on the same side of the center line as the server (the so-called Australian formation). From that position he moves across to intercept returns, either by an instantaneous decision or by plan, accompanied by signals exchanged with his partner. Usually, this formation is employed to prevent the receiver from using his effective cross-court returns; it forces him to return down the line. Occasionally, however, it is used to combat effective net play by the receiver's partner, who may be good at poaching on the server's first volley. In this unconventional formation, the server's first volley is being played from the opposite side of the center line from the opposing poacher. From there the volley can easily be kept out of his reach and placed to the receiver.

Although our discussion of poaching was dealt mainly with its use in advanced play, intermediates and beginners can also learn to poach effectively. They can

Figure 10–5 An example of a reverse formation adopted by the serving team used to "take away" a receiver's effective cross-court return or to minimize the effectiveness of his partner's poaching to intercept the server's first volley. With the formation shown, the receiver is forced to return down the line (supposedly his weaker shot), and the server's first volley can easily be placed out of reach of the receiver's partner.

increase the range of their reach by making frequent, well-timed moves to the center line. At the early levels of play, however, we stress what we call "stepping out" rather than the wilder, all-or-none dash across the line seen so often in advanced play.

In "stepping out," the net man simply skips sideways, toward the center, as the opponent makes his hit. From this new position close to the center line, he can reach across the line with a crossover step to intercept a return, or can reach back toward his alley (with a crossover step) to protect his half of the court. As players develop skill at this, they seem to naturally expand their reach so that soon they are moving across the line in one continuous dash. The one big drawback to poaching at the elementary levels of play is that the server cannot always place his serve down the center line. If the serve is wide, of course, the net man must hold his position to protect his alley. Nevertheless, "stepping out" can be done effectively in such a case provided players learn to return to their starting position if the receiver aims there.

Spontaneous poaching and stepping out is likely to be more successful when it is done in response to various cues given inadvertently by an opponent. Sometimes a player's stance, or his backswing, or even his eyes will reveal his intention and will enable the poacher to react to his shot. When an opponent appears to be having difficulty handling a particular shot, such as a hard serve straight at him, a high bouncing serve to his backhand, or a half-volley from midcourt, he is not likely to be able to place his return accurately. Usually, troublesome shots such as these are played carefully and safely to the conventional aim point—away from the closest net man. The net man, knowing this, is often able to move across the center line to intercept such returns. Players who are known to be "percentage minded" (they seldom take chances) often fall into a pattern and return in the conventional manner on certain crucial points. Knowing an opponent's attitude and philosophy toward doubles often enables a net man to predict his reaction in such "clutch" situations. As a result, he is often able to estimate correctly when to poach and when to hold his ground.

Chapter Eleven

ADMINISTRATIVE PROCEDURES FOR TEAM COACHING

The importance attached to school tennis programs varies among communities and school districts, and consequently the caliber of instruction and coaching in the sport varies as well. Many schools have well-rounded programs in which tennis is a major sport. At some schools, however, tennis is the least important of all sports offered in the program. It gets less administrative support, and the players get less recognition and publicity than are given to athletes in other sports (which may, incidentally, have fewer benefits to offer).

Generally, such second-class status results from disinterest in the community toward the game itself. If parents, sportswriters, and radio and television commentators are not interested in tennis, then children are not likely to be interested either. Nor are school principals, supervisors, and athletic directors. Understandably, they will stress activities favored by residents of the community, who are asked to provide financial support for school programs.

Unfortunately, negative attitudes toward tennis often can affect school tennis coaches. Sensing the attitude of the community and of their own supervisors, inexperienced coaches often regard tennis as a minor sport, and since their tennis duties are usually secondary to their duties in some other sport or activity, they inadvertently begin to act accordingly. Such attitudes prevent coaches and players alike from deriving maximum benefit from their programs.

Of course, enthusiastic, energetic tennis coaches who understand and appreciate what a well-run program can offer often overcome the apathetic attitudes of others and manage to make wholesome learning experiences out of daily practice and competitive play. In the discussion that follows, we describe coaching methods used by experienced, successful coaches. We hope, in this way, to motivate inexperienced coaches to organize and conduct programs that provide training and development not only in the physical skills basic to the game but also in the many related areas that well-run school athletic programs encompass.

THE TENNIS COACH'S PHILOSOPHY

In any sport, a coach's attitude and conduct toward his players is determined by his philosophy. To a certain extent, a tennis coach's philosophy should resemble that of an academic teacher; the tennis program should be regarded as part of the educational process. The justification for it in the school program is, after all, its contribution to the total education of the participants. The coach, therefore, should be as much an educator as are teachers in other areas.

In tennis, where squads usually consist of only 8, 10, or 12 players, the coach can become more than simply an acquaintance of the students. He can become a friend, a counselor, and a confidant. In such relationships he may be able to contribute more than just technical knowledge of the game. Because the coach is able to observe and evaluate his players not only in competitive athletic situations but in social situations as well, he may be able to affect their attitudes, temperaments, and personalities along with their games.

By his attitude and conduct, a coach conveys to his players his interpretation of his role. He shows that he cares as much about their feelings as about their playing skills, as much about their welfare as about the team's record. He considers their social and psychological needs as he plans and conducts the program. The coach spends time socializing with his players in order to recognize and understand those needs as well as their interests, ambitions, and aspirations—and their frustrations. Only in this way can he provide for the development of desirable behavior patterns for the many stress situations that occur in practice and in competition. It is solely through this approach that he can meet his responsibilities as an educator and as a teacher of skills.

In tennis, as in other sports, we see students "out for the team" for a variety of reasons. For some it is their major interest; their aim is to achieve state, regional, or even national recognition. For others it is simply a seasonal sport. For still others it is merely a pleasant way of fulfilling the credit requirement for Physical Education. We know of students who have chosen tennis because it is traditionally a relaxed and loosely structured sport run by an academic teacher who uses laissez faire methods that allow players to practice or play as they choose, and even when they choose. Obviously, the coach must recognize many different attitudes if he is to establish an effective relationship with his players.

Usually, tennis is considered to be an individual sport. We suggest, however, that it should be regarded as a combination individual *and* team sport, which in its administration requires a combination of democratic and autocratic methods. Because players compete as individuals, they often expect to be permitted to make many of the administrative decisions themselves. This often results in confusion; leadership by all usually means poor leadership. Certainly, however, the opinions and ideas of the players should be considered. Players should be permitted to discuss procedures and methods with the coach, and they should be encouraged to offer suggestions and to solicit help so that instruction can be individualized as much as possible. In the final analysis, though, the coach is the authority who must make the major decisions.

In contrast to most tennis players, participants in popular team sports expect the coach to conduct a highly organized program in which he directs the activity completely. He is expected to designate practice procedures, to make time allotments, to devise game strategy, to establish training rules, and to control all of the other many facets of the sports program. Team players are usually willing to accept the coach's decisions and in most cases attempt to conform to his methods. They realize that as team members they are granted certain privileges not enjoyed by less skilled players. They understand that in exchange for these privileges they have certain duties and obligations that are imposed on them by the authority, the coach. They obey authority not because they are forced to do so, but because they want to. They have learned that this kind of behavior is necessary for a winning team.

The tennis coach is not likely to establish an effective relationship with his team unless he can engender similar attitudes toward discipline in his players. He cannot control and direct the practice sessions unless his players let him do so—or more precisely, unless they want him to. The desire on their part will not be present unless he gains their respect. Respect does not come automatically to new coaches; it must first be earned. We submit that the basis for earning respect lies in the coach's attitude and enthusiasm, in his ability to organize and plan, in his skill in dealing with team members, and finally in his technical knowledge of the game.

THE FIRST SQUAD MEETING

The coach's enthusiasm for his sport and his eagerness for the season to begin are first revealed to his players in the opening squad meeting. The coach must conduct a good meeting because he will be new to some players, and the impression he makes is likely to be lasting. The players' attitude toward him and his program could very well be determined by what they see and hear in the first team session. Experienced coaches prepare the agenda for the opening meeting with the same amount of care that they devote to formulating lesson plans in their favorite academic subject. To guide the inexperienced coach in the preparation and conduct of his first squad meeting, we present a list of items usually covered by experienced coaches in their meetings.

The Introduction

The coach introduces himself, his assistants, and returning team members. He reviews recent records of the team, mentions any individual accomplishments, and describes each player's best performance. If the group of new players is not too large, they are each asked to stand and describe their tennis background, listing their rankings and rating on their former team or in their region. They mention their previous coach's name and the record of their school or club.

The Information Sheet

Both old and new candidates are asked to fill out information sheets listing such items as name, home and campus address and phone number, class schedule, course of study, grade point average, tennis experience (including titles won and ranking attained in city, state, regional and national play), name of previous professional or school coach, high school attended, and other sport experience or special ability in other fields.

One of the coach's responsibilities is to publicize his program and his players. To do so he must have essential information available for newspaper releases and even for his own publicity releases. For his team's home matches, for example, he can increase the interest and enthusiasm of the spectators for the team by distributing a team roster in which he includes the information we have cited. The team members' backgrounds are listed as a courtesy to both the players and to their previous coaches; at the same time, such a listing is a good public relations gesture. There are stronger reasons for gathering this information, however. Every bit of knowledge that a coach acquires about his players will help him understand them better; he is more likely to recognize their problems, to understand their behavior, and to appreciate their degree of commitment to the sport. As a result, he is more likely to be able to communicate with them, and to provide what they want and *need* to be effective players and contributing members of the group.

It is not unusual for last-minute changes in schedule, departure time, or starting time to occur in school play. A coach will need to spread the word about a change in plans during the school day. Knowing where each of his players is at every hour of classes, and knowing how to get in touch with families of players, often helps avoid many of the difficulties that arise from disrupted situations.

Eligibility Forms and the Physical Examination

Academic teachers who are new to coaching often minimize the importance of checking players' status and familiarizing themselves with school and conference rules for competing. These rules vary among schools and among conferences, but almost always they prescribe a minimum grade as a prerequisite for student participation in extracurricular activities. In addition, either a physical examination or a doctor's certificate is usually required before a student is permitted to participate in vigorous activity. The coach who ignores the physical and academic requirements is negligent and not worthy of the trust placed in him by the school authorities, by the players, and by their parents.

Lockers and Equipment

Tennis team members benefit from dressing together in their own private section or room (as do most school athletic teams). Admittedly, this is not always possible because of administrative limitations, but we feel that this privilege can be attained more often than is generally known simply by the coach requesting it. A separate section of the locker room will provide the coach with an opportunity to post such items of interest as the team's schedule, a description and record of previous and future opponents, the practice schedule (daily, and perhaps even weekly), teaching points for individuals, general remarks meant for the entire group, newspaper and magazine clippings illustrating techniques of play, and whatever other motivational items the coach *and his players* can devise.

In school tennis, the amount of equipment that is available and the schedule of distribution of it is determined largely by the athletic director. Traditionally, tennis is a minor sport and is not always allotted enough money to support a well-dressed, well-equipped, well-traveled, and well-fed team. We feel that most coaches can forestall criticism from their players and nullify their complaints (which will follow inevitably if other teams are treated more generously) by making at least a show of satisfaction with the tennis budget, while at the same time taking every precaution to avoid unfairness in the distribution of equipment.

No rules can be set down here to govern coaches' actions. Even guidelines are of uncertain value, because each team's situation is unique. Nevertheless, in regard to equipment, a few points are worth noting. The home team provides balls for an interschool match, and each coach must therefore preview his schedule and estimate the number of balls needed to last the season. New balls will be required for each individual match in the team match, in both singles and doubles. Many conferences require that three balls be used in play, and that they be discarded for replacement at some definite point, usually at the start of a third set. These details are not specified in USLTA rules; each tournament director is permitted to make his own policies. Consequently, in circuit tennis tournaments, balls are changed more frequently in a match (after 11 to 13 games, for example). Usually, however, in school play, coaches agree to—or are compelled to—change balls at the start of the third set, unless rough or wet courts wear or soil balls so quickly as to make play difficult. This often occurs when there is a long, high-scoring set (12–10, for example). Clearly, coaches should be prepared to offer new balls earlier than the third set when necessary. The precise point of change should be agreed upon by both coaches before play begins. As for another essential, the racket, we can only say that availability and supply varies with each coaching situation. The coach provides whatever amount of equipment to whatever number of players his budget allows.

Wearing apparel is usually of less importance to the coach who is on a limited budget, for many schools issue standardized underclothes to all athletes. In addition, even in the "major" sports (with the exception of football), players are required to provide their own shoes. Although traditionally white is worn for tennis, including white outer apparel (warm-up jackets), it is not unusual to see even top-flight high school teams and some college teams dressed in conventional school warm-up clothes with the regular school colors. Often, this equipment is allotted to the tennis team for seasonal use only. The wrestling team, gymnastic team, or some other team may have priority for its use during the appropriate season.

The Season Schedule

Printed copies of the complete season schedule are issued to all players. Players are reminded of their obligation to meet the schedule requirements. They are expected to know the schedule so that they can plan their social activities accordingly. They should know at the beginning of the season how many classes they are likely to miss because of tennis matches, and they should be reminded of their obligation to make up any class assignments that are missed. The coach explains to them the procedures for obtaining official class excuses when participating in tennis travel or play with the team.

For the benefit of the new players, the coach describes and explains the schedule. Conference matches are indicated, neighborhood rivalries are pointed out, and new opponents are described. The procedures for determining the conference champion and for selecting representatives to state and district meets are also explained.

Requirements for a Letter Award

Many coaches find it best to distribute mimeographed sheets listing requirements for an award after they have explained them at a team meeting. At intervals during the season the coach can meet individually with players who need guidance toward fulfilling the requirements. He discusses each player's attitude and potential and tries to motivate him to work with the established requirements always in mind.

Practice Procedures

The "meaty" part of the team meeting is in the coach's presentation of practice procedures. Here the coach sets the tone and determines the pattern for the season practice schedule. He describes his methods, discusses the drills he intends to use, and establishes the procedure by which he intends to convey his knowledge of the game to his players. As he does so, his philosophy begins to unfold. He describes his interpretation of his role and what he expects of his players. He stresses that he expects regular attendance at practice, and that he expects practice to start promptly at the appointed time. He lists acceptable excuses for missing practice and for early departure from practice, and closes the meeting with a question-and-answer session in which he clears up any points left unresolved and any misunderstandings that might have occurred. He tries to create a mood and to engender enthusiasm for the season about to begin by showing that he, personally, is impatient and eager for the first sessions on the court.

SELECTING THE TEAM

Many experienced coaches rely on their judgment, on their subjective rating, rather than on the results of tournament matches, to choose new players. They feel that they can better predict the potential of new players by watching them in action, as opposed to merely noting the results of matches played.

Most experienced coaches, however, choose team members from among new candidates on the basis of some kind of competition arranged to help them make their selection. A round robin tournament in which each new candidate plays the others is common. Players with the best records of wins vs. losses are then chosen to join the squad. In some instances, when the squad is large and space is limited, winners of the round robin are made to play the lower ranked returning members of the squad to determine whom among the two groups are to be selected.

In many cases, records and results of matches played during the previous summer are available to the coach. Some of the new candidates may have played well enough in regional tournaments to have earned a USLTA ranking. In such cases the coach can use this information to supplement and to reinforce his opinions.

When looking at new candidates, a coach must be careful not to attach too much importance to stroke technique. Strokes alone do not win matches. The coach must look for other necessary qualities to go along with them. Match play temperament and attitude, speed and quickness, and general athletic ability must also be considered. The student's status as a freshman, sophomore, junior, or senior and his potential to learn and develop are other important points. The coach must evaluate the player's summer activity as well. A student who can arrange to play regularly in good competition during the summer is more likely to improve than is a student who must travel or work. The possibility of tournament play and instruction from a professional coach must also be taken into account. All of these factors enter into the matter of selecting team members; all of them must be considered by the coach if he is to develop a good, long-range program.

INTERSCHOOL COMPETITION

There are no specific rules for the conduct of team matches in the USLTA official rules of the game. Consequently, procedures for conducting interschool play are usually determined by each particular conference or league. As one would imagine, procedures vary among the different conferences. We see inconsistencies in such matters as placing players in the line-up, submitting line-ups, coaching during play, maintaining continuous play, and handling defaults resulting from injuries.

Placing the Players

Once his team has been selected, and at some appropriate date prior to the first interschool match, a coach must determine the playing order of the team members. Procedures vary on this point. Some conferences require coaches to establish and maintain a challenge ladder throughout the season and to place players in the line-up in the same order in which they appear on the ladder. Rules are sometimes so explicit as to require coaches to send to the conference office the results of challenge matches played on specified dates. The line-up, then, must remain the same until and unless challenge match results sent in at the next specified date indicate that changes are in order. Most conferences, however, let coaches determine for themselves exactly how they place their players for interschool play. Most experienced and successful coaches use a combination of the methods described earlier in our discussion of team selection. United States Lawn Tennis Association rankings, attitude and temperament, recent performances, and the coach's subjective rating often provide enough information for making an accurate placement of players. Special challenge matches are assigned when there is doubt or uncertainty about the relative abilities of certain players.

Many inexperienced coaches make the mistake of permitting or requiring too many challenge matches. Players are often so busy challenging or defending that they have little time for real practice. Certainly, there is no substitute for competition for providing match play experience, but challenge match competition is often mis-

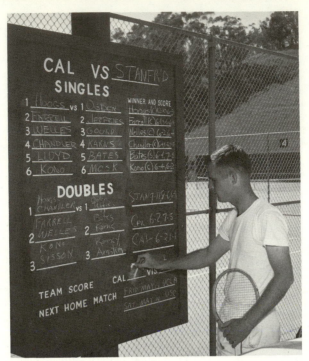

Figure 11-1   Dressing-up a school tennis match to make it appealing to players and spectators is every coach's responsibility. Shown above is a team scoreboard which keeps spectators informed about the progress of the match. In addition, individual scoreboards at every court are essential for effective conduct of a match.

leading. It is not unusual to find a player who competes well in intrasquad matches, but who plays less effectively against outside competition. The reason for this is difficult to determine, but most experienced coaches have witnessed such contradictory play.

Regardless of the different methods used by coaches and conferences for placing team players, there is one generality that governs interschool play. Coaches are expected to place their players in the order of their abilities, irrespective of the opposing team's line-up. Coaches are not expected (nor are permitted, in some cases) to place their players in positions to match certain players on an opposing team. Such a procedure, in which a coach places his better men lower in his line-up than is proper in order to ensure some wins, is known as "stacking the line-up," and is considered unethical. A school match is really meant to pit one team's best player against the other's; the second best against the opponent's second best, and so on. This procedure is to be carried out even for doubles, although here each coach can determine his best combinations in any way he chooses. Once they are chosen, however, he is expected to place teams in the order of their abilities, in the order of their strength. Players in adjacent positions on the challenge ladder (the numbers one and two men, for example) need not necessarily be teamed together. A number one man may play with the number five man, and they may play in the number three doubles position if the coach judges them to be only his third best team.

Most experienced coaches feel that the question of the proper placement of players is governed by an implied coaches' honor system or by conference regulations. The latter is seldom the case, however. Although one seldom hears the honor system discussed, the foremost authority in the game in matters of rule interpretation and enforcement stresses its use and need in interschool play. In personal correspondence with the authors, Jack Stahr, chief umpire of the USLTA, made the following remarks:

> Not infrequently the USLTA Umpire's Committee receives an inquiry about the propriety of a coach, in a team match, deliberately ranking one or more of his players in a sequence that does not coincide with their actual relative abilities—the objective being to "sacrifice" perhaps the No. 1 and No. 2 matches (which his team is quite sure to lose anyway) and let his true top players contend with lower-rated players of the opposition.
>
> Let there be no doubt about it: This tactic is a dishonest one! It is contrary to the whole spirit of sportsmanship that should prevail in any game, and especially in tennis. No coach or pro should encourage the idea for a moment.
>
> Of course, it can happen that there is, honestly, no discernible difference in skill between the No. 1 and No. 2 men. In such a case (heeding that adverb "honestly"), it is allowable to try to put them opposite those (expected) players of the opposition against whom each would be likely to fare best because of playing styles, but that's as far as anyone should go.

Submitting Line-ups

The theory that school tennis play should match one team's best player against another's carries over into doubles play. Each coach is expected to form his three best combinations and to place them in the order of their ability. The coaches' honor system implies that "jockeying" doubles line-ups is not permitted. It is customary, therefore, for coaches to exchange line-ups simultaneously for *both* singles and doubles *before* the singles play begins. This procedure prevents a coach from making a last-minute switch to form one very good doubles team (if he needs only one doubles win to win the team match) after he has first placed his players in a way that distributes his strength among all three teams.

Coaching During Play

The United States Lawn Tennis Association rules do not forbid coaching during play except in certain divisions.* Most tennis authorities, however, interpret the USLTA rule regarding "continuous play" in a way that precludes coaching. As Rule

---

*As of February, 1973, the USLTA rule on coaching during play reads as follows: "Excepting formal rest periods, coaching in all forms is now prohibited in Junior and Boys' and Girls' matches."

Figure 11-2 A well-planned college tennis facility: nine courts built above a parking lot, with a permanent bleacher seating 800 people. Note courtside details for championship tournament play: umpires, linesman, ball boys, nets flush to ground, and singles sticks in place.

30 states, "Play shall not be suspended, delayed, or interfered with for the purpose of enabling a player to recover his strength or his wind, or to receive instruction or advice." Some authorities interpret Rule 30 more loosely and feel that coaching is perfectly legal and permissible. They contend that it is possible for a coach, a teammate, or a parent to offer brief advice between points in a way that does not interfere with play. At the odd-game changeovers, they say, a few quiet words need not cause a delay in the action of the match.

Despite these different interpretations of the rule, however, custom and tradition dictate that once players take the court to play, they are "on their own," so to speak, and any advice from outside the court is a violation of the spirit of the game. It is probably correct to say that this is the more common attitude and opinion among experienced school coaches. Consequently, coaching during play is not usually considered ethical unless it is expressly permitted by conference rules. It must be noted, however, that two of the more prestigious conferences in the country now permit coaching during play. Both the Big Ten and the Pac 8 (formerly the Pacific Coast Conference) have recently revised their rules to permit coaching at any time if it is done without delay. In addition, a two-minute delay for coaching is permitted at the end of a set.

Continuous Play

United States Lawn Tennis Association rules state that play must be continuous. In most college play, therefore, no "break" is permitted at any time, not even after the second set when the set score is one-all. The inadvertent delay that often occurs at this point to provide new balls for the third set is often misinterpreted as permission for a rest. Unless special league rules provide for a break here (as in the

Big Ten and the Pac 8), such a delay should be brief, and players should not be permitted to leave the courts.

Many *high school leagues* provide specifically for an intermission after the second set to enable players to recover strength and wind. This rest is provided as a precautionary measure, just as it is in National Boys', Women's, and Girls' play. Many college players, most of whom have come up through the ranks of high school play, mistakenly assume that this procedure is to be followed in college play.

Defaults

Official rules do not specify procedures for settling matters relating to defaults resulting from injuries and from players failing to appear. There is some question as to what should be done, therefore, it a team's number two man, for example, is hurt and cannot play, or fails to show up for the match. Does his team default at the second position while all other players remain where they are? Or do all players below number two move up one notch?

The most commonly accepted procedure is to move all players up a notch to present the best possible line-up for the day's matches. If a team runs out of players, the defaults are at the bottom. The opinion of Jack Stahr, Chairman of the USLTA Umpire's Committee, is again offered as a guide to conduct in this area. In personal correspondence with the authors, Mr. Stahr offers the following advice:

> *In any team match (school, college, industrial leagues, etc.) when there is any absence or known-in-advance inability to play, the available player of the next ranking below the absent player should be moved up to fill that spot in the line-up, and others moved up accordingly.*
>
> *Of course, ethics and sportsmanship must play a strong role in any such competitions. The line-ups of players in honest descending order of ability should be simultaneously exchanged by the captains. Of course, it would be possible for a coach to designate as No. 1 a player who, he knew, would default after hitting only a few balls (thus letting the team "escape" the obligation of moving up the other players a notch), but this would be, of course, a blatant violation of the ethics involved.*

Deciding How to Score

Although reference to scoring procedures may not seem appropriate in a discussion of administrative duties, recent USLTA options for scoring are important and have implications for coaches for both practice and match procedures. Any body of coaches acting as policy makers for a league or conference should consider the possibility of improving or at least expediting tournament and match play by adopting one or the other of the scoring options now permitted. The National Collegiate Athletic Association adopted both options for use in its 1974 tournament. As a consequence, most major collegiate conferences now use these methods for their dual match and tournament play.

The USLTA rules now permit any sanctioned tournament to employ a "sudden death" tie-breaking procedure after the set score reaches six-all. The procedure may be used at the option of the tournament committee, either throughout the tournament or in designated rounds.

A second major change permits use of a "no-ad" game, wherein a player need win only four points to win a game. If the score goes to three points all (deuce, in the conventional system), the winner of the next point wins the game. The receiver has the right to choose to which court the opponent serves on the deciding point. Here, the scoring terms love, 15, 30, and 40 are not used. Instead, points are called simply one, two, and three.

If a no-ad set reaches six games all, a tie-breaker should be used. Two such tie-breakers are authorized: 5 out of 9 points, and 7 out of 12 points. In the first, at six-all in games, the player whose turn it is to serve the thirteenth game serves two points; his opponent serves two. Players change sides and again alternate serves for the next four points.* If the score reaches four points all, the second player serves the ninth point to the right or left court at the election of the *receiver*. The player winning five of the nine points wins the set, seven games to six. Usually, the score of the tie-breaker game is indicated in parentheses: (5–2), for example. In the 7 out of 12 point tie-breaker, players alternate serving two points each for six points, after which they change sides and continue to serve two points alternately for six additional points. When one player wins seven points, the set is recorded as seven games to six in his favor. If the score of the tie-breaker game reaches six points all, players change sides and continue to serve, alternating *on every point* until one player establishes a margin of two points.

Readers are reminded that use of the no-ad and tie-breaker procedures is discretionary and not mandatory. The new procedures are recommended for use in situations in which limitations in the number of courts available and in the amount of time available make it difficult to run an event with conventional procedures. An implication for coaches is that their players should be made to *play for practice* under these revised conditions to prepare them for serious play later.

We conclude this discussion of administrative procedures in coaching by reminding the reader that USLTA rules do not cover all controversial areas. The continuous play rule has implications that apply in some cases, but different opinions exist all the same. Some conferences have their own special rules. We suggest that when there is an absence of specific rules, coaches should communicate with one another for the purpose of correcting this oversight. We know from experience that Big Ten and Pac 8 coaches have succeeded in just this way. Sensing differences among themselves and anticipating continued problems, they needed to send only a few letters to their directors to gain approval of guidelines in areas of concern.

---

*In doubles the same format used in singles applies, *except* that players continue to serve from whichever end of the court they have served during the set.

Chapter Twelve

TEAM PRACTICE PROCEDURES

In tennis, as in other sports, game participation does not always provide a great deal of practice in the many separate parts needed to play the total game well. An entire match, for example, may provide only eight or ten opportunities to hit an overhead smash, hardly enough chance to develop the habit of hitting smashes well. Most players must be given the opportunity to repeat a shot time and time again — in practice — to be able, eventually, to use it properly in play. This, after all, is what learning a sport is all about: developing habits so that actions are performed automatically and properly when there is no time for thought on these actions.

Since competition itself does not provide adequate practice, experienced coaches use drills to instill certain proficient habits in players. Some drills are designed to provide practice on form, some on tactics and strategy, and others on a combination of the two. As drills vary in purpose, likewise the setting, atmosphere, and procedure for conducting them vary. Wise coaches are always looking for new and interesting drills to offer their players in an attempt to maintain interest and enthusiasm in the learning tasks.

When planning for drills in their practice schedules, most tennis coaches are faced with the same problem confronting coaches of other sports: there never seems to be enough time, nor enough space, to work on all of the many facets of the game. Consequently, they must be selective; they must decide which are needed most and which must be fitted into the practice schedule. To do this, they must consider the level of their players and the level of their competition, and then after considering the team's time schedule, they must select only those drills that will give maximum return for the time spent on them.

Of course, regardless of the level of play or the caliber of competition of a particular group, certain skills are necessary for effective performance. Serving and returning the serve are required of players on every point; the ability to sustain a rally from the backcourt is essential and sooner or later at all levels, skill at passing a net man is required. These may be regarded as *basic* skills and should be practiced daily to ensure that players can regularly bring them to bear, within the limits of their ability, even under the stress of high pressure competition.

185

In addition to providing daily instruction in these basic skills, coaches must also provide practice on various *special* parts of individual players' games. One player, for example, may need work on hitting low balls, another on lobs, while still another may need special attention on making approach shots. Each of these needs must be recognized and attended to. At the same time, coaches must weigh various objectives against each other when planning practice schedules. Specifically, they must decide how much time to spend teaching strokes, for example, and how much time to allot to tactics and to play. If possible, each day's practice should include work on both the basics and on the special skills we have described, and students should be allowed to play each day *after* the practice. In other words, they practice *and* play daily.

ORGANIZING PRACTICE

There are several ways to organize daily practice sessions. Perhaps the most common is to provide opportunities for practice on the fundamentals of strokes first, followed by work on tactics and strategy. Play comes afterward, either in full-scale versions or in modified versions designed by the coach.

Stroke Practice

The coach can provide a daily review of form by playing the role of a practice partner for the players. Stationed at a teaching court, the coach tosses balls for his players to hit. Players take turns working with him at his station. He places each ball carefully to provide precisely the kind of practice needed. Later, when a particular player is ready for advancement, the coach makes a careful drop-and-hit from a distance more similar to that encountered in actual play. Still later, the coach rallies carefully with the player to provide even more realistic practice. Alternatively, the coach can appoint one of his players to act as a practice partner in his place.

Another approach to providing practice is to designate several courts or parts of one court as stations at which players practice specific skills. Players move from station to station on the coach's signal, and he passes among them offering suggestions. This method ensures that most of the basic items — and even many of the special points devised for specific players (or for specific opponents) — will be covered. Six or eight players can be practicing strokes on one court, for example, while at the same time, two or three others can be practicing some point of tactics (such as when and how to go to the net) on another court. With careful planning of this kind, the coach can best prepare his players for intensive work under game-like conditions.

By spending only a few minutes each day on the necessary drills, the coach can "nail down" his teaching points. Usually, however, he must first have a longer starting session with each player, during which time he introduces, explains, and analyzes the particular teaching point under discussion. Often a teaching point applies to several members of the group or to the total group. In such cases, the coach saves time by calling the entire group together and making only one presentation. Later, a brief review is given to each player as he takes his turn working under the coach's supervision on the teaching point.

Strategy Practice

For work on tactics and strategy—which should be done at the same time as work on form—a slightly different approach is necessary. Players should be permitted to practice in simulated competition to work on the kinds of shots and the sequence of moves used in match conditions. Specific play situations must be duplicated as closely as possible if players are to develop skills and habits that can be carried over into competitive match play.

Play for Practice

The discussion so far has centered on drills designed for the purpose of developing specific responses in players. It should be recognized that drills will provide only part of the kind of training needed by inexperienced players; they are not substitutes for competition. Players learn to play better by playing more. Countless hours of practice do not guarantee that players will perform as well in competition as they do in practice. Conversely, neither will endless competition without special practice lead to total skill development. Continuous competitive play often leads to bad habits. A player may avoid a certain weak point, for example, and thus never improve in that area. Moreover, he will eventually meet an opponent who exploits his weakness; at that point, the player suffers the consequences of having neglected special practice. Obviously, what is usually needed is a combination of practice and play. We suggest a great deal of "play for practice," in which players ignore the score and concentrate instead on the strokes, shots, and tactics practiced separately earlier. In a sense, the players will then be putting into play the techniques they have practiced in drills.

DRILLS

Most experienced coaches have available on their clipboards—at their fingertips, so to speak—a list of activities or drills to which they can refer to meet a need as it develops. We now list several such drills that can be used regularly in practice sessions. For convenience, some are given a descriptive name. Players soon learn the names and learn to change quickly from one to another as the coach suggests. No recommendations on specific time allotments are made for these drills. Instead, we suggest that each coach decide what his players need most and provide more of that kind of practice.

At intervals, a coach should evaluate his program, noting the results of practice to date and measuring the effectiveness of his procedures. He can often be guided toward correct conclusions on these matters by conferring with his players to ask their feelings. Their opinions are at times surprising to the coach. A player may be lacking in confidence in a particular shot or move that his coach thinks of as his strong point. Another player may be miscalculating percentages and inaccurately tabulating results from certain of his shots or moves. When the coach and his players can settle their differences on such matters, they can then plan together for more beneficial and more realistic practice sessions.

Basic Drills

Practice in each of the following areas is essential to a well-rounded tennis training program: (1) backcourt rallying (offensive and defensive play), (2) serving, (3) returning the serve, (4) going to the net, and (5) playing against a man at the net. At any given moment in a match, a player is likely to find himself in one or another of these specific situations, depending on his own—and his opponent's—tactics and strategy. We recommend that coaches set up their practice and their "play for practice" in a plan that permits players to spend considerable time drilling on each situation.

In Chapter 9, we described in detail some teaching points to be stressed in basic drills. We suggest that the reader now review that material and that he combine it with the brief descriptions offered here.

RALLYING FROM THE BACKCOURT

When used at the beginning of practice, this drill prevents players from hitting carelessly as they warm up. Two players rally with each other from the backcourt, either player starting the rally with a bounce-and-hit. One player (assigned to practice offensive shots) tries to move the other; he tries to make his opponent run along the baseline to create an opening before finishing off the point. He uses whatever mixture of shots he can: cross-courts or down-the-lines, short or deep. Meanwhile, the other player retrieves and practices defensive play. He tries to stay out of trouble by choosing the right shot and by moving into proper position after each shot. Net play is not permitted; players are urged to remain in the backcourt to practice their groundstrokes. After a suitable time, players reverse their roles.

SERVING AND RETURNING THE SERVE

In this drill, one player serves in the regular manner, attempting to serve effectively enough to draw a weak return. If the server does not serve or volley well enough to safely follow his serve into the net (as is often the case in high school tennis), he stays back and simply notes the kind of return. He is not permitted to rally after having served; this is serve and return practice only, until such time as the coach permits a play on the return.

The receiver, meanwhile, tries to return to the server's weak stroke (if possible) and to a "deep" area marked in the server's court (an area within six feet of the baseline, marked by a line drawn across the court at this point). It is best initially to restrict this drill to just two shots—the serve and the return. In this way the player's attention is directed to the importance of these two shots. Later, when this is understood, players can be permitted to rally and to play the point out to its finish.

If the server does serve or volley well enough to play safely in the net position, he follows every serve in when permitted to do so by the coach. He tries to make a winner or a preparatory shot for a winner on his first volley. In this situation, the receiver tries to return low in order to force the server to hit at a low ball.

Here, too, the rally ends after the first volley to emphasize the importance of the serve and return. Soon, when players understand this, they are permitted to play each point out to its conclusion. If players later appear to be minimizing the importance of the serve and return, the rallies are again shortened to just three shots — the serve, the return, and the first volley. This advanced version of the serve and return drills can thus be called "serve and first volley."

GOING TO THE NET AND DEFENDING AGAINST A NET RUSHER

Although forehand and backhand approach shots are groundstrokes, many players who are normally very steady from the backcourt have trouble making effective approach shots. For them, special practice often must be provided in which they learn precisely when and how to go to the net. The drill described here provides that practice and can follow conveniently after backcourt rally practice.

The two players rallying with each other from the backcourt are again assigned separate roles; one attacks, the other defends. The attacker is permitted to go to the net behind any forcing shot made from inside his baseline. The defensive player tries to make the attacker hit from behind the baseline: he tries to hit deeply enough to prevent the opponent from advancing to the net.

After a short return by the defensive player, the attacker follows his own drive into the volleying position at the net. He makes a jump-stop to the ready position just as the defender's racket meets the ball. He then moves to intercept the drive and tries to volley to win the point.

When the attacker has come in to volley, the defensive player tries either to pass him outright or to keep the ball low while waiting for a safer chance to pass. He uses the kind of shots he would use in match play — drives (down-the-line or cross-court, flat or topped), slow chops to make the volleyer hit up, and defensive shots (even lobs) when appropriate.

Special Drills

THE DEEP GAME

In the deep game, the players rally against each other, each hitting from his backcourt area and trying to place his shot in the opponent's "deep area" (the area between the baseline and a line drawn across the court six feet inside the baseline). Either player starts the rally with a drop-and-hit shot. The rally ends and a player loses a point whenever his ball does not land in the opponent's deep area. The next rally is begun by the player who can do so most conveniently. No net play is permitted.

Several variations are possible. Players may be permitted to start the rally by hitting to the opponent's backhand if the coach thinks this is appropriate for their level. Players may be required to rally only forehands, only backhands, or to alternate forehands and backhands. In all cases, emphasis is on control, both side-to-side control and depth control; the purpose is to develop steadiness along with effective pace.

NO-SERVE TENNIS

Inexperienced players often mistakenly overlook the importance of baseline play when analyzing their matches. Many of them attach too much importance to serving and returning the serve, and even use these as cover-ups for bad all-around play. A coach can help his players recognize their lack of ability in backcourt play (and thus encourage improvement) by implementing "no-serve" tennis. A player begins the game with a drop-and-hit shot into his opponent's court. Play continues in the normal manner, with either player staying in the backcourt or going to the net as necessary. Emphasis is on maintaining the rally and on playing defensive or "neutral" tennis while waiting for a safe chance to attack. With experienced players, emphasis is on controlling the rallies by hitting hard enough, deep enough, and accurately enough to draw errors and to get safe chances to attack.

THREE-SHOT TENNIS

In all but the highest level of competition, school players who try to play the full-court game make most of their errors on three particular shots: the approach shot, the first attempt to pass, and the first volley. The drill for practice in these three shots begins with one player making a drop-and-hit shot from the baseline and running to the net to volley. His opponent returns as well as he can, and the first player attempts to make an effective volley. The rally always is stopped after three shots to allow players to analyze the point. The baseliner tries either to pass the net man or to hit low to his feet. He may even defend with a lob when appropriate. Whatever the shot, the emphasis throughout is on avoiding errors rather than on shooting for "winners."

A variation for experienced players is to have one player start a rally with a feeder shot that is purposely hit short in order to permit the opponent to make an approach shot and a dash to the volley position. Again, the baseliner either passes or lobs. This version of the drill can be used to provide practice at attacking an opponent's weak stroke; alternatively, when no "built-in weakness" exists, practice at creating a weakness by moving the opponent to a difficult position is provided.

VOLLEYING THROUGH MIDCOURT

This drill affords the player practice at volleying after moving in, at volleying from several positions in the court, and at controlling the depth of volleys. Two players face each other on opposite baselines. One starts a rally with a bounce-and-hit and then moves up two steps. He tries to hit deep into the opponent's court. The second player returns and moves up two steps; he tries to hit to his opponent's feet. The rally continues with each player moving up two steps after each hit. Each ball is aimed at the opponent's feet to make him volley upward. Players try to work their way into the safe volleying position by keeping the ball low. This requires taking the speed off some volleys. When they can hit down, they hit harder and attempt to finish off the rally.

A variation of this drill provides excellent doubles practice by developing in the players both a feel for working their way into the net and a respect for the importance of protecting their partner. In this variation, each deep player has a partner at the net. The deep players rally cross-court, moving in two steps after each hit. They try to keep the ball low and away from the opposing net man (to protect their partner) and to hit hard at the opposing net man when hitting from up close.

PASSING SHOTS: ONE AGAINST TWO

Two volleyers take a position at the service line, one on each side of and about a half-step from the center service line. Another player takes a position on the baseline at the far side of the net. The rally begins with a feeder shot from either side. When the ball is in play, the baseliner tries to pass the net men. He plays out every shot as if it were a point in match play. He hits cross-court and down the line; he lobs when appropriate; he moves forward to handle short, weak returns and volleys when necessary. The volleyers simply return to him and permit him to have several chances to return in each rally. They practice making the proper moves to reach the ball. They hit softly enough to control their low hits and hard enough to attack on high ones.

Figure 12-1 A backcourt player tries to pass two net men in a passing-shot drill. The net men stand close to the center line as shown so that they have to make a proper move—a crossover step—to reach the short corners, the baseliner's targets.

PASSES AND VOLLEYS: "RING-AROUND-THE-ROSEY"

Three players form a line, with the first player standing midway between the service line and the baseline, the two other players standing behind him. A fourth player stands at the opposite baseline. The rally begins with a feeder stroke from either side. The baseliner drives at the first man in line, who moves up to volley and then quickly goes to the end of his line. Meanwhile, the second man in line moves up to volley the next return from the baseliner. The rally continues in this way with the volleyers taking turns at continually moving up to volley. They first hit directly back to the baseliner to give him several consecutive shots. Later, they aim away from him to cause him to move. The baseliner first hits directly back to the volleyers; later, he tries to pass them.

PROTECTING YOUR PARTNER

Two players line up at opposite sides of the net, taking positions on the baseline and on opposite sides of the center mark. Each has a partner at the net, in a volleying position, on the other side of the center line. The deep men rally ground-strokes, attempting to keep the ball away from the opposing net men. The net men attempt to poach, to intercept, and to put the ball away.

Baseliners are urged to protect their net man by keeping the ball deep. To provide opportunities for poaching, they should hit aggressively at short balls. Net men are encouraged to move aggressively to protect their alley when necessary, to intercept, to look ahead of the ball as their partners make a return, to move back to a modified net position when the opponents attack, and to retreat and play defense when their partner lobs.

LOBS AND SMASHES

Two baseliners lob to a net man, who practices hitting with speed and control. The lobbers first give him short, easy balls to hit. Later, they lob deeper and higher to make it more difficult for him. Still later they mix lobs and drives; they try to push the net man back with a lob, then drive the return at his feet. It is often necessary to provide experienced players with three lobbers to return hard, angled smashes. The smasher is given several very high lobs which he lets bounce before hitting.

Another variation, used to develop teamwork for doubles, has doubles partners either lobbing or smashing together. Two baseliners lob to two net men. The baseliners try to dislodge the net men by lobbing and driving, after which they close in to volley.

SPEED VOLLEYING

Two players face each other across the net, each standing in the ideal volley position. Either player starts the rally by volleying a ball released from his left hand. Players attempt to force a "miss" from the opponent by hitting faster and more quickly than the opponent can manage. Here, players must be cautioned not to rally at a convenient speed; instead, they should attempt to rally faster than the speed they are accustomed to.

PRACTICING THE FIRST VOLLEY

Two baseliners provide practice for one volleyer, who stands at the intersection of the service lines to make his play. The rally starts with a bounce-and-hit feeder shot. In the first stages of the drill, the backcourt men hit directly to the volleyer; later, they make him stretch to reach balls. They try to keep the ball low, as they would in actual play. The volleyer concentrates on hitting deep, as he would in play in preparation for moving up to a better location for his second shot. In the drill, however, he stays at the service line to get continual practice at playing from the first volley location.

FUN IN FUNDAMENTALS

In the first few weeks of practice at the fundamentals, it is not necessary to inject the element of competition into the various drills, nor is it necessary for the players to have fun at practice. Usually, the challenge of being out for the team and the feeling of working under supervision are enough to stimulate the players to serious effort. Of even more importance is the fact that the initial practice drills should be done carefully and thoughtfully so that players are really concentrating on items of form suggested by the coach, e.g., the position of the elbow, the correct follow-through, or the proper footwork.

Later in the season, however, players begin to lose interest in practice. Many of them become weary of drills and bored with playing the same teammates day after day. To maintain their interest and enthusiasm, the coach may have to alter his early season plans and provide some sort of activity that is realistic, beneficial, *and* fun. Along these lines we suggest friendly competition in drills, conducted in a congenial, relaxed atmosphere. When they are planned with the needs and interests of the players in mind, such drills can be made to function as motivators for continued practice.

Youngsters want to compete; they want to compete against themselves and against others. They want to know the results of their competition as well, and the results must occasionally, at least, be satisfying. The coach's task, therefore, is to devise drills in which everyone, even the lowest squad member, will sometimes win. In some cases "winning" may simply be a matter of a less adept player improving his score on a drill. Better players will want actual win or lose situations. In any case, the competition itself will often motivate players to practice further the skills covered by the competitive drills.

We will now describe several drills we use to lighten the tone of practice when we feel such an approach is necessary to maintain interest. The procedures presented here will require some preliminary planning by the coach, and some will require that a record-keeper be active during the drill and afterward, tabulating scores and changing standings. The advantages gained by these fun-and-practice procedures will outweigh such technical disadvantages.

In all of these drills, squad members are competing against one another, sometimes as individuals, other times as members of small groups. We recommend that scoring be a main part of these drills, and that players and the coach call the score loudly enough and frequently enough to motivate the players. As fun drills, these activities should be conducted in an atmosphere where players joke and kid with one another, heckling opponents and praising partners — even though this kind of behavior violates the tradition that tennis is a game of quiet efficiency.

THE LONGEST RALLY

Two players rally groundstrokes from the backcourt, trying to sustain the rally as long as possible. They play as a team, competing against other twosomes on the squad, trying to make the highest number of consecutive hits. Net play is not permitted; balls must be played on the first bounce. Emphasis is on rallying *with* a partner, not *against* him.

The coach can modify the rules to make them appropriate for the skill level of his players. For example, he can permit each rally to begin with either a serve or a bounce-and-hit. He can decide that balls are to be played indiscriminately with the forehand or backhand, or that a ball is only "good" when it lands in a deep area. He may even set a limit to the height of net clearance (when practical, a string may be stretched across the court above the net) to prevent players from hitting with unrealistically high trajectories. Clearly, the quality of the shots in the rally can be improved by all sorts of special requirements (especially provisions that players hit from behind their baselines and that balls be considered "out" unless they land within the deep area).

ANGLED GROUNDSTROKES

In a variation of the preceding drill, each player is required to hit forehands and backhands alternately. In order to continue to rally, the players will be compelled to hit a mixture of cross-court and down-the-line shots and to be in position to reach their partner's shots.

CONSECUTIVE VOLLEYS

Two players play as a team and *volley* back and forth to each other from assigned net locations. As in the preceding drills, they try to "beat" other twosomes by making the highest number of consecutive hits. In one variation on the drill, the coach may determine that one or both players will hit either forehands or backhands exclusively; in another, he may require them to hit forehands and backhands alternately.

FASTEST VOLLEYS

Play begins as in the previous drill, but in this case players seek to hit the highest number of volleys within a specified time limit. All twosomes are set to start

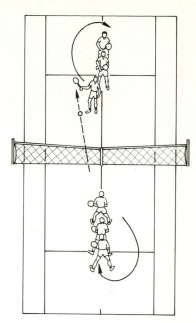

Figure 12-2   Ring-around-the-rosey volleys.

simultaneously on a given signal and continue to attempt to rally (with volleys) until a finish signal is given. When a miss occurs, either player makes a toss-and-hit volley with a second and third ball held in his hand.

HALF-VOLLEY GAME

This drill is similar to the volley game, with the exception that players attempt to hit consecutive *half*-volleys. Players count the number of times the ball crosses the net, but the count ends and a new one begins when either player hits a groundstroke or a volley (only half-volleys are counted). Players must stand behind a boundary line (the service line is convenient), but they can move up or back as necessary in order to play the ball on the short hop as a half-volley.

GROUNDSTROKE ACCURACY: TWO AGAINST TWO

This drill pits one twosome against another on one court. All the contestants stand at their baselines, one player of each pair in the right court ready for a forehand, the other in the left court ready for a backhand. Either of the right court players starts the rally with a bounce-and-hit, hitting down the line to the opponent's backhand. The backhand hitter hits cross-court to *his* opponent's backhand. He in turn hits down the line to the other opponent's forehand, who returns cross-court. Consecutive hits by each twosome are counted until a miss occurs. Scoring is similar to that used in ping pong, with 11, 15, or 21 points needed for victory. Players will naturally hit as hard as they can (while still controlling their shots) in order to make an opponent miss.

DRIVE-AND-VOLLEY RALLY

Four players on a court (or if space is limited, on half a court) rally for the longest number of consecutive hits. One participant plays as a baseliner. His "teammates" on the other side of the net take turns moving up to volley. The volleyers start in "no man's land" and run up and make a "check" just as the baseliner makes his hit. All volleys must land in a "deep" area (or perhaps beyond the service line, or to the forehand or backhand, as specified by the coach). Groundstrokes must be normally paced drives or slices.

TEAM VOLLEY RALLY

Four players compete against other foursomes, as in the preceding drill, with one important variation: the single player also volleys.

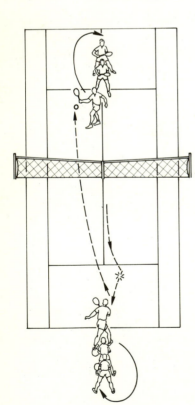

Figure 12–3 Ring-around-the-rosey groundstrokes and volleys.

Figure 12-4 Three players volley as a team against one player. The object is to make him miss by volleying at him faster than he is able to defend. He may place his shots as he chooses or, by order of the coach, hit alternately to the left, center, and right opponent.

VOLLEY TRIANGLES

Three players line up *across the court* in volley positions, facing an "opponent" who is in a volley position on the other side of the net. The ball is volleyed back and forth with the threesome trying to make the single player miss. He tries to sustain the rally for the longest number of successive hits. He may be required to hit to each player in turn or be permitted to place his shots as he chooses. Players rotate at intervals.

VOLLEY SQUARES

This drill is similar to the preceding drill, but in this case two doubles teams oppose each other. In addition, players may be required to make their opponents hit alternately or they may place the ball randomly.

VOLLEY LADDER

Two players (preferably doubles partners) face each other across the net in volley positions. They volley to each other trying to make the highest number of con-
(*Text continued on page 201*)

PERSONAL FORM ANALYSIS CHART FOR _____

GROUNDSTROKES   Footwork
   Forehand

   Backhand

   Application—steadiness, speed, accuracy, control of depth,
          control of rally

VOLLEYS   Footwork
   Forehand

   Backhand

   Application—consistency, placement, crispness,
          reduction of speed

SERVE

   Application—consistency, variety, placement, depth, effectiveness

---

RETURN OF SERVE

   Application—consistency, defense, attack, variety (control of speed and direction)

OVERHEAD SMASH—consistency, speed, placement, movement

LOBS—variety, control of depth, height, and   DROP SHOTS—control of depth and
     direction; defensive, offensive   direction

Tactical use   Tactical use

READINESS, QUICKNESS, AGILITY, MOVEMENT

A

Figure 12–5   A Personal Form Analysis Chart helps a coach individualize his instruction. Each player's game is analyzed and described by both the coach *and* the player. The player's game is then "pictured" graphically to show strong and weak points, as in *B*.

(*Illustration continued on opposite page.*)

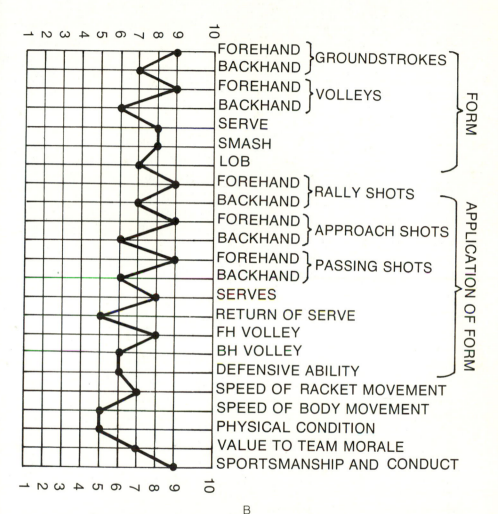

Figure 12–5 *Continued.* B, The graph is based on a 0 to 10 scale, with 10 representing an excellent score (an excellent stroke or shot) at the particular level of competition that applies to the player.

											JONES	BROWN	SMITH	PLAYER'S NAME	DRILLS FOR SKILL	
															Going to the net	Serving
															Staying in the backcourt	
															With opposing net man	
															Deep to backhand	Return of serve
															On the rise	
															Going in after it	
															Rallying from the backcourt	Ground-strokes
															Moving your man	
															Defense—sustaining the rally	
															Passing shots 2vs 1	Pass-shots
															Passing on the approach	
															Volleying for quickness	Volleys
															Volleys to backcourt 2vs1	
															Volleying through midcourt	
															Lobs	Lobs
															Mixed lobs and drives	
															Lob return of serve	
															Smash for consistency	Smash
															Mixed smashes and volleys	
															Smash with doubles partner	
															Poach on return of serve	Doubles
															Signals	
															Odd formations	
															Basic positions and moves	
															Protecting your partner	
															Returns against poacher	
															Half-approach & mixture	
															1st volley to feet or deep	
															Half-volleys	Touch Shots
															Drop shots	

MASTER PRACTICE CHART

Figure 12-6 A Master Practice Chart helps a coach tabulate the frequency of each player's attendance at practice sessions on various specific parts of the game. When attendance at practice is not regular, such a chart is necessary to ensure that players do not consistently miss some particular drill or item.

secutive hits. Three pairs can work on each court. The duo with the best score after the first rally moves up (to the right) to the number one position next to the coach's position. Other pairs take their respective positions in the order of their scores. After each rally the pairs realign themselves. If the rallies are excessively long, the coach requires alternate backhands and forehands, or all backhands, or even an occasional half-volley (required on a whistle signal).

OFFERING INDIVIDUAL INSTRUCTION

In addition to providing the opportunity for practice in drills and play, coaches should provide as much individual attention as each player needs. In this regard we recommend the use of Personal Form Analysis Sheets and a Master Practice Chart. The coach prepares a separate sheet for each player on which he presents his analysis of that player's game. He indicates both the strong and weak points and indicates practice procedures that will be helpful. When particular players appear to be resisting the coach's suggestions, it often helps to have several better players analyze the games of such players for the purpose of reinforcing the coach's opinions. Few players are able to comfortably ignore the opinions of their teammates; most will be made receptive to suggestions offered by them.

The Master Practice Chart shown in Figure 12–6 can be useful in ensuring that the coach does not overlook any of the important parts of any player's game. By checking his chart at intervals and by analyzing the performances of his players, he can plan his practices to provide the kind and amount of activity most needed by each individual.

A coach who plans his practices using Personal Form Analysis Sheets and a Master Practice Chart to tabulate the amount of time spent on basic drills, on special drills, and on play for practice is more likely to be thorough in his work than is a coach who uses less of a plan or a more rigid one. Again, we may say that flexibility is a mark of a good coach, just as it is of a good teacher.

Chapter Thirteen

CONDITIONING FOR TENNIS

Every experienced coach at one time or another has seen his players become involved in a match that was as much a test of endurance as it was an exhibition of shot making, tactics, and strategy. These tests of endurance occur at every level of play, in Boys' and Junior divisions, in Girls' and Women's events, and in high school and college play. True, there is some difference of opinion among medical authorities regarding the wisdom of subjecting youngsters to strenuous play under competitive conditions. "Adolescence," they tell us, "is the time to build endurance, not to test it." It remains a fact, however, that tournament tennis is an active game that makes many demands on the participants, some in the form of physical endurance, others in the form of muscular strength, at whatever level it is played. For this reason, a serious tennis player ought to condition himself physically in order to play with maximum effort—to play "all out" for the length of a tennis match. A properly conditioned player will not have to pace himself to conserve energy for crucial points or for the final set. If match play were a continuous activity, such as swimming, running, or rowing, pacing would be essential. In tennis, however, the frequent breaks between points and at the end of each game provide sufficient time for a properly conditioned player to recover. For most players, the "properly conditioned" state can be attained only through the regular performance of special exercises designed to develop endurance, agility, and strength in the form required in match play.

Some teachers and coaches may question the need for special conditioning programs for tennis players. "Have we not had national champions who were slender and not athletically developed," they might ask, "and did they not succeed without special work aimed at the development of endurance, strength and agility?" In reply, it should be pointed out that one of the reasons for improved performances in many sports where objective measurement is possible (track, swimming, and rowing, for instance) is improved training. Specifically, there is increased emphasis on interval training, overloading, and specificity when selecting training events or activities. Tennis players who apply these methods to their conditioning programs are more likely to play up to their capabilities and fulfill their potential than are players who simply let fitness develop as a by-product of actual play.

ORIENTATION

Generally, it can be said that the foundation for strenuous competitive sports is laid in childhood as the child runs and plays in whatever game or activity he or she enjoys. That is to say, those youngsters who are the most physically active during childhood develop their bodies to the highest degree—and they are also the youngsters with the most potential for becoming fine athletes. Unfortunately, however, few children develop enough strength and endurance through just their everyday activities to enable them to compete later in highly specialized sports. Few of them ever attain the level of physical condition necessary for championship play without first undergoing a vigorous, sound conditioning program. The factors of training and hard work play an important role in the success of most truly fine performers.

The tennis teacher or coach must do more than recognize the necessity for and the value of hard work in preparing for competitive tennis; he must decide what kind of training is likely to be most beneficial. In facing this problem, he must first realize that tennis requires a great deal of endurance, speed of bodily movement, agility, coordination, and range of movement. Furthermore, he must realize that playing competitive tennis itself develops most of these attributes. It also develops strength in the form that is needed in match play.

Clearly, if competitive tennis requires certain attributes and also *develops* these attributes, then the training program should include a great deal of tennis. It is equally clear, though, that tennis is only a *slow* developer of such items as strength and endurance. Consequently, the training program should include certain exercises designed specifically to develop these attributes more quickly. We will describe several exercises we use for just such a purpose. A few are done with weights and dumbbells, others are done with tennis rackets. Still others are modifications of ordinary running exercises commonly used as conditioners in sport. All are intended to serve as supplementary exercises to the normal tennis practice routine as conditioners for competitive play.

Some Practical Considerations

In general, it may be said that a conditioning program should aim at development and improvement in six areas: (1) cardiovascular endurance, (2) muscular endurance, (3) strength, (4) speed of bodily movement (footwork and agility), (5) flexibility, and (6) dexterity with the racket. The exercises we describe here were selected because they provide development in one or more of these areas.

It is impossible to prescribe an exercise that will single out one muscle and develop it independently of all others. In the normal human being, muscles do not work alone. They are always coordinated with and helped by other muscles or groups of muscles. For this reason, no attempt is made here to prescribe exercises for any individual muscle.

In order for a training program to be of maximum benefit, each player must know his own strong points and weaknesses. A player with a particular failing in one area might do well to spend a great deal of time on exercises designed for development in that area. At the same time, he could eliminate exercises dealing with muscle groups in which he already is well developed.

In addition, players must understand and apply the principle of *overloading*.

Simply stated, overloading refers to the fact that a player must tax his muscles over and over again by engaging in practice or exercise activity which requires an output *beyond that needed in the actual contest* (the player therefore must exercise beyond the initial onset of tiredness). Stopping at the first sign of fatigue — the convenient level of fatigue — is wasteful of time and energy. Players must push themselves beyond this point and continue to work until closer to their actual limits in order to achieve maximum benefit from exercises. This process creates a reserve which may be tapped in an emergency, enabling the performer to maintain a steady pace throughout the contest.

Running for conditioning ought to be done in a manner that utilizes the principles of *interval training.* Interval training is a process by which graduated periods of vigorous effort and rest follow each other in fairly rapid succession. A player does a certain amount of work (sprinting for 30 yards, for example) and then repeats it at small time intervals, either resting or doing less work (such as jogging for 30 yards) between sprints. Then, either by progressively increasing the length of the work period or by decreasing the length of the rest period, one gradually increases the amount of work done, which leads to increased endurance for that kind of work.

A word of warning is necessary here: the level of fitness that is attained is likely to drop off quickly if the training program is discontinued. For tennis players who are not regularly pushed close to the limit of endurance in match play, this means that the exercises, particularly the running drills, should be continued during the tennis match play season.

In addition to the theories of overloading, interval training, and maintenance of condition, we feel that the theory of *specificity* in training has implications for all serious tennis players. The theory of specificity holds that the development of any skill or attribute — quickness, speed, strength, or endurance — will follow more closely from practicing the actual skills or movements to be used in competition. Tennis players, for example, ought to spend considerable time practicing the actual footwork movements and the racket movements used in match play. In addition, they should run for conditioning in the manner in which they must run in match play.

Lastly, one must understand that any training program is only as strong as its weakest link. For this reason the athlete must get an adequate amount of sleep and rest. Regular living and training habits must be established, and the diet must be a sound one, providing for regular intake of the proper amount of protein, carbohydrates, fats, vitamins, and minerals. Disregarding any of these factors will minimize the effectiveness of the program.

CONDITIONING EXERCISES

Running

Running is an integral part of any conditioning program. Tennis is primarily a leg and heart exercise; therefore, running is one of the best means of conditioning for it. Daily running around a track, a gymnasium, or a battery of courts will undoubtedly develop cardiovascular endurance, and for this reason it should be done by all players as the competitive season approaches. Players may obtain still greater benefits from a running program if they incorporate into it the kinds of quick stops and changes of direction, along with the lunging and stretching, that occur in match play. The practical procedure for tennis team players to follow is to run around the circumference of the court space (around four, five, or whatever number of courts are in a block) in the backcourt area for a prescribed number of laps (it will vary depending on the number of courts). Players run for 10 yards, come to a ready hop, and immediately lunge to their right and then left with crossover steps, as if reaching for wide volleys. They recover to the ready position and sprint forward 10 yards to repeat the crossover steps. They continue this way around the courts until well beyond the point of initial fatigue. We have found that players are more likely to "push" themselves in this drill—and thus get maximum benefit from it—if it comes as the last item in the conditioning program after practice. We believe that the helpfulness of this drill derives from its resemblance to actual play conditions; players get tired here from the identical moves that make them tired in play: quick starts and stops, changes in direction, and lunges and reaches. Running in this way as a conditioner for tennis is far superior to conventional running. Moreover, players seem to relate this exercise to play and to appreciate it as having greater value than ordinary running.

If running space is limited, the crossover steps alone may be performed with beneficial effect. We also recommend crossovers for general warmup exercise, preceding practice. Here, however, players should be cautioned to begin slowly and carefully and to increase only gradually the tempo and intensity of the movements.

One running exercise designed for the development of endurance *and* agility is known as "spot-running." Players simply run in place, sometimes slowly, with their knees raised to waist height, other times as fast as possible, with the feet scarcely leaving the ground. Initially, the exercise should continue for about 50 counts (one count each time a foot touches the ground), but as stamina develops, the running period should be lengthened. A rest period of 10 or 12 deep breaths (approximately 20 seconds) follows each running period, after which stationary running is resumed. As fatigue sets in, the length of the rest periods may be increased.

Both of the running programs we have described should provide for a progressive increase in the amount of work done. Players should continually try to increase the length of the work periods, the speed at which the work is done, and the distance over which it is done. The exercises should be continued beyond the point of initial fatigue; the action should be sustained by each player until he is thoroughly tired.

Agility

In addition to developing basic all-around physical capacity and endurance, a conditioning program should be so designed as to develop a player's agility and speed of foot. The crossover step exercise described in the preceding section, *when conducted at maximum speed*, can be used for this purpose. In addition, rope-skipping exercises and various running exercises (up and down stairs, forward and backward, in the semisquat position, etc.) can be helpful. Two additional drills for the development of agility can also be followed.

To perform the first drill, the player gets into the ready stance, midway between two marks or lines drawn on the floor to his right and left, 12 feet apart. He glides and skips sideways to his right until he touches the right mark with his right foot. He stops quickly, reverses direction, and glides sideways to his left until he touches the left mark with his left foot. He continues to glide and skip sideways back and forth between the marks, moving as fast as possible.

To perform the second exercise, the player stands in a stride position, with his left foot advanced slightly from the right foot, which is set on a mark. Using his left foot as a "reaching foot," he steps around in a circle with that foot, moving it as quickly as he can while pivoting on the toes of the right foot. After fatigue sets in, he rests briefly, then reverses the position of his feet to repeat the drill. The wider the stance, the more difficult the exercise.

Flexibility

Flexibility is unquestionably one of the essentials of fitness for tennis, and for this reason the training program ought to include exercises that develop and maintain it. General body flexibility can best be attained by performing stretching exercises such as those illustrated in Figures 13–1 to 13–3. In addition, certain weight exercises (to be described) promote flexibility around specific body joints. For best results, these exercises should be done slowly and steadily, with a slight pause at each full extension of the range of motion.

Weight Training

Training with weights (barbells, dumbbells, or pulley-weights) is considered to be an excellent manner of providing the body with many of the vigorous repetitive movements needed for all-around fitness. When done regularly and enthusiastically, weight training will lead to the development and maintenance of flexibility (range of movement) in key joints and of strength in key muscles.

There are two general theories regarding the use of weights. Some coaches ad-

Figure 13–1   The player stands erect, then steps and lunges to his right, bending and stooping to grasp his right ankle. He returns to his starting position. He then lunges to his left to grasp his left ankle.

Figure 13-2 The player stands with legs spread and arms extended, as shown. He then twists to his left and bends at the waist to touch his right hand to his left foot. He returns to his starting position and repeats the exercise to his right.

vocate the use of heavy loads with a small number of repetitions, while others advocate moderate loads with a larger number of repetitions. In either case, the athlete is encouraged to attempt to increase continually and progressively either the amount of weight lifted or the number of repetitions.

Choosing one or the other of the two general systems of weight training seems to be largely a matter of individual preference. For the athlete with no previous experience in weight training, the following plan is recommended. The coach selects an amount of weight that permits 10 to 12 repetitions before fatigue sets in (for an average-sized man, 35 to 50 pounts will suffice in the exercises listed here). The

Figure 13–3 The player stands erect and lunges forward with his right foot. He bends at the knees and at the waist and reaches down to grasp his right ankle with both hands. He returns to his starting posture and then lunges forward with his left foot to grasp his left ankle.

player then lifts this weight daily or as often as possible, attempting to increase the number of repetitions. When he can do 15 repetitions before he is fatigued, he adds an amount of weight that again permits only 10 to 12 repetitions. He continues to increase the number of repetitions and the amount of weight in this manner.

A word of caution is necessary: in order to ensure the development and mainte-nance of flexibility, each exercise should be performed through the full range of movement of the body joint involved. Whenever possible, the arms should move from full extension (completely straight) to full flexion (completely bent).

For tennis players, six simple and conventional exercises, two each with bar-bells, dumbbells, and pulley weights are recommended and described here.

Barbell press: The player stands comfortably holding a barbell under his chin at chest height, with his palms turned upward. He presses the weight upward until his arms are fully extended. He returns to his starting position and repeats the up-ward press.

Barbell curl: The player stands comfortably holding the barbell in front of his thighs, hands spread to shoulder width and palms facing away from his body. He raises the bar to his upper chest, flexing his biceps fully. He then lowers the bar to the starting position and repeats the exercise.

Simulated serve: The player holds a five-pound dumbbell in his serving hand in a position directly overhead with his arm straight. He bends his arm at the elbow and lowers the dumbbell behind his back as far as he can, keeping his upper arm vertical. He then pulls the dumbbell straight up until his arm is again completely extended.

Sideways-overhead swing: The player stands with his arms relaxed at his sides, holding a five-pound dumbbell in each hand. He straightens his arms and extends them sideways and upward until his hands meet overhead. He returns to his starting position and repeats the exercise.

Back-to-wall: The player stands with his back toward a set of pulley weights.

He holds the weight handles at shoulder level with his arms extended to the rear as far as possible. Keeping his arms straight, he swings the weight handles forward in an arc, until his hands meet in front of his body. He returns to his starting position.

Facing the wall: The player stands with his body facing the pulley weights. He holds the handles at shoulder height with his arms fully extended forward. He swings the weight handles backward as far as possible, keeping his arms straight. He returns to the starting position and repeats the exercise.

Arm, Hand, and Wrist Strength

Modern tennis, with its booming serves and quick exchanges at the net, requires a great deal of skill and dexterity with the racket. Although rackets weigh only ounces, a certain amount of strength is required to overcome the inertia of the racket during the swing. Ranking players all have firm grips and well-developed muscles in their hitting arms, particularly in the forearm. One often hears it said of such players that they move the racket so quickly as to make it appear to be part of their arm. Such racket control comes only with the development of strength in the grip, the wrist, and the muscles of the forearm.

For development in these areas we strongly recommend that the student use a covered racket in rally practice against the wall. The cover adds enough weight and provides enough air resistance to require the player to hold his grip and wrist firm throughout the practice exercise. As he does so, he develops strength in his grip, wrist, and forearm. Most importantly, he uses his racket in the drill just as he uses it in play, and consequently he develops the kind of strength he needs in play and in the places where strength is necessary. The teacher or coach should continually prompt the player to use grips in this drill that are identical to those he uses in play. This is essential if maximum benefit is to be derived from this practice.

Figure 13–4 Volleying against a backboard with a covered racket is a good exercise for developing strength in the grip, wrist, and forearm. Because the strength that is developed here corresponds to that needed in match play, we consider this routine to be more beneficial than exercises designed for specific muscle groups.

Figure 13-5 The player sits with his knees drawn up toward his chest so that his feet are flat on the floor. With arms raised and hands clasped behind his head, he twists his trunk to his right to touch his left elbow to his right knee. He then twists in the reverse direction to touch his right elbow to his left knee.

Leg Strength

An expression familiar to many coaches and players is the maxim that "an athlete is only as good as his legs." Although this may not be completely true, it must be admitted that leg strength is an important item for any athlete competing in activities requiring sustained running, bending, and stretching. An exercise for strengthening the legs was described in an earlier section on flexibility. In addition, half-knee bends, as described earlier, help strengthen legs.

A word of caution is necessary here. The *deep knee bend* and "duck waddle" which have been used traditionally as training activities for sports are now generally disapproved by medical authorities, because they have a high potential for serious injury to the internal and supporting structures of the knee joint.

Abdominal Strength

Abdominal strength plays an important role in nearly every athletic activity, especially in those requiring maximum endurance. Many experienced athletes believe that the amount of firmness in their stomach muscles is an accurate indication of their degree of overall fitness. The exercises we recommend for "toning up" the abdominals are shown in Figures 13–5 and 13–6.

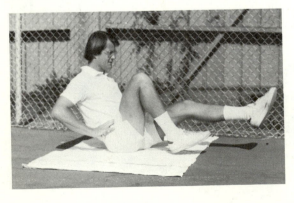

Figure 13–6 The player sits on the floor with his legs extended together in front of his body and his heels held just off the floor. He draws one knee in toward his chest, then quickly extends that leg by straightening it and forcing the foot out. While extending, he draws the other knee in toward his chest, and then quickly extends and straightens that leg. He alternates drawing his knees in and extending his legs.

CIRCUIT TRAINING: ONE WAY TO FITNESS

Despite the obvious advantages of being properly conditioned for tournament play, and despite statistical proof (where measurement is possible) that strength and endurance can be developed through special exercises, many tennis players question the need for a special fitness program. They feel that play alone is sufficient to develop the degree of fitness necessary for the sport. As a result of this attitude, coaches are faced with the problems of devising an appealing and interesting conditioning program and of presenting it in a way that motivates their players to participate willingly and enthusiastically in it. We suggest that circuit training offers at least a partial solution to this problem.

Circuit training offers as a unique feature the introduction of a time element into the performance of specific exercises. It requires athletes to do progressively more and more work, in the form of special conditioning exercises, in progressively less and less time.

The procedure is simple. An athlete (or a group of athletes) is timed by a coach or trainer in order to determine the amount of time required to perform a certain number of repetitions of specific exercises. The athlete tries daily to reduce his time, because a decrease in the amount of time required to do a fixed amount of work is presumably an indication of improved fitness for that kind of work.

When presented properly and organized efficiently, a program of circuit training offers several distinguishing features that usually motivate players to participate enthusiastically in it. First of all, the manner in which the circuit is laid out, so that players move from "station" to "station" to perform various exercises, is in itself more appealing than is working on one spot in the conventional manner. Secondly, the fact that each player knows that he is to work at his own rate—at a rate which is, at the moment, suited to him—removes much of the fear and embarrassment felt by timid and less confident performers. Thirdly, the fact that each player is able to experience some success early in the program (the teacher plans it this way) and is able to gauge the rate at which he is improving appears to serve as added incentive for continuous work. Lastly, the fact that individuals are free to work on their own, inconspicuously among other team members and free from constant supervision by the coach, seems to appeal to most youngsters. These points, together with the fact that differences in levels of performance and degrees of fitness become obvious as team members work daily on the circuit, seem to engender an attitude of respect for fitness and an appreciation of the amount of work necessary to attain it.

Circuit training was intended originally for the purpose of developing all-around fitness, with no special consideration made for specific sport activity. Many coaches have adopted it, however, after modifying it to suit their particular requirements, and they are now using it to condition athletes for specific sports. We present our modifications for tennis here, in the hope that tennis players and coaches will benefit from a description of the use of these modifications in a school tennis program.

The General Nature of Circuit Training

A circuit, consisting of several "stations," is marked out on a gym floor or court surface, either by chalk marks on the court or by posters on the fence or wall. The markers indicate the kind and amount of exercise to be performed at each station.

Stations are spaced so that several team members can perform without interference. Each performer works his way around the circuit three times, moving from station to station upon completion of the prescribed number of repetitions—the "dose"—of each exercise. The number of repetitions, which is determined by the coach, varies, depending on the kind of exercise, the length of the circuit, and the physical condition of the athletes. At the first station, for example, the performer may be required to do 10 pushups; upon completion of these, he moves on to the second station, where he may be required to do 20 Burpees, and so on. The activities are so arranged in the circuit that different muscular areas are exercised in turn. Since each performer's repetitions do not exhaust him (the number of repetitions is set low enough to avoid exhaustion), he can proceed immediately and without rest to the next station to perform the prescribed dose of the next exercise. He tries continually to reduce his time for three laps of the circuit. On the final lap, because of fatigue having set in, the prescribed dose at each station will be fairly close to the maximum he is capable of doing.

There are several ways of determining the doses and the estimated time for three laps of a circuit, but for team procedures the "fixed dose" method is probably best. For the entire team a certain number of repetitions is set for each station, and a certain time—a target time—is arbitrarily established for three laps. It is essential that this target time be low: no one should reach it until after a few days' work on the circuit. Each performer must have a goal toward which he is working, a goal that requires intensive work.

Players all begin the circuit at once and go through three laps of it. The amount of time required by each individual for completion of the three laps is recorded and posted daily. When an individual succeeds in finishing the circuit in the target time, he goes to work the following day on a new circuit at which the number of repetitions at one or more stations is increased. For convenience and for motivational purposes, each circuit may be given a descriptive label: "Gold One" for the first, "Gold Two" for the second, and so on. When a performer reaches the target time set up for the second circuit, he moves on to a third, "Gold Three." Any additional circuits developed for the more fit individuals can be labeled appropriately. While some players are still attempting to reach the target time on "Gold One," others are working on "Gold Two" or "Gold Three." Any number of additional circuits can be devised, each having a progressively greater work load. Thus the stronger, fitter individuals may work toward higher levels of fitness, while the not so fit may work initially and for a longer period of time toward lower levels before moving up. While the ultimate goal of being a superbly fit tennis player is still far away, the athlete can be satisfied with having made numerous small steps.

The Tennis Player's Circuit

The exercises selected will depend on the conditioning effects sought. A tennis conditioning program should aim at development and improvement in five areas:
1. cardiovascular endurance,
2. speed of bodily movement (agility) or footwork,
3. flexibility,
4. strength and power, and
5. dexterity with the racket.

Cardiovascular endurance can be developed by performing work of a general kind which places a load on the circulatory and respiratory systems rather than work

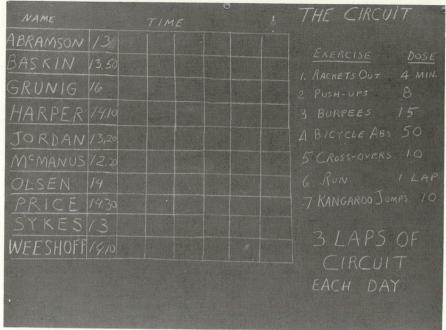

Figure 13-7 A sample circuit for team tennis conditioning. Each player performs the seven-event circuit three time in succession, performing at his own rate but trying to reduce the amount of time he spends on the events. Later in the season, after a general state of conditioning is established for the entire team, individuals work at increased dosage at various events. A slow mover may do a greater number of crossovers, for example, while a player lacking upper body strength may do more push-ups. The circuit is modified to meet each individual's needs; he competes against himself only, trying to work faster and (later) to increase the dosage and still work at an improved rate of speed.

of a specific kind which places a strain on a particular group of muscles. Since each participant will be attempting to decrease the amount of time required to perform his exercises, he will be increasing the intensity of his work and will thus ensure the building of general endurance. Agility and footwork can be developed by continual practice at quick starts and stops and changes of direction. Skipping exercises and crossover steps, when performed correctly, provide such practice. Flexibility can also be brought about (to some extent, at least) by the crossover steps, but the Windmill and Jumping Jack exercises are useful to augment its development. Strength and power can be developed by working a muscle group slowly against heavy resistance and quickly against lighter resistance. Fingertip push-ups and abdominal exercises involve heavy resistance; the Kangaroo Jump and certain weight exercises involve lighter resistance.

In selecting exercises for a circuit, the principle of specificity should always be kept in mind. Coaches and players developing a circuit ought to include several exercises that closely resemble movement in play. The skipping and crossover step drills are examples of suitable exercises.

Exercises in a circuit must meet two other requirements in addition to that of specificity: (1) they must be easy to perform so that players need not spend a great deal of time learning to do them, and (2) they must be standardized so that they can be done in the same way, requiring the same amount of effort each day. One must not expect, however, that all of the exercises will be done exactly alike by all performers. There may be slight modifications in the Burpees, for example. Such variations are not necessarily important, because the players are not really competing against each other. It is important, however, for any particular performer to do the exercises in the same fashion each day, for only in this way can he measure his performance on a day-to-day basis.

Another matter for consideration when setting up a circuit is the length of time required to perform it. Initially, this can be determined by trial and error. Experience has shown us that a group of top-flight college tennis players can get a good "workout"—one strenuous enough to be beneficial—in about 15 minutes. Later, as players improve in fitness, the length of time can be increased to as much as 25 or 30 minutes.

It is quite possible that some players could eventually be working on an advanced circuit requiring 30 minutes for completion, while other boys, less fit, would still be working on a shorter form of the circuit, perhaps one requiring only half as much time. Herein lies the reason for the strong appeal of circuit training: each participant competes only against himself, at a rate that is compatible with his own general state of fitness and with his kind of physique. One individual, for example, might not be able to progress as rapidly as would another. But the fact that the first requires more time to perform the same circuit than does the second does not mean that the slower boy is less fit. If the first boy manages to reduce his time, one can say that he probably has become more fit than he was previously—more fit for the kind of work done in the circuit. For this reason, the coach must select exercises carefully. He must select exercises that provide specifically for the development of fitness for tennis. Of equal importance is the need to display an enthusiasm for fitness that will communicate itself to the players and inspire them to undergo willingly a vigorous program aimed at developing maximum efficiency.

We offer the following principles as guides to be used when developing a circuit for tennis players.

1.   The exercises selected to be performed should provide for the specific development of those qualities considered to be essential for tennis players. The principle of "specificity" suggests that these qualities can best be attained by performing exercises closely related to actual movements required in match play.

2.   The program of exercises selected should provide for progression; a gradual reduction in time should be possible, and it should be followed by a gradual increase in the amount of work done. Over a period of time, although not necessarily at every day's trial, the work rate (i.e., the amount of work done per unit of time) should be increased.

3.   The exercises selected should be adapted to the group's tolerance for work. It is important to remember that the athletes are likely to be in poor condition in the early stages of the program and, therefore, should not be exercised too severely at the start.

4.   It is important, for motivational purposes, that everyone achieve some success, some reduction in time, in the early stages of the program. This can be ensured by making certain that the initial circuit is easy enough to perform without excessive fatigue.

5.   It is essential that each performer be permitted to work at a rate which is

fixed according to his own capacity for work, a rate which is, for him, the best rate. This requires that the program be highly individualized, with the exercises so designed that they are easy to perform and yet strenuous enough to be beneficial.

6.   It is important for the performer to know the rate at which he is working each day; he should know at intervals how he stands in regard to his target time. This requires that a clock be visible or that the coach call out the elapsed time at intervals.

7.   It is equally important for the performer to know the rate at which he is progressing toward his target time over a period of days. This requires regular recording and posting of the times of each performance.

The exercises that follow, with the time or number of repetitions indicated, are examples of suitable tennis conditioning exercises.

1.   "Rackets out" (time: four minutes): Players spread out on the court surface so as to have ample room for skipping sideways, forward, and backward. One team member is selected as a leader and takes his place at the front of the group, with his back turned to the group. All players hold the racket in their playing hand with the volley grip. For four minutes of continuous action, the players mimic the leader, who skips forward, backward, and sideways at random, with occasional crossover steps in a simulated volley movement. At the end of four minutes' time, all players move quickly to the next station.

From this point on in the circuit, the "dose" for each "stunt" should be adjusted for each individual to fit his needs. Here we see the true value of circuit training: it is individualized. The coach and player together decide what kind of stunt will best make up for a certain inadequacy or deficiency. The "dose" of a stunt for one player may be higher than for another (who may not need special work in the exercise involved in the stunt). Specifically, a player who is working on a stunt to tone up his abdominal muscles and who is weak in this regard needs more total repetitions of that stunt than does one already possessed of good abdominal development. The weaker one may first be able to perform only a few "bicycles" before fatigue sets in. (We have seen players become ill when pressed too fast at these.) Gradually, and very slowly, the number of repetitions can be increased, although they may never equal the number done at one trial by a stronger player. All of the exercises we describe should be planned in much the same fashion as the bicycle stunt. Only "Rackets out," which itself is timed, should be performed by all the players on the team for the same amount of time. The "dose" we list here for each exercise is offered only as a guide. The coach and his players may find more or fewer of these repetitions to be more suitable for certain individuals.

2.   Fingertip pushups: Players perform eight push-ups, modified to the extent that only the fingers of each hand rather than the palms are in contact with the ground.

3.   Burpees: Fifteen four-count Burpee exercises are performed in the following sequence: hands down, (one); feet back (two); feet forward (three); and stand up (four).

4.   Bicycle abdominals: Players sit on the court with their hands clasped behind their heads and with their elbows extended sideways. Both heels are lifted off the ground and the knees are bent. Twisting and leaning forward, the players

touch alternately the left elbow to the right knee and the right elbow to the left knee. Each touch is one count; the exercise continues for 50 counts.

5.   Crossover steps: Standing at the center service line with rackets in hand, players simulate volley movements, reaching first for an imaginary wide forehand volley, recovering to the ready position, and then reaching for a backhand volley. Each reach is one count; the exercise continues for 10 counts.

6.   Run, with crossover steps: With rackets in hand, players run across the courts, pausing at each doubles alley and center service line to do two crossover steps, as if reaching for wide volleys, with first a backhand and then a forehand. Players do one lap of the court, which brings them back to the starting position (this may be modified depending on the number of courts).

7.   Kangaroo Jumps: Players leap from the ground, jumping as high as they can, drawing the knees up and in toward the chest at the high point of the leap. The feet are then quickly extended so that the players land on the balls of their feet ready to leap again. Exercise continues for 20 jumps.

8.   Jumping Jacks: Standing erect with arms at their sides, players jump to a stride position and at the same time swing arms sideways and upward until hands touch above their heads. Players then quickly jump back to their original stance while lowering the arms to the side position. Exercise continues for 25 counts.

9.   Windmill: Standing erect with feet spread as wide as their shoulders and with arms extended sideways, players twist, turn, and bend at the waist so as to touch the left hand to the right foot. After returning to the starting position, they twist and turn so as to touch the right hand to the left foot. Alternating left to right, the exercise continues for 20 counts.

10.   Weight exercise: With a three to six pound dumbbell in their playing hands, players extend the arm and weight vertically above their heads. Keeping the upper arm vertical, they bend the elbow so as to lower the weight behind their backs until it touches the shoulder. The arm is then extended vertically again. Exercise continues for 20 counts.

11.   Volley against wall (with cover on the racket): Standing behind a restraining line, players volley alternately forehands and backhands against a wall or backboard. Three balls are provided at each station so that no time will be lost for retrieving a bad shot. The player simply picks up another ball and continues his count. Some young players will tire quickly, within 10 to 15 hits. We find an appropriate dose for college players to be 25 hits.

By way of summarizing the concept on which circuit training is based, it can be said that if it becomes apparent over a period of time that a player is doing more and more work in a shorter period of time than was previously necessary, and if the work is the kind of work that tires him in tennis play (bending, stopping, stretching, running, starting, and stopping), then he is becoming more fit for tennis. For this reason, circuit training can be a valuable adjunct to a school tennis program.

Chapter Fourteen

TOURNAMENTS

One of the most important ingredients of any successful tennis program is the variety of events and activities it includes. The experienced instructor knows that his ability to teach the strokes and the strategy of the game must be supplemented by an attractive and interesting general program of activities to encourage and maintain eager and enthusiastic participation in the game.

KINDS OF TOURNAMENTS

There are several different kinds of tournaments and special events that can be effectively used to add to the appeal of the tennis program. The most popular are the following:

1. single elimination
2. double elimination
3. consolation
4. round robin
5. ladder
6. pyramid

The single elimination, the double elimination, the consolation, and the round robin are generally used to determine a champion and runner-up. The ladder and the pyramid tournaments are generally used for two purposes: establishing a ranking of players, and maintaining a ranking list over a prolonged time period.

Frequently, the elimination tournaments or round robin matches are used early in the season by a school coach to determine the positions of the players on the challenge ladder or pyramid, which are then run off during the remainder of the season.

Elimination Tournaments

MAKING THE DRAW

When the number of entrants in an elimination tournament is any power of two (2, 4, 8, 16, 32, and so on), they meet in pairs in a simple "match-up" system in which

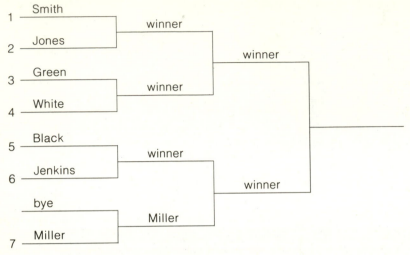

Figure 14–1   Elimination tournament with one "bye."

there are no "byes" (a "bye" is a pass from the first round into the second, as in Figure 14–1). When the number of entrants is not a power of two, byes are necessary in the first round to bring into the second round a number of competitors that is a power of two. The number of byes is determined by subtracting the number of entries from the next highest power of two. For example: if there are 12 entries, a bracket of 16 is necessary, and there will be four byes (to determine the number of competitors in the first round, subtract the number of byes from the total number of entries). In the tournament shown in Figure 14–1, only seven players were entered; accordingly, one bye is necessary to provide an even number of players in the second round. The bye is placed as shown and goes to the last player drawn (Miller).

The players' positions on the numbered lines in Figure 14–1 are determined by draw. The players' names are written on separate cards and placed in a suitable receptacle, and they are then withdrawn one by one and copied on the draw sheet in the order drawn.

If there is to be an even number of byes, half of them should be placed at the top of the draw and half at the bottom. If there is an uneven number of byes, there should be one more at the bottom than at the top. The names drawn first are given the byes in the top half, while those drawn next play in the first round. The names drawn last have byes in the bottom half of the draw.

Seeding the Draw.   To avoid having the best players meet in the early rounds of a tournament, it is common practice to separate them in the draw. This procedure is called "seeding" and is determined by ranking, record, and reputation. The rules permit seeding one player for every four participants, but no minimum number is specified (the most usual number is one for every eight players). The list of seeded players, in the order of their seeding, should be posted when the draw is posted. If two players are to be seeded, numbers one and two should be drawn by lot; the first drawn should then be placed at the top of the upper half of the draw, the second at the bottom of the lower half. If four are to be seeded, numbers three and four should be drawn by lot, also, with the first drawn being placed at the top of the second quarter of the draw and the second drawn placed at the bottom of the third quarter.

THE SINGLE ELIMINATION TOURNAMENT

The simplest type of tournament is the single elimination tournament, in which the winner of each match advances in the tournament and the loser is eliminated. As the name implies, one loss eliminates a player with no provision being made for an "off day" or bad luck. This type of tournament is most convenient when a large number of contestants are entered in the tournament and only a short time is available for play. In the draw, all names are placed in a receptacle and withdrawn blindly for position on the draw sheet. The first name drawn is placed on the second line, and so on, assuming that provision has been made for seeding and for byes.

THE DOUBLE ELIMINATION TOURNAMENT

The double elimination tournament, in which a player must lose twice before he is eliminated, is superior to the single elimination tournament when a small number of contestants is involved, in that it makes allowances for players having an "off day." Byes are given as specified in the rules. If a large number of players are entered, separate tournaments may have to be run, in which case the winners of each meet for the championship.

FLIGHT TOURNAMENTS

A variation of the elimination tournament that has proved successful, especially when a large number of players is involved, is a match-up in which contestants are divided into flights according to their ability. Flight A, for example, would include the best players, Flight B the next best, and Flight C the poorest. Players thus compete with others who have similar degrees of skill and experience. The winners of the flights are sometimes made to play off for the top prize, with handicaps being devised as necessary (as will be described). The flight system can be used for either singles or doubles tennis.

Consolation Tournaments

Consolation tournaments are offered to provide additional competition for first-round losers in elimination tournaments. The names of first-round losers are placed to the left and directly opposite their first-round match. They continue to advance to the left as they win matches. Losers are eliminated. Winners of the consolation tournament are generally awarded less valuable prizes than are winners in the championship bracket.

The Round Robin Tournament

In one kind of round robin, each player or team plays all the other players or teams once, and the winner is determined by the number of *matches* won. For convenience, tennis scoring may be revised to make a match consist of some arbitrary number of games, possibly six, eight, or ten, or even a "pro" set. For doubles, eight is a suitable number of games because it allows each player to serve twice. If the score is four-all, some kind of tie-breaker is needed. For example, each man or woman can serve four points, and the team winning the majority of the eight points played in the tie-breaker wins the match.

Such a scoring system, which permits a strong team or individual to lose a few games and still win the match, encourages friendly, social play. As a result, weaker players usually find this to be the most enjoyable kind of round robin.

For variety in a program, another kind of scoring system may be used. The winner of each match is determined by the number of *games* won. Each player or team is awarded whatever number of games was won in each match (0 to 8) and their scores are totaled after they have played every team in their bracket or flight. The disadvantage of this kind of scoring is that it forces the participants to play seriously and to win as decisively as they can in each match. As a result, some players are likely to lose badly (8–0, or 7–1) and become discouraged and disheartened. Since round robins are usually used in social situations for the purpose of encouraging participation and providing enjoyment, this second scoring system often defeats the purpose.

One efficient and convenient way to "draw" the round robin is in chart form. All the participants' names are written along a horizontal line at the top of the chart and along a vertical line and in the same order along the left side of the chart. Lines are then penciled in vertically and horizontally to form squares opposite each name. Scores are recorded in the appropriate squares.

If the "*matches* won" system is used, the lower half of the chart can be discarded and the match scores recorded in the squares at the intersection of lines extending from the names of the respective opponents. For example, if Jones beats Smith 5–3, that score is recorded (along with the winner's name or initial), as shown in Figure 14–2.

If the "games won" system is used, the entire chart is used. To record his score, each player reads *across* from his name to the square at the intersection of the line extending vertically from his opponent's name. If Jones beats Smith 5–3, Jones gets his five in the third square opposite his name, as shown in Figure 14–3; Smith gets his three in the first square opposite his name. At the end of the tournament, the

	Jones	Brown	Smith	White	TOTALS Won	Lost
Jones		Jones 7–1	Jones 5–3	White 6–2	2	1
Brown			Smith 5–3	White 7–1	0	3
Smith				Smith 5–3	2	1
White					2	1

Figure 14–2 Scoring in "matches won" system.

	Jones	Brown	Smith	White	TOTALS
Jones	XXXXXXX	4	5	7	16
Brown	4	XXXXXXX	6	5	15
Smith	3	2	XXXXXXX		
White	1	3		XXXXXXX	

Figure 14-3 Scoring in "games won" system.

player reads across from his name to total the number of games won. In case of a tie, the result of the match played between the tied teams determines the winner.

Round robins can be used in club play, in parks and recreation programs, and in competitive school team situations. Usually, it is best to separate competitors into flights, depending on their abilities. If the "matches won" system is to be used, it is best to place all the better teams in one flight (call it "A" flight), the poorer teams in "C" flight, and the intermediate teams in flight "B". A play-off between the winners may or may not be appropriate, depending on the attitude of the participants and the purpose of the tournament.

If the "games won" system is to be used, it is best to place one or two strong teams in each flight. When they realize they can beat a team easily, they will relax a bit and soften their play to make it more enjoyable for the opponents. They will play only well enough to win, not to win decisively; they may even play at "half speed" to save energy for the play-offs with stronger teams and with winners of other flights.

The Ladder Tournament

In a ladder tournament, players are listed according to ability or ranking, with the best player at the top of the ladder. Competition is arranged by challenge, with a player being allowed to challenge either of the two players immediately above him on the ladder. If the challenger wins, he takes the place of the loser, who drops down one notch. If the challenged player wins, he is allowed to challenge someone above him before he must accept another challenge. All challenges must be accepted and played within a mutually agreeable time period. Specific rules should be posted concerning the ladder tournament in order to avoid disputes and to keep the tournament running smoothly.

The ladder tournament is ideal for maintaining a continuous ranking of players over a long period of time.

The Pyramid Tournament

The pyramid tournament is similar to the ladder tournament in that it is ideal for maintaining continuous, prolonged competition. It allows for more challenging and

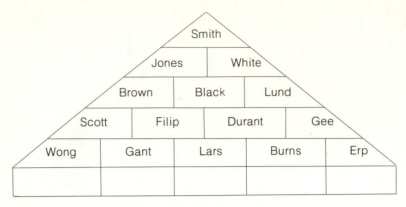

Figure 14–4 A pyramid tournament.

CHALLENGE LADDER RULES

1. A player may challenge any player in the line above him.
2. After having accepted and played a challenge, a player is privileged to challenge before accepting another challenge.
3. If the challenger wins, he and the challenged player exchange positions on the ladder. (This is an alternate method to that recommended in the text.)
4. All challenges must be posted on the schedule chart.
5. All challenges must be accepted within a set number of days.

participation and can include a larger number of participants than the ladder tournament.

After the original drawings are made, any player may challenge any other player in the same horizontal row. If he wins, he can then challenge any player in the row above him. When a player loses to someone on the row below him, he changes places on the pyramid with the winner.

Again, as in the ladder tournament, clear, concise, and specific rules should be posted with the pyramid in order to avoid disputes about challenge matches (as in Fig. 14–4).

The Point-Pyramid Tournament

In club work and in parks and recreation programs, where players are available daily, a variation of the scoring in a ladder is often used effectively. Points are awarded for each match played—two points to the winner, for example, and one point to the loser. Since in these club and community programs the purpose of the ladder is to encourage play (and in that way to lead to improvement and development), less importance is attached to winning than is the case in school situations. Often each player is required to play a prescribed number of matches within a specified period of time (e.g., three matches a week, or a match each day). The length of all matches is determined beforehand. Sometimes it is a "pro" set, other times 10 games, or even a regular set. At prescribed intervals, points are totaled, and the winner is the player with the highest number of points scored during the time interval. Additional points may be awarded for various positions on the pyramid at stated time intervals. For example, every Saturday at noon (at which time many clubs require youngsters to give up the courts to adults) points may be totaled and prizes offered; additional points for positions on the pyramid (fewer points for each line in descending order) and for wins *and* losses can then be included.

The Move-in, Move-out Tournament

When court space is limited and it is necessary to assign three players to a court, a rotational plan can be used effectively. Two players play normally while the third player waits his turn. At the end of two games, he takes the place of the player who served the last game. The new player receives the serve in the first game each time he goes in to play. Players continually move in and out this way, each sitting out for one game and playing two (except in the very beginning, when the third player must sit out for two games before going in for the server). Players count the number of games won. The player with the highest number won after a prescribed time or the first player to reach a prescribed number is declared the winner.

The Move-up, Move-down Tournament

A tournament in which players move up a court (from court 5 to 4 to 3, and so on) when they win a match, with each player trying to reach court 1 and to stay there throughout the tournament, is fun in a friendly group situation. Players are paired as opponents and assigned to numbered courts. Play starts on a signal from the instructor. After some arbitrary time period, play is stopped. The number of games won by each player is then recorded. The winner on each court moves up to the next lowest numbered court. The loser on each court stays where he is. The winner on court No. 1 remains there; the loser on Court No. 1 moves to the last court (the highest numbered court). Another round is played, after which changes in position are again made. (In doubles, players change partners after they change courts.)

VARIATIONS OF THE BASIC TYPES OF TOURNAMENTS

There are many variations of the standard types of tournaments that can be used to add variety to a tennis program and to create interest in it. Play conducted in men's or women's doubles divisions, or in father and son, mother and daughter, parent and child, and mixed doubles divisions can be stimulated through use of the following tournaments.

Handicap Tournaments

Frequently, when a regular elimination or round robin tournament is used, the results can be anticipated and predicted. One can almost predict the exact scores of matches that involve players who have played against each other several times before. In cases where two players have not met each other in competition, but have met some common opponents, comparative scores will give some indication of the probable result of a match between these two players.

A player is easily discouraged when he is scheduled against an opponent to whom he has lost several times before, and against whom he feels he has little chance of winning. The better players get little fun out of playing against someone they have beaten easily several times before, and whom they know they can beat easily again. In order to provide close, exciting competition, therefore, tournaments in which players are assigned handicaps on the basis of their records and rankings are used.

One of the most common handicap events assigns to each player a rating of +3, +2, +1, 0, −1, −2, or −3, to indicate his score from love. The poorest player in the tournament is given a +3 rating, which means he starts every game with three points—that is, he has 40. The strongest player is rated −3; he has to win three points just to bring his score up to love. Other players are rated at whichever of the five intermediate scores are appropriate, +2 or +1 for the weaker players, love, −1, or −2 for the stronger.

Keen competition develops when players' handicaps are carefully assigned. A top-flight player with a minus handicap playing against a less adept player with a plus handicap cannot afford to make many errors during play, nor can he afford to loaf. He must play his best at all times in order to win.

The Bridge-type Round Robin Tournament

A bridge-type round robin doubles tournament is often used to provide informal competition for club or school players. Its value is that it provides a wonderful opportunity for players to gain experience playing with different types of partners.

The number of entries in a bridge tournament is determined by the number of courts available for play, there being four entries per court. Players draw for partners and courts, with Player No. 1 teaming with No. 2 against Nos. 3 and 4 on Court 1. Players No. 5 and 6 play against Nos. 7 and 8 on Court 2, and so on. Each match consists of some arbitrary number of games, generally 4, 6, or 8. At the completion of all first-round matches, the number of games won by each player is recorded, and players change courts. The winning team on each court moves up a court, except for the winners on Court 1, who remain there. The losing team on each court remains on their court, except for the losers on Court 1, who move to the last court.

Before the second round of play begins, players change partners. For example, if Players 1 and 2 won on Court 1, and Players 7 and 8 won on Court 2, the latter move to Court 1, and Player 1 teams with either Player 7 or 8.

The "Screwball" Tournament

An informal tournament that provides much fun and enjoyment for the participants is a "screwball" tournament, in which various types of obstacles and gadgets are used to provide unusual and humorous playing conditions. This type of tournament is especially enjoyable to junior and intermediate players when played as a mixed doubles event.

Teams are assigned numbers from 1 to 6 (if six teams are entered in the tournament) and are then assigned to courts in numerical order in clockwise fashion for first-round matches. For example, Team 1 plays on the north end of Court 1; Team 2 plays on the north end of Court 2; Team 3 plays on the north end of Court 3; Team 4 on the south end of Court 3; Team 5 on the south end of Court 2; and Team 6 on the south end of Court 1.

Each round of play consists of some arbitrary number of games, usually four. At the completion of each round, each team moves in a clockwise direction to the next court and plays according to the rules of that court. Teams move clockwise after every round until each team has played on both ends of every court. The number of games won by each team is recorded, and is totaled at the completion of the tournament. Winners are awarded some unusual type of trophy (a huge screw imbedded in an old tennis ball and mounted on a plastic base is a good novelty award).

The rules of play on each court can vary according to the imagination and ingenuity of the tournament director. One set of rules that has proved highly successful follows:

Court 1.
South end—*Players use specially provided rackets which are tied together at the handles by a 12-ft. rope. Each racket has a cluster of three or four small balloons tied to the end of the frame; if a balloon breaks during play, the point is lost.*
North end—*Players wear special sunglasses (inexpensive glasses can be purchased at a local five-and-dime store). One lens of each pair of glasses is covered with adhesive tape or paint so that the players cannot see through it.*
Court 2.
South end—*Ball must be played on the second bounce only, except for the delivery of the serve.*
North end—*One player uses a fisherman's landing net in place of a racket. The player must catch the ball in the net before it bounces, and then must throw the ball over the court net. The player is allowed to take only one step after catching the ball in the net. The catcher's partner plays left-handed or two-handed, except for delivery of the serve.*
Court 3.
South end—*One player carries a small Easter egg or tomato basket, filled to overflowing with tennis balls, at all times except when actually delivering the serve. If a ball falls out of the basket during play, his team loses the point. His partner must play inside the service line at all times.*
North end—*Team must at all times play behind a line drawn across the court six feet inside the baseline but ball does not have to be played on the volley or on the first bounce. It can be played on any bounce.*

The Costume Tournament

A modified version of the "screwball" round robin mixed doubles tournament has been used with success by many teachers to provide unusual and humorous activity. It is very similar to the regular "screwball" tournament with its different set of rules applying to each court. Players, however, are asked to appear in a costume which is appropriate to the theme of the tournament (Independence Day, Gay '90's, or Club Founders Day, for instance). Trophies can be awarded for the most unusual costume, the most appropriate, the most original, and to the team that wins the greatest number of games.

The Strong-Weak Tournament

Many successful teachers modify their program by pairing good players with less skilled players. Participants are given ratings of 1, 2, 3, or 4, depending on their playing ability, with a 1 rating given to top-flight players, 2 to the next best, and so on. Teams are then equalized by pairing a No. 1 with a No. 4, a No. 2 with a No. 3.

The results of such a tournament are often surprising. Quite frequently, two average players will play their hearts out and enjoy a rare victory over the local "star," who is playing with a "weak" partner. On other occasions, the "star" may play so well that his low-ranked partner may also enjoy a seldom achieved victory over a more skilled player.

The Tennis Carnival

An event that is particularly attractive to very young, unskilled players is a Tennis Carnival, or Field Day, in which tennis equipment is used by participants in carnival-type events. Participants can be divided into teams (three or four players to a team) and points awarded to the teams on the basis of their performance in each event. The team that scores the highest number of points is declared the winner. Some events that can be used in a Tennis Carnival are described on the following pages.

Balloon Hit for Distance.   Each team is provided with a balloon that is weighted with a coin placed inside of it. From a starting line, each team tries to advance its balloon the greatest distance in the following manner. Player No. 1 tosses the balloon into the air and strikes it with his racket. He lets the balloon fall to the ground, advances to it, picks it up, and strikes it again. Player No. 2 on the team then advances to the balloon and also strikes it twice, after which players No. 3 and 4 each strike it twice in the same manner. The team that has moved its balloon the greatest distance after each team member has participated is the winner of the event.

Dribble Relay.   Teams take positions about five yards apart along one doubles sideline, with members of each team lined up behind a team captain or No. 1 player. At a starting signal, the No. 1 player on each team drops a tennis ball and dribbles it across the court to the opposite sideline by striking the ball with his racket. When he returns to the starting line (still dribbling) Player No. 2 on the team then dribbles the ball to the opposite sideline and back; Players No. 3 and 4 then follow suit. The team that finishes in the shortest time is the winner.

Dribble Marathon.   Team members form a circle inside each service court with each member standing just inside a line that bounds the court. The captain of the team drops a ball and strikes it with his racket so that it bounces to the team member on his left. As the ball comes up from the bounce, this player strikes it so that it bounces to the player on his left, and so on clockwise around the circle. The ball must be kept in play by each player striking it on the first bounce, hitting the ball to the team member on his left. Each team keeps its own count of the number of times the ball is struck before a miss is made. After a miss, the count is started over, with the player who made the miss starting the new count. The team that scores the highest number of consecutive good hits without a miss between the "start" signal and the "stop" signal (about three minutes) is the winner.

Air-dribble Marathon. In this variation of the preceding activity, the ball is passed from player to player by being hit while it is still in the air. Players merely hit the ball upward into the air, and, keeping it from touching the ground, pass it along in a clockwise direction. The count starts over when the ball strikes the ground.

Tennis Bowling. Empty tennis cans are placed near the net in ten-pin fashion, with the back row of cans three feet from the net, the front can about six feet from the net, and each can about six inches from any other can. Members of each team line up behind their team captain, who is standing on the baseline. Regular bowling procedure is followed, with each team member getting two chances to knock the cans over by dropping a tennis ball and striking it with a racket so that the ball rolls along the ground. The cans are placed upright after each player "bowls" two balls. The total number of cans knocked over by a team is its score for the event, and the team with the highest score is the winner.

Basketball. A circle with a 15-foot diameter is drawn on court and is divided into four quarters by lines extending from its center to one foot beyond its outer rim. Three bushel baskets or tubs are placed in the center of the circle, with edges touching each other. The baskets are given pre-selected point values that are unknown to the players. Each team member is assigned one segment of the circle. He stands behind the outer rim of the circle and is given six balls which he must drop and hit into the baskets. If a ball is hit or rolls or bounces outside of the circle, it is "dead" and cannot be used again, but a ball that stops inside the circle can be retrieved by a player in whose segment the ball lies if he can drag it back by extending the racket. He cannot step into the circle but merely reaches with his racket.

When all balls are either dead or are in the baskets, the event is completed. The point value of each basket is then multiplied by the number of balls in that basket, and the total point value for all three baskets is computed. The team with the highest score is the winner.

The instructor or person in charge of the carnival can use his ingenuity in conducting each event. Some events can be run off with two to four teams competing simultaneously in different sections of a tennis court.

Target Shoot

Another exciting event for both club and school programs is called a target shoot. Players test their accuracy and try to outscore one another by hitting at balls tossed or fed to them by an instructor or a ball-throwing machine. They use a different stroke at each station and move from station to station after having had a prescribed number of attempts at each stroke (we often set it at 25). At the right sideline, for example, a player may be hitting forehands, attempting to hit into the dou-

Figure 14–5 A weekly target shooting contest is always a popular club and school activity. Pupils start in "shotgun" style at various stations and move on to another station after having had the allotted number of tries. Shown above are a boy serving, a girl preparing to hit forehands, a boy with a tether ball, and a girl volleying against a volley board.

bles alley beyond the net. His score at that station will be the number of "good" shots he makes out of 25 attempts. Meanwhile, another player may be hitting backhands at the left sideline, aiming into that alley. A third person may be serving spin serves from the left of the center mark, while a fourth may be hitting flat serves from the right of it. Each player's score is recorded after he performs at a station and he moves on to another station. At the completion of the circuit the player with the highest number of accurate hits is declared the winner.

For convenience, the "shot gun" start may be used with as many players starting simultaneously as there are stations. Other players wait their turn at whatever station they prefer to start.

If a second court is available, volley stations and lobbing stations may be set up to test players in similar fashion. If a backboard is available, targets may be indicated on it and players may be allowed to rally against it for the highest number of consecutive hits. Boundary lines are advisable in this activity; players may be required to hit from behind the lines at distances adjusted to the various levels of ability.

A GLOSSARY OF TERMS

Ace: an outright winning shot by virtue of speed or placement, in contrast to a winning shot scored on an opponent's misplay (used most frequently to refer to a served ball that the receiver cannot make a reasonable play on).

Ad: a contraction of the scoring term "advantage"; refers to the first point won from deuce.

Alley: the area between the singles and doubles sideline on each side of the court (the singles court is made 4½ feet wider for doubles by the addition of the alley).

All-court game: a style of play that combines net play with baseline play.

American Twist: a type of service in which overspin and sidespin cause the ball to bounce high and fast to the receiver's left.

Approach Shot: the shot after which a player moves into the volley position (usually applied to a groundstroke).

Backcourt: the area in the vicinity of the baseline as contrasted to the area close to the net (the forecourt).

Backhand: a stroke made from the side of the body away from the player's hitting arm.

Backspin: spin imparted to the ball by hitting down on it or under it. The front edge of the ball moves up and the ball rotates in that manner during flight.

Backswing: the preparatory phase of the stroke in which the racket is carried back, from the ready position, to prepare for the forward swing.

Baseline: the line 39 feet from the net and running parallel to it at either end of the court.

Baseliner: a player who prefers to remain in the backcourt and attempts to win by using his groundstrokes.

Break: to win a game served by the opponent (the receiver breaks his opponent's serve).

Bye: a pass through the first round of a tournament to the second round without having to play a match. Usually occurs when the number of entrants is not a power of two, and is awarded by chance in the drawing.

229

Cannonball: a hard, flat service in contrast to a slower spin serve.

Center Mark: the mark in the center of the baseline. It is equidistant from the side-lines and is meant to indicate the server's permissible locations; he may stand anywhere between the mark and the sideline.

Center service line: the line under the net and perpendicular to it that serves as one of the boundary lines for the service court.

Center strap: the strap at the center of the net that holds the net securely at the required height—3 feet.

Chip shot: a groundstroke made slowly to apply underspin for control and accuracy (a variation of the chop).

Chop: a groundstroke in which the racket is drawn sharply down against the back of the ball to impart backspin (a variation of the chip and synonymous with "cut").

Close: to move in nearer to the net in preparation for a "kill" shot on the inter-ception of the opponent's return.

Consolation: a kind of tournament in which first-round losers continue to play other losers.

Cross-court: a shot made by hitting the ball diagonally over the net and across the court from one sideline to the other.

Cut stroke: a stroke in which the racket strikes the ball sharply and obliquely to impart backspin and often sidespin.

Deep area: the area within and close to the line being used—i.e., the baseline on groundstrokes and volleys, the service line on the serve.

Default: the victory awarded to a player for his opponent's not showing up or declining to play.

Deuce: the score of a game when each player has won three points or when the score is tied after that point. Also the set score when the number of games won by each player is five or when the games are even after that point.

Dink: a soft, delicate shot in which the ball has little pace.

Double elimination: a kind of tournament in which a player or team is not eliminated until losing twice.

Doubles: two players playing as partners opposing two others.

Draw: the chance pulling of names from a receptacle to determine the order of play in a tournament. Also the chart or diagram showing the pairings for the tournament.

Drop shot: a soft, delicate shot intended to cause the ball to barely clear the net and to drop and bounce more vertically than horizontally close to the net in the opponent's court.

Fault: a served ball that is either hit illegally or does not land within the proper service court.

Fifteen: the first point won by a player.

Five: a scoring term used to designate that number of games won or the number of the set. Also used unofficially in social play (as a contraction of fifteen) referring to the first point won in a game.

Flat service: a serve in which the ball has little or no spin, used mainly as a first serve in top-flight play.

Foot-fault: a served ball declared illegal because the player has violated the rule pertaining to the location of the feet when serving.

Follow-through: the part of a stroke occurring after contact.

Forcing shot: 1. usually used synonymously with approach shot to refer to the shot after which a player advances to the net. 2. a shot that places an opponent in difficulty because of either speed or placement.

Forecourt: the area of the court between the service line and the net.

Form: the manner in which a player strokes the ball, usually applied to the total pattern of a stroke.

Forty: the third point won by a player.

Game: a unit of scoring awarded to a player when he has won four points and is two points ahead of his opponent.

Groundstroke: a stroke made after the ball first hits the ground, in contrast to a volley, which is made before the ball hits the ground.

Gut: the stringing in a racket.

Half-volley: a shot made by hitting the ball on the short hop, immediately after it bounces.

Kill: a put-away, a ball hit so hard or placed so accurately that the opponent cannot possibly return it.

Let: a replay of a shot or a point; a let usually occurs on a served ball that lands in the proper service court but touches the net as it sails across. "Let" also refers to replays resulting from interference or from some misunderstanding between players and officials.

Linesman: an official whose function it is to determine whether balls are in or out on a specific line.

Lob: a ball lofted high into the air, usually used against a net man.

Love: a scoring term used to designate no score or zero for a player.

Love game: a game in which one player (or team) fails to score a point.

Love set: a set in which one player (or team) fails to win a game.

Match: the term used when referring to the complete contest. A match may be the best of three sets (2 out of 3) or the best of five sets (3 out of 5). A match is comparable to a game in baseball or a meet in track.

Match point: a point which, if won by a player, will make him the winner of the match.

Midcourt: the area midway between the sidelines, the net, and the baseline.

Mixed doubles: doubles play in which a man and a woman (or a boy and a girl) team up to oppose another man and woman.

Net game: an individual's technique for play in the forecourt, including his volleys, half-volleys, and overheads.

No man's land: the area just inside the baseline up to the service line. A player caught here is vulnerable to balls landing at his feet.

Out: a ball landing outside the playing area.

Overhead (smash): a shot played against a lob, usually hit much like a serve with an overhead swinging motion.

Pace: synonymous with speed, used to refer to the rate of travel of the ball through the air and after the bounce.

Pass: to hit a ball so that it flies out of reach of a volleyer.

Place: to direct the ball accurately to a particular section of the opponent's court.

Placement: an accurately directed shot that causes an error by the opponent.

Poaching: used to describe the manner in which a doubles player extends the range of his reach by moving into his partner's territory to make a play.

Rally: a series of good hits made successively by both players. Also refers to the practice procedure in which players hit continually back and forth.

Ranking: a listing of players in the order of their ability based on their previous records. Also a judgment made about a player's ability based on comparative records with other players.

Referee: the chief official at a tournament who supervises play and makes technical decisions when asked to do so by players or umpires.

Round robin: a kind of tournament in which each participant plays all other players entered.

Seeded (player): a player whose record suggests that he is likely to advance far in a particular tournament (the act of seeding refers to the manner in which players are separated in the draw so as not to meet in early rounds of a tournament).

Service line: the line drawn across the court 21 feet from the net and parallel to it, on either side.

Set: a scoring term used when a player has won six or more games and also has a two game lead over his opponent.

Set point: a point which, when won by a player, gives him the set.

Short ball: a ball landing short of the baseline in the vicinity of the service line.

Slice: a stroke that imparts backspin to the ball.

Slow court: a rough-surfaced court on which the ball bounces relatively slowly.

Spin: the action imparted to the ball by striking it an oblique blow.

Thirty: a scoring term, the second point won by a player.

Top spin: spin imparted to the ball by an oblique blow; the front edge of the ball moves downward.

Twist: usually refers to a kind of serve in which the ball spins and takes a high bounce.

Umpire: an official who governs play from a chair at courtside.

Underspin: spin on the ball in which the front edge of the ball moves upward.

Unseeded: players in a tournament whose records do not warrant special placement in the draw.

Volley: a ball hit before it has touched the ground.

Volleyer: a player who prefers to play from the forecourt, in contrast to a baseliner.

WHERE TO STAND

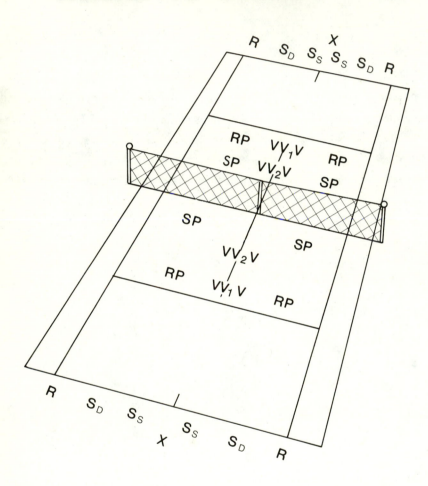

Figure A-1   Positions on the tennis court.

Ss—position when serving in singles
Sd—position when serving in doubles (in the middle of each player's half of the court)
  R—place where player waits to receive serve (the player moves up or back a step

234

depending on speed of serve; he moves left or right depending on server's position bisecting the angle of possible returns)

V_1 — spot for the player to occupy when he wants to get inside the service line for his first volley after an approach or a serve

V_2 — ideal volley position; the "V" on either side of this position is where the player should stand if his opponent is hitting from a sideline

SP — location of server's partner in doubles (halfway between net and service line and in the middle of the appropriate half of the court)

RP — location of receiver's partner in doubles (one step inside service line and in the middle of the appropriate half of the court); as an alternative the receiver's partner plays back at the baseline for stronger defensive position.

X — home base for rallies, one step behind center mark (off-center to left or right if opponent is hitting from an alley)

THE RULES OF PLAY

The official rule book of tennis contains 14 pages of regulations. It is not necessary for a teacher of elementary or intermediate tennis to know and understand the correct interpretation of all the rules. He must, however, know those that apply to play at the lower levels, and he must see that his players can properly apply them in situations that occur in their play. Specifically for this purpose we present here, in simplified manner, a few basic rules. An understanding of them will enable inexperienced teachers to answer most of the questions and problems that arise in their work. Coaches and teachers of advanced players are advised to study the complete list of rules and to familiarize themselves with the following USLTA publications: The Umpires Manual, A Friend at Court, Rules of Lawn Tennis.*

The regulations as they appear in the rule book are intended for umpired matches where all decisions on technical matters are made either by an umpire (working from a high chair beside the court at the net) or by a linesman, each official being assigned to call "out" balls on a particular line. Yet the very large majority of matches are played without such supervision. Instead of relying on officials to make such calls, players themselves must make all the decisions. To do so accurately they must be aware of several instances where decisions on technical matters, or on moral judgments, or even on a simple act of courtesy are not covered by the rules and are determined, instead, by custom and tradition. One example of a tennis tradition is the kind of clothing that players wear. The rules do not specify what is to be worn.† Custom and concern for personal comfort dictate that white, or at least pastel colored clothing, is most appropriate, though it is becoming increasingly common to see a variety of colors.

The unpleasantness that often develops between opponents over the foot-fault rule is another result of the omission in the rules of procedures for un-umpired matches. In such matches, players make their own calls, but it is not proper, by custom, for a receiver to call foot-faults on his opponent. About all the receiver is expected to do is to request that the server serve legally, but there is no provision in the rules for forcing the server to comply or suffer a penalty. Presumably, in the absence of a linesman or an umpire who would normally make such decisions, a

---

*The cost of these booklets is nominal (certain of them are free). They can be obtained from the United States Lawn Tennis Association, 51 East 42nd Street, New York, New York.

†Although the rules do not require players to dress in white clothing, many clubs request that players conform to standards set by custom—i.e., that they wear white apparel.

player may be his own watchdog and change his methods if they are illegal, or he may choose to ignore his opponent's request and continue to serve as he always does, illegally or otherwise.

Another point of confusion is found in the differences in procedures and rule enforcement in friendly, social play and in serious, competitive play. The teacher must make his pupils aware of these differences and should encourage them to make distinctions in procedures in their play at different levels. In the discussion that follows we indicate several instances where these differences occur.

Tossing for Side or Serve

The matter of which player serves first, and from which side of the net, is determined by a "toss" of the racket. One player places the tip of his racket on the ground, holding the end of the handle, and spins the racket rapidly, letting it fall to the ground as its spinning speed decreases. While the racket is spinning, the other players calls "rough" or "smooth," referring to the manner in which the trimming silk is wound around the main strings of the racket at the top and bottom of the racket face. The player who "wins the toss" has his choice of serving or receiving, *or* the choice of side, *or* the option of having his opponent make the choice of serving or receiving or of choosing a side.

If the winner of the toss chooses to serve, his opponent then has his choice of side. If the winner chooses a side, his opponent then has the choice of serving or receiving.

Not all rackets have trimming silk wound around the main strings of the racket. In the absence of trimming silk, the manufacturer's label or trademark, usually found on the butt end of the handle, can be used for spinning, with a call of "right-side-up" or "upside-down" being used to refer to the position of the trademark when the racket comes to rest after the spin. A third method makes use of an identifying mark or label found only on one side of the racket frame (a crest, an insignia, a trademark, or a signature can often be used for this purpose). Players call "signature up" or "crest down" as the racket is spun.

In social play, players are usually less formal; courtesy rather than legality determines who serves and from what side. Each player generously offers to let his

Figure A-2 Spinning for side or serve.

opponent have his choice of sides and suggests that he begin by serving. In doubles, tournament players usually let the stronger server of their team serve first because by doing so he may get to serve one more game than his weaker-serving partner. In social play there is no definite policy; the stronger or the weaker server may serve first either for the advantage we have mentioned or for courtesy's sake. In either case, the opposing team usually follows the procedure selected by the team that serves first.

Warming up

After the spin or toss of the racket, players (or teams) go out to their respective sides of the net and warm up by rallying the ball back and forth. It is customary for both players to hit the ball deep and down the middle of the court directly to each other during the warm-up. Each must give the other whatever practice shots he wants. After about three or four minutes of rallying, one player might decide that he is ready to begin play as soon as he has practiced some serves. "I'm ready," he will tell his opponent, who might decide that he too has hit enough volleys and groundstrokes. Each player will then practice some serves (usually five or six) and finally, when both players are completely warmed up, play will begin. If one player is not ready, however, the other must give him whatever warm-up shots he wants. To this extent, the warm-up is cooperative; this is true in both social play and competitive play.

The rules do not prescribe a time limit for the warm-up. Many tournament committees set a limit, however, to ensure getting matches started without prolonged delay. Nor do the rules specify the number of practice serves allowed. Players may try as many practice serves as they need, within reason. Six to eight is the usual number, but in tournament play, most participants have warmed up on an outside court long enough to get truly "loosened up" before making their appearance on the match court.

In a doubles match, it is customary to keep two balls in play simultaneously during the warm-up. The balls are hit parallel to the sidelines, one on each side of the center line, so that all four players are in action.

Delivery of the Serve

Play is begun by the server, who stands behind the baseline and between the center mark and the right sideline. He tosses the ball into the air in any direction and, before the ball hits the ground, strikes it with his racket. He cannot step on or across the baseline into the court until after he strikes the ball, nor can be walk or run into the act of serving. In delivering the serve, he plays the first point from the right of the center mark and serves the ball diagonally across the net to his left to the receiver's right service court (the right service court is also called the *forehand* court, the *deuce* court, and the *even* court). The server delivers the next point from the left of the center mark into his opponent's left service court (often called the *backhand* court, the *ad* court, or the *odd* court) and then stands alternately behind the right and left courts until the game is finished.

For each point, the server is given two chances to make a good serve. A serve that is not good is called a *fault,* and if the first serve is a fault, the server is given another chance to make a good serve. If the second serve is not good, he has served a *double fault* and he loses the point. It is a fault if the server swings at the ball and misses it, but if he tosses the ball, changes his mind, and catches it or lets it drop instead of swinging at it, it is not a fault. If the served ball touches the top of the net and lands within the proper service court, or on a line bounding the service court (line balls are good), it is called a *let* and does not count. It must then be played over. There is no limit to the number of lets that can be served, and the server continues to serve into the same court until he makes a successful serve or serves a double fault. If the first serve is a let, the server gets a replay on it and is still allowed his second serve. If a fault has been served and the second serve is a let, it alone is replayed and the server is allowed only one serve.

As he gets ready to serve each point, the server need not call out "Ready?" or "Service," as many inexperienced players do. Since the rules forbid him from serving until the receiver is ready, the server must determine from the receiver's location and position whether or not he is ready.

"First one in."   The rules limit the server to just two serves on each point; he has two tries to get one in. There is seldom any variance from this requirement in tournament play. Only when the server has been delayed between first and second tries (by a ball rolling into his court from an adjacent court, or by spectators moving about, or by any other distraction or interruption) is he permitted to have an additional serve. In social play, however, it is customary to allow each server to have as many tries as he needs to get the ball in play *the first time he serves in the match*. This custom, known as "first one in," is of fairly recent origin and has become common in the last ten years.

Receiving the Serve

The receiver may stand anywhere he chooses: in front of, on, or behind the baseline; inside, on, or beyond the sideline. His position will vary somewhat depending on the speed of the serve; he should adjust his position in order to play each serve conveniently after it has bounced once. The rules require that he make a return after one bounce and before a second bounce.

The receiver is also required to be ready to receive quickly—without delay—after each point and after each missed first try in a point. He cannot delay nor leave his position to retrieve a fault if the server is ready to serve his second try.

It is customary for the receiver to call "Out!" or "Fault!" when a serve lands out, either allowing the ball to go back against the backstop fencing at the rear of the court or hitting the ball softly into the bottom of the net. If the serve is good, the receiver should say nothing and make a return. The fact that the receiver does not call "Out!" indicates to the server that his serve was good and that he must then play the return of serve. Silence means "good"; only out balls are called.

On some occasions it is difficult for the receiver to determine whether a serve is in or out before he hits it back. This usually occurs when the serve is hard and fast. The receiver's first concern is to return the ball, and there is no restriction against his doing so and then calling the serve "Out!"—provided he makes the call immediately after he has determined that the ball is out. Such a "play it and call it simultaneously" procedure is permitted on any ball landing close to a line, *at any time during a match*.

After the Serve

The receiver must play the ball on the first bounce and return it over the net and into the area bounded by the net, the sidelines, and the baseline. His opponent can then play the ball "on the fly" or on the first bounce (that is, he may hit either a volley or a groundstroke) and must return it over the net into the other court (from then on in the point *both* opponents may hit volleys or groundstrokes as they choose). Play continues until one of the players fails to return the ball into the proper area or fails to play it before it bounces twice. If the ball strikes the net on or after the service return and lands in the proper court, it is a good ball and is in play (remember, though, if a served ball strikes the top of the net and lands in the proper service court, it is a *let* and must be replayed).

Each player is responsible for determining whether balls that land on his side of the net are in or out. If they are in, he says nothing and returns them; if they are out, he calls "Out!" as quickly as he can, in order to let his opponent know not to chase his return and hit it back.

Changing Sides

To avoid giving one player the advantage of having the sun at his back or of playing with the wind, tournament players change sides after every odd-numbered game (after the first game, the third game, the fifth game, and so on). Social players often modify the rule, however, sometimes to permit the weaker or less experienced player to have whatever side offers an advantage, at other times to avoid the delay caused by making frequent changes of sides. They often agree to change after every *three* games, or possibly only after each set.

Reaching over the Net

A player cannot reach over the net to hit a ball *before it bounces;* he must hit the ball on his side of the net, although he can follow through with his racket, letting his racket pass over the net *after* he has hit the ball. A player can reach over the net to hit a ball *that has bounced backwards over the net* provided he does not touch the net with his racket, his clothing, or his body. A player must play such a backward-bouncing ball to win the point. If he does not make a play on it, he loses the point.

Swinging beyond the Net. Although a player may never touch the net while a ball is in play, he may follow through with his racket beyond the net. If his proximity to the net or to an opponent making a play on the ball interferes with the opponent in any way, the point must either be awarded to the opponent or be replayed, depending on whether the interference was deliberate or unintentional.

In all play whether competitive or social, players are expected to call any of these violations against themselves.

Stopping "Out" Balls

A ball is considered to be good until it strikes the ground or the fence or bleachers outside the lines of the court. If a player catches or stops a ball that is in flight before it strikes the ground or the fence outside the court, he loses the point, whether he is standing inside or outside the lines. The ball must hit the ground or the backstop before it is legally out.

In social play, this rule is often ignored. Players are permitted to catch or stop out balls before they land out, provided the catch or stop is made outside the lines of the court. Presumably, the ball would have gone out if it had not been stopped or caught. The player is merely avoiding the bother of chasing and retrieving wildly hit shots from the opponent.

Line Balls

A ball that strikes any part of the line (outside edge, middle, or inside edge) is considered good. If no call is made on a ball landing close to a line, the silence must be interpreted as a call of "good." To avoid confusion and misunderstanding, however, players should be urged to make an audible call on all balls landing close to a line. As stated earlier, a call and a play may be made simultaneously, and in such a case the call is in effect.

Interference

When a player has been interfered with by a ball rolling into his court from an adjoining court, by moving spectators, by a piece of paper that has been blown on the court, or by other such distractions, it is courteous and customary to allow the affected player to decide whether or not the point should be replayed. (Replaying a point is called a *let.*)

Doubles

When playing doubles, opposing teams take turns serving. Teammates serve in order; one player serves the entire first game, and his partner serves the third game. A player from the other team serves the second game, and his partner serves the fourth game. This procedure is followed throughout the set. At the start of a new set a team may change the order of service from that followed in the preceding set.

In doubles as in singles, the server delivers the first point from the right of the center mark. He then serves the second point from the left of the center mark, the next from the right, and so on in alternation during the entire game. The server may stand anywhere between the center mark and the doubles sideline when serving.

The receiving formation of a doubles team may not be changed during a set. If Player A on the receiving team plays the right-hand court for the first point of the match, he must play that position whenever service is made by an opponent during the set. Once the ball is in play, players may roam around their own court at will, but to receive the next serve they must return to their respective sides, to either the right or left court, as they were positioned on the first point of the set.

SCORING IN TENNIS

The scoring method used in tennis is often confusing to beginners; the terms are unusual and the progression of points seems to make little sense because the numbers don't "add up" properly (youngsters often ask why 15 plus 30 equals 40).

An effective way to teach scoring is to have pupils play hand tennis on a tiny court drawn in with chalk for just that purpose. Any smooth surface can be used; if only dirt and clay are available, lines can be scratched in with a stick. Make the court about 2½ paces long and 1½ paces wide. Place two sticks end to end across the center of the area to simulate a net (or simply draw a net line) and draw in the service courts by extending service lines across the court on each side of the "net," midway between the net and the baseline. Next, print the scoring terms in the order in which they occur (love, 15, 30, 40, game) in large letters on one side of the court so that players can refer to them as necessary while they learn.

To play, pupils bat a ball back and forth across the "net," attempting to make each hit land in the opponent's court. The open palm is used as a racket; form, style, and technique are not required. Smaller players may even be permitted to catch and throw the ball. To serve, a player merely drops the ball out of his hand and slaps it with the other hand, aiming for the proper service court. Players continue to rally, using either hand to slap the ball back and returning all "good" balls after one bounce.

Figure A-3 Hand tennis helps the players learn scoring.

THE GAME

Points in tennis are called love, 15, 30, 40, deuce, advantage, and game. Zero is called love. The first point won by a player is called 15, the second 30. The third point won by a player is called 40. The fourth point gives the player the game, unless each player has won three points, in which case the score is deuce. A player must win two points in a row from deuce to win a game. The first point after deuce is called advantage for the player winning it. If he wins the next point, giving him two in a row from deuce, he wins the game. If he loses the point after advantage, the score reverts back to deuce, and play continues until one or the other player wins two points in a row from deuce.

The term "all" is used to describe a tie score: 15–15 is called 15-all 30–30 is called 30-all, but 40–40 is called deuce.

The score should be called loudly and clearly after every point. Either player can call the score, but the server's score is always called first: 15–love means the server has won one point and the receiver has won none; 30–40 means the server has won two points and the receiver has won three; 40–30 means the server has won three points and the receiver has won two.

Advantage is called "my advantage" by the player who has the advantage, and "your advantage" by the player who does not have the advantage. An umpire or spectator would call "Advantage, Mr. Jones!" or "Advantage, Mr. Smith!"

The score in games should be called after every game so that no confusion results. Here again the server's score is usually called first: 4–love means the server is leading, four games to none; 5–4 means the server is leading five games to four. "All" is used here, also, to describe a tie: 4–all means each player has won four games.

Experienced players often use abbreviations when calling the score. They will sometimes use the term 5 instead of 15, and "ad" for advantage. Often they call "ad-in" for server's advantage, and "ad-out" for receiver's advantage. They may refer to 40–30 as ad-in and to 30–40 as ad-out, for the reason that these scores are similar to advantage in that the player who has 40 needs to win only one more point to win the game. Similarly, 30–all is sometimes called deuce. These abbreviations are not technically correct, however, and are used in friendly, informal matches only.

The Set

The first player to win six games wins a *set,* provided he is at least two games ahead of his opponent. Set scores can be 6–love, 6–1, 6–2, 6–3, 6–4, but not 6–5. When each player has won five games (5–all), play continues until one player gets two games head of the other. The set might finally end at 7–5, or 8–6, or 9–7, and so on.

The Match

A *match* usually consists of two out of three sets. The first player who wins two sets wins the match. A match score, for example, can read 4–6, 6–4, 7–5, which indicates that the player who won the match lost the first set 6–4, but he won the next two sets 6–4 and 7–5. This would be called a three-set match; the winner would be described as having "won in 3 sets," or as winning "at 7–5 in the third."

A straight-set match might have a score such as 6–0, 6–1 (the winner won by "love and 1"), or 6–3, 6–4 (the loser lost by "3 and 4").

All girls' and women's matches are two out of three sets, as are all matches for young boys. Championship matches in the men's and older boys' divisions, however, are often three out of five sets. An example of the score in a three out of five set match is 2–6, 6–3, 6–4, 2–6, 7–5, with the winner of the match having lost the first set (2–6) and the fourth set (2–6) but having won the second set (6–3), the third set (6–4), and the fifth, or final, set (7–5).

The most recent innovation in scoring is the "sudden death" rule, which can be used at the discretion of each tournament committee. Players use sudden death in order to reduce the amount of time required to conclude long sets. When the set score is 6–all, for instance, the opponents play best-out-of-9 points to break the tie. If it is Player A's turn to serve the thirteenth game, he serves two points, Player B serves two, A serves two, and B serves the remaining three if necessary for either player to reach the five-point majority. (It must be noted that this tie-breaker procedure is discretionary — not mandatory — and that the set score shall be recorded as seven games to six).*

A second scoring change permits use of a "no-ad" game system, in which a player need win only four points to win a game regardless of how many points his opponent has won. If the score goes to three points all (deuce, in the conventional system), the winner of the next point wins the game. The receiver has the right to choose to which court his opponent serves on the deciding point.

---

*A 7 out of 12 points tie-breaking method is also permitted but is not described here. The USLTA strongly recommends the 5-of-9 version because of statistical evidence of its fairness (see USLTA Yearbook, "Tournament Regulations").

EQUIPMENT AND FACILITIES

THE RACKET

Tennis rackets vary in price as they vary in quality and design. A cheap, poorly made racket can be bought for less than five dollars. A top-grade wood racket costs about 20 dollars for the frame alone, while the newer metal rackets cost about 50 dollars. Most manufacturers have a complete line ranging from inexpensive models to top.quality designs. Beginners and low intermediate players need not select the more expensive kind, until they develop at least enough "feel" to recognize the differences in the weights and handle sizes of rackets.

Rackets are usually marked "light," "medium," or "heavy." The grip size—the circumference of the end of the handle—is usually indicated, also. Preferences for one or another grip size vary as strength and hand size vary. An average adult man should use a medium-weight racket with a 4¾ or 4⅞ inch grip. Men with small hands should use a 4⅝ inch grip; tall, strong men can use a "medium" or "heavy" frame with a 4⅞ inch grip. Most adult women will find a light racket with a 4⅜ or 4½ inch grip most comfortable, as will most young players (boys and girls 10 to 15 years old). Older teenagers should move up to a larger handle (4⅝ or 4¾) and a medium weight.

Rackets are also "head heavy" or "handle heavy," depending upon how the overall weight of the racket is distributed in relation to the balance point of the racket. The total length of a racket is about 27 inches; thus the balance point will be about 13½ inches from the end of the handle. Balance the racket at this point: if the head falls, the racket is heavy in the head; if the handle falls, the racket is heavy in the handle. The weight of the strings will add a little weight to the head of the racket (about ¾ oz.)

Beginners will find a handle-heavy racket easiest to use. Many experienced players, however, prefer a racket that is either evenly balanced or slightly head-heavy.

The strings used in a tennis racket can vary in price and quality, just as the frame itself can vary on these points. Top-grade "tournament" split lamb gut, which is preferred by almost all experienced players, costs from about 12 to 24 dollars. The cheaper synthetic strings, usually made of nylon, range in price from 8 to about 14 dollars; these cheaper strings are adequate for beginners and inexperienced players.

Figure A–4 A convenient way of measuring the height of the net at the center strap is shown above: one racket's length plus one racket's width equals three feet, the standard height of the net at the center.

When buying a top-quality racket, it is customary to select the frame alone and then have it strung to order with the desired string. Gut can be strung very tight (about 55 to 65 lb. on a standard stringing machine).

The cheap and medium-priced rackets are in most cases pre-strung with nylon by the manufacturer, usually at about 50 lbs.

We would like to warn you about a practice that is all too common and that we have found to be a real handicap to beginning young players. We refer to the practice of a young beginner, boy or girl, using an adult's "hand-me-down" racket. It is very likely that such a racket, if it was originally bought by an adult for his own use, will be too heavy and have too big a handle for the youngster to swing properly. We have seen many youngsters in clubs, schools, and parks become discouraged and learn to dislike the game because they tried to learn to play it with a heavy, large-handled racket that was made for a strong adult.

BALLS SHOULD BE "HEAVY"

The matter of tennis balls for the beginning player and the tournament player is an important one. It is practically impossible to develop a good, sound tennis stroke by continually using old, light, worn-out tennis balls. By light balls we mean balls on which the fuzzy wool cover has been worn down to a smooth, thin, skin-like cover. The fuzz on a new or slightly used ball is what keeps the ball from curving or sailing wildly when hit; it keeps the ball on its course. So important is this fuzz that in most important local and sectional tournaments—and in all national tournaments—three new balls are used every seven or nine games. Good players sometimes use as many as a dozen balls in a long match.

The heavier balls will give a better feel of the ball on the racket, which is a very important factor in developing a good tennis stroke. We have seen many players who have tried to play with old balls ruin their strokes or ruin their chances of learning good, sound strokes. Old, worn, light balls do not fly accurately; they "sail" or "float," making it necessary for the player to resort to all forms of spin shots, cuts, slices, or to a "patty-cake," pushing tennis stroke to keep the ball in the court.

TENNIS SHOES

Standard tennis shoes are of the low-cut oxford style, with canvas tops and rubber or crepe soles. Tennis shoes are usually white in color. The soles of tennis shoes are smooth, without the rough notches sometimes found in basketball and softball shoes. Court regulations usually require smooth-soled shoes on a clay court, because rough, notched soles will tear up the clay or make dents and holes in the surface which will cause the ball to bounce badly. On a hard cement or asphalt surface court, however, usually any kinds of shoes are allowed, whether they are tennis sneakers, basketball shoes, or rubber-soled loafers. Nonetheless, players are still advised to wear regulation low-cut, white tennis shoes for maximum comfort and safety.

TENNIS CLOTHING

Tennis committees and tennis clubs usually insist that players wear the clothing associated with the game. A polo shirt or a T-shirt, white shorts, and wool sweat socks are standard garb in most tennis clubs. Public parks and municipal courts usually have no restrictions on the color or type of clothing worn, but most players choose apparel that permits freedom of movement as they run, twist, leap, reach, and turn during the course of the game (the apparel should also be comfortable when one begins to perspire). A medium-weight sweater or jacket comes in handy after the match to keep oneself from cooling off too quickly and thus stiffening up.

TYPES OF TENNIS COURTS

The dimensions of a tennis court and the height of the net are standardized according to the official rules of the game. There is no official or standardized surface for tennis courts, however. A visit to several different tennis clubs, each located in a different geographical area of our country, would reveal many variations in the materials that make up the actual courts. Court surfaces likewise vary considerably, and one can find several different types within one locality.

In general, there are five basic types of tennis courts: (1) cement, (2) asphalt, (3) clay (dirt), (4) grass, and (5) wood. Each of these surfaces has its own peculiar characteristics, and each causes the ball to react differently than do the others.

Cement (or concrete) courts, which are very popular on the West Coast, require practically no maintenance or care other than an occasional sweeping to remove dust from the court. There are "slow" cement courts and "fast" cement courts, depending on whether the finish is rough or smooth. On all types of cement, however, the ball tends to take a faster bounce than on the softer dirt courts.

Asphalt courts, while similar to cement courts in many respects, also differ from them. They are usually a trifle softer than cement, and as a result the ball gen-

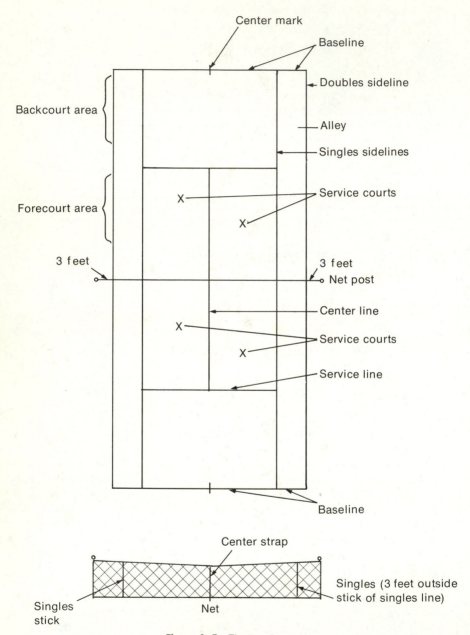

Figure A–5 The tennis court.

erally does not bounce as high as it does on a harder court. Asphalt courts may be faster or slower than cement courts, depending on the type of construction used. In most cases, asphalt courts are faster than dirt courts. Various tradenames for asphalt courts include *Lay-Kold, Grass-tex,* and *Plexi-Pave.* These names are applied by different companies, but the courts are very similar to each other in playing quality. Some are green in color, others are two-tone red and green, and others are green and dark grey or black.

Clay courts, of which there are many varieties, are found in the East, the South, and the Midwest. They usually require a good deal of upkeep and maintenance because the soft clay scuffs up very easily. One often sees dark red or dark green clay courts at private clubs or at schools and colleges. They are generally made of a mixture of clay and brick or stone-dust and are identified by a variety of tradenames (e.g., *Har-Tru, En-Tout-Cas,* and *Tenico*). The red or green color, of course, cuts down the reflection of the sun and decreases the glare from the courts. The courts are constructed in such a manner that they dry quickly, often being playable an hour or two after a heavy rain. However, they tend to get a bit slippery and dusty when dry, and bumpy and rough after a great deal of play, unless they are watered, brushed, and rolled often. They are the slowest of all the different types of courts.

Common, unmixed clay makes a good surface for a tennis court, and it is often seen in the courts at parks and recreation centers. The bounce on these clay courts is about the same as on a quick-drying court, although often a little faster. The unmixed clay court dries very slowly, and it sometimes takes a day or two for such a court to be playable after a heavy rain.

Grass courts are found only on the East Coast, usually at exclusive, private clubs. The bounce on these courts is low and fast—much faster than on clay and much lower than on cement—because the ball skids as it strikes the grass. The grass provides excellent footing when dry. Many of our major tournaments are played on grass.

Wood, on which the bounce is fast and low, is used for indoor courts. Most wood courts are located in armories or school gyms. Wood is a difficult surface to play because the bounce is a fast one, but at the same time, its true bounce and good footing make it a pleasure to use.

KEY WORDS AND CUES FOR TENNIS INSTRUCTION

I. The Grip
  1. Shake hands with the racket (FH).
  2. Point of V slightly to the left of the midline of the flat edge of handle facing you (FH)
  3. Thumb around the handle and against the big finger (FH)
  4. First finger spread slightly from the others (FH)
  5. Palm of hand facing the net (FH)
  6. Turn hand about ¼ of a turn to the left, or counterclockwise (BH).
  7. Palm of hand facing the ground (BH)
  8. Knuckles facing the net (BH)
  9. Point of V on midline of left edge (BH)

II. The Groundstrokes
  A. The Stance:
    10. Face the net.
    11. Stand as you would if you were an infielder in baseball, waiting for the ball to be hit to you.
    12. Hold the racket in front of your body, resting the racket: racket throat in the left hand, the racket head about even with your head, and the right hand (gripping the racket) about even with your chest.
    13. Turn from a baseball fielder's position to a baseball batter's position.
    14. Stand sideways.
    15. Face the sideline.
    16. Pivot on the right foot.
    17. Swing the left foot forward.
  B. The Backswing
    18. Take the left hand off the racket throat and let the racket head flow back naturally as you turn.
    19. Your racket should be pointing toward the fence at the left rear of the court.
    20. Racket should be over 7 on the clock face.
    21. Racket head should be about shoulder high at backswing position.
    22. Keep your wrist firm during the backswing.
  C. The Forward Swing
    23. Step toward the right net post with the left foot.

24. Step into the ball; shift your weight from the rear to the front foot.
25. Step as you would in batting in baseball.
26. Hit the ball flat.
27. Hit a line drive.
28. Thrust the racket head through the ball.
29. Swing the racket head into the ball.
30. Flatten the arc of your swing.
31. Move your elbow away from your body.
32. Swing toward the net, then toward the left net post.
33. Point and reach toward, or just beyond, the left net post.
34. The racket head should be high (about head high) and the wrist should be low (about chest high) at the finish of the stroke.
35. Hold the finish position—pose for a picture.
36. A high, firm finish
37. Your shoulders should be facing the left net post at the finish.
38. *Stroke* the ball, don't slap at it.
39. Keep your wrist firm.
40. Watch the ball carefully.
41. Try to see the seams on the ball.
42. Bend your knees slightly during the swing.

III. The Serve

43. Use the forehand grip, but hold the racket slightly more in the fingers.
44. Your toes should be pointing toward the right net post.
45. A line across your toes should be pointing toward your target area.
46. Hold the racket out in front of your body.
47. Point the racket toward the court to which you're hitting.
48. Rest the left hand against the racket throat of handle.
49. Racket head held high, your wrist should be low.
50. Move your arms down, then up, together.
51. Let the racket *fall* over your shoe tops, then drag it back toward the top of the rear fence.
52. Swing the racket down then up, away from the net, about head high.
53. Use a smooth motion when tossing the ball—just "lay" the ball up.
54. Toss about as high as you can reach with the top edge of the racket about a foot or two forward of your body, toward the net.
55. Drop the racket head low, behind your back.
56. Scratch your lower back with the racket head.
57. Let the ball "hang" in midair before you swing at it.
58. Throw the racket head *upward* and over into the ball. Flip it.
59. Hit the ball on its top right quarter.
60. Give the ball a ¾ spin.
61. Everything is loose and wobbly during the swing.
62. Think in terms of throwing a baseball.
63. Let your weight shift naturally from the rear to the front foot.

COMMON MISTAKES IN STROKING

I. The Grip
  A. Forehand
    1. Hand too far under the handle; too far to the right
    2. Fingers too close together
    3. Thumb extended along the top of the handle
    4. Racket not held firmly
  B. Backhand
    1. Hand too far to the right; first knuckle not on top of the handle
    2. Fingers too close together with the thumb extending along the handle farther than the first finger
    3. Loose, wobbly grip; racket not held firmly enough
II. The Swing
  A. Forehand
    1. Body not sideways to the net; body facing the net too much
    2. Loose, floppy backswing; racket flipped back with a loose wrist
    3. Racket taken back too far, with right arm too far from the body and too straight
    4. Racket not taken back far enough, with right arm too close to the body and bent too much
    5. Weight not back on the rear foot when racket is back
    6. Racket back too high or too low, not at waist level
    7. Weight not shifted to front foot as forward swing is begun
    8. Loose, wobbly swing; grip and wrist not held firm during the swing
    9. Racket face turned under or over during the forward swing
    10. Swinging across the ball, rather than through it and out toward the net
    11. Knees not bent enough during the swing
    12. Poor timing: Ball met too far in front of the left hip or too far behind it
    13. Right arm bent throughout the swing; right arm doesn't straighten out as it should during the swing
    14. Racket head allowed to "droop" during the swing; wrist not firm.
  B. Backhand
    Most of the errors that occur during the forehand swing also apply to the backhand. A few additional faults should be noted:
    1. Right elbow bent too much during the backswing

2. Right arm extended too far from the body during the backswing
3. Right elbow leading on the forward swing, with racket and forearm being flipped forward at the ball
4. Loose grip and wrist during the forward swing, with racket head being allowed to droop
5. Racket head swung under the ball and upward excessively; racket does not meet ball in a "line drive" swing
6. Top edge or racket face turned back during forward swing, resulting in an undercut shot or a high shot
7. Racket head lower than the wrist at the finish of the stroke

III. The Serve
   A. Bad toss; ball tossed too far right, left, forward, or backward; ball tossed too high or too low
   B. Jerky motion of left arm during the toss; ball not being "laid" or "placed" up in proper hitting position
   C. Right wrist and elbow not loose enough during backswing and forward swing
   D. Right elbow not bent enough at farthest point in backswing; racket head not dropped behind the back
   E. Weight shifted forward too soon during the swing, or weight not shifted forward at all during the forward swing
   F. Wrist too firm at moment of impact; racket head not being "thrown" up and into the ball
   G. Ball not being hit at full extention of the right arm; ball allowed to drop too low

IV. The Volleys
   A. Swing too long because of excessive body action; ball not "punched" or "jabbed" but stroked too much
   B. Weight not shifted forward during the short stroke
   C. Wrist and grip not firm at moment of impact
   D. Knees not bent enough during the stroke
   E. Stepping with wrong foot, ending any chance to reach wide balls
   F. Raising the elbow on high backhands

OUTLINE FOR TEACHING BEGINNING TENNIS

I. Introduction to the Game
   A. Explain the idea of the game; using a diagram on the floor or the blackboard will be helpful.
   B. Demonstrate basic strokes (forehand groundstroke, backhand groundstroke, serve, volley, overhead smash, lob).
   C. Classify group into smaller homogeneous groups of 2, 3, or 4 members through the use of a simple wall test. (Player hits ball against a wall as often as he can in one minute, standing behind a line 20 feet from the wall. Ball must strike wall above a three foot line. Divide players into small groups on the basis of scores on this test.)

II. Handling Groups
   A. Simple Swing Drills
      1. Group merely spreads out on floor, keeping 8 to 10 feet apart (left-handers to the right side of group when working on forehand swings and to the left side of group when working on backhand)
      2. Instructor stands facing group for instruction and demonstration
      3. Instructor walks among group making necessary correction in strokes
      4. Players check each other's swings (buddy system).
   B. Hitting Drills (dropped and tossed balls)
      1. Work individually or in pairs or in groups of three or four, depending upon the size of the group and the space available. (No. 1 hits, No. 2 coaches or tosses; No. 1 hits, No. 2 tosses or drops, No. 3 coaches, No. 4 retrieves balls. Rotate positions so that all get equal hitting time.)
      2. Players hit against a wall or fence.
      3. On a court, players hit from sideline to sideline (one court can accommodate 16 to 20 players easily).
      4. Instructor walks from group to group to give individual attention.

III. Steps in Teaching the Ground Strokes
   A. Drills for Developing Readiness for Tennis
      1. Footwork drills
         a. side shuffle, left and right
         b. crossover step, left and right
         c. forward shuffle (galloping), forehand and backhand
         d. backward shuffle, forehand and backhand

254

      e. oblique (angle) running, left and right, and stopping with good balance (for forehand and backhand)

  2. Hand and ball drills

    a. buddies play underhand catch (on first bounce and "on fly")

    b. stationary hand dribble

    c. self-toss and catch with tossing hand (toss opposite left foot)

    d. self-toss and catch at waist level with hitting hand ("wall-to-wall" or "fence-to-fence" swing of hand)

    e. self-toss and right-hand hit against wall or fence or to buddy with right foot anchored and left foot used to reach

    f. buddy toss and right-hand hit to buddy (6 feet away)

  3. Racket and ball drills (using choke grip, with hand at racket throat)

    a. stationary racket-dribble

    b. stationary air-dribble

    c. stationary air-juggle ("pistol grip" or racket on edge)

    d. self-toss and hit against wall or fence

    e. self-toss and hit to buddy (20 feet away)

    f. buddy-toss and hit to buddy (20 feet away)

 B. Levels in Development of the Groundstrokes:

  1. The swing

  2. Hitting a dropped ball (self-drop and buddy drop)

  3. Hitting a tossed ball (buddy toss)

  4. Running to hit a tossed ball (buddy toss)

  5. Rallying (against a wall or on a court)

 C. Five Points of Form for the Groundstrokes:

  1. The grip

  2. The ready (waiting) position

  3. The turn and backswing

  4. The step and forward swing

  5. The finish position

IV. Teaching the Serve

 A. Levels in the Development of the Serve:

  1. The swing

    a. toss-and-let-ball-drop practice

    b. delayed toss and catch with hitting hand (catch before, at, and after peak of toss)

    c. delayed toss and hand-hit against wall or fence (6 feet from wall or fence)

  2. Serving against wall or fence (with racket; 6 feet away from the wall or fence)

  3. Serving to target man (buddy) who stands against wall or fence, 15 yards away from server

  4. Serving on court from service line; moving back to baseline

 B. Points of Form for the Serve

  1. The grip and stance

  2. The starting position

  3. The backswing and toss

  4. The forward swing

V. Teaching the Volleys
  A. Levels in the Development of the Volley
    1. The swing
    2. Hit buddy-tossed ball to buddy (12 feet away)
    3. Volley a drop-and-feed ball on court (feeder at baseline)
    4. Rally on court with buddy (one at net, one at baseline)
    5. Both at net, volleying together
  B. Points of Form for the Volley:
    1. The grip
    2. The ready (waiting) position
    3. The hitting position
    4. The backswing
    5. The forward swing
    6. Footwork
VI. General Class Progression
  A. Progress from one level to the next when a majority of group is ready for advancement. Use simple tests to prove readiness (hit 10 balls in a row to tosser or target with good form).
  B. Let group rally at close of each period (to learn timing and judgment). Use short court, bounded by service lines, with lowered net in early stages. Move the students back and raise the net when they become more skilled.
  C. Start backhand after the second or third lesson; start serve after the third or fourth lesson; then teach all three together.
  D. Teach scoring after the fourth or fifth lesson in order to enable the group to play. Use of a simple chart showing scoring terms and sequence, combined with hand-tennis (on court 8' × 4') is an effective method.
  E. If players are small (7 to 9 years old), let them serve from point midway between baseline and service line, then move them back to baseline when they become more skilled.

THE CODE FOR PLAYERS

Although the Code is intended primarily for players, we consider it appropriate for inclusion in any manual for teachers and coaches. Relatively few players will bother to read the Code in its entirety, despite the fact that it is one of the most important and informative presentations of procedures and policies in match play ever offered. Tennis coaches, on the other hand, should be completely familiar with every point discussed in it, and should acquaint their players with their responsibilities for fair and just procedures as they apply the points of the Code in their play.*

We express our appreciation to the author of the Code, Colonel Nicholas E. Powell, and to the United States Lawn Tennis Association for permission to reprint the Code here.

1. Before reading this article you might well ask yourself: Since we have a book which contains all the rules of tennis, why do we need a code? Isn't it sufficient to know and understand the rules?

2. An overall answer to these questions could come from this hypothetical situation. Two strangers, A and B, are playing a tightly contested tournament match without officials. On one of B's shots A says: "I can't be sure if it was in or out; therefore, the point is yours." Three games later, on one of A's shots B says: "I'm not sure how it was; let's play a let." In two identical situations there are two different decisions. If no one else is in favor of a code that works the same on both sides of the net, you can be sure that A is!

3. There are a number of things not specifically set forth in the rules that are covered by custom and tradition only. For example, everybody knows that a "carry" results in loss of the point, but can you find some place in the rules where this is mentioned? Everybody knows that in case of doubt on a line call your opponent gets the benefit of the doubt; can you find that in the rules? Further, custom dictates the manner in which players will proceed in reaching a decision in order that there will be a generally understood pattern that all follow. These, then, are the reasons why we have and need a code, the essential elements of which are set forth below.

4. One of the unfortunate aspects of tennis is that when a match is played without officials the players themselves have the responsibility for making decisions, particularly line calls, but there is a subtle

---

*Use of the *Code for Players* is now required in all non-officiated sanctioned USLTA matches.

difference between their decisions and those of an umpire or a linesman. A linesman does his best to resolve impartially a problem involving a line call with the interests of both players in mind, whereas a
player must be guided by the unwritten law that any doubt must be
resolved in favor of his opponent. Sadly, there seem to be more and
more players who are inclined to disregard this tradition.

5. A corollary of this principle is the fact that a player in attempting to be scrupulously honest on line calls will find himself frequently
keeping in play a ball that "might have been out" and that he discovers
—too late—*was* out. Even so, the game is much better played this way.

6. In making a line call a player should not enlist the aid of a
spectator. In the first place, the spectator has no part in the match and
putting him in it may be very annoying to an opponent; in the second, he
is liable to offer a call even though he was not in a position to see the
ball; in the third, he may be prejudiced; and in the fourth, he may be
totally unqualified. All these factors point decisively toward keeping all
persons out of the match who are not officially participating.

7. It is both the obligation and prerogative of a player to call all
balls in his court, to help his opponent make calls *when the opponent
requests it,* and to call against himself (with the exception of his partner's first service) any ball that he clearly sees out on his opponent's
side of the net.

8. The prime objective in making line calls is accuracy, and all
participants in a match should cooperate to attain this objective. When
a player does not call an out ball against himself when he clearly sees
it out—whether he is requested to do so by his opponents or not—he
is cheating.

9. All players being human, they will all make mistakes, but they
should do everything they can to minimize these mistakes, including
helping an opponent. No player should question another's call unless
he is asked, but a player should *always* ask his opponent's opinion
when the opponent is in a better position to see a ball; obviously aid
from an opponent would not be available except on calls that ter-
minate a point. The laws of parallax being what they are, the opinion
of a player looking *down a line* is much more likely to be accurate than
that of a player looking *across a line.*

10. Any call of "out" or "let" must be made instantaneously which
means that the call is made before either an opponent has a chance to
hit the return or the return has gone out of play.

11. The requirement for an instantaneous call will quickly eliminate
the "two chance" option that some players practice. To illustrate, C is
advancing to the net for an easy putaway when he sees a ball from an
adjoining court rolling towards him. He continues his advance and hits
the shot, only to have the supposed easy putaway fly over the baseline.
C then makes a claim for a let, which is obviously not valid. C could
have had a let when he first saw the ball rolling towards him, but
when he saw it and then continued on to hit the easy shot he forfeited

his right to a let. He took his chance to win or lose, and he is not entitled to a second one.

12. Another situation eliminated by the instantaneous call requirement is that where a player returns the ball over the net, at the same time yelling: "I don't know." This sort of call constitutes a puzzle which should not be thrown at any opponent.

13. In living up to the instantaneous call requirement it is almost certain that there will be out balls that are played. On a fast first service, for example, sometimes the ball will be moving so rapidly that the receiver has hit the ball and it has gone into play (maybe for a placement) or into the net before an out call can be made. In such cases, the receiver is considered as having taken his chance, and he is entitled to only one, whether he made a putaway or an error. Likewise, when the server and his partner *thought* to be out the ball which *was* good, if they didn't play their opponents' return they lose the point. The purists' argument that a ball that is out cannot be played under any circumstances falls before the practicality of the player's responsibility to make calls. Otherwise, after a point involving a long rally had been concluded a player could discover an out mark made at the beginning of the point and ask that the point he had just lost be awarded to him. It is only fair that any time you cause your opponent to expend energy he should have a chance to win the point; and when you fail in your duties as a linesman you pay by letting an out ball stay in play. *From strictly the practical view, the instantaneous call rule will eliminate much indecision and unpleasantness.*

14. Any ball that cannot be called out is presumed to have been good, and a player cannot claim a let on the basis that he did not see a ball. If this were not so, picture your opponent at the net ready to tap away a sitter. As he does so your back is to him. Can you ask for a replay because you didn't see where his shot landed? If you could, the perfect defense has been found against any shot that is out of reach.

15. One of tennis' most infuriating moments occurs when after a long, hard rally a player makes a clean placement and hears his opponent say: "I'm not sure whether it was good or out. Let's play a let." Remember that it is each player's responsibility to call all balls on his side of the net, and if a ball can't be called out it is good. When you ask for a replay of a point because you say your opponent's shot was really out but you want to give him "a break," you are deluding yourself; you *must* have had some small shred of doubt, and that doubt means the point should be your opponent's.

16. When time and the court surface permit, a player should take a careful second look at any point-ending placement that is close to a line. Calls based on a "flash look" are often inaccurate, and the "flash look" system has a high probability of being unfair to an opponent.

17. In doubles when one partner calls a ball out and the other one good, the doubt that has been established means the ball must be considered to have been good. The reluctance that some doubles players have to overrule their partners is secondary to the importance of not

letting your opponents suffer from a bad call. The tactful way to achieve the desired result is to tell your partner quietly that he had made a mistake and then let him overrule himself.

18. Normally, asking for a replay of a point is a sign of weakness and of failure to exercise line calling responsibilities, and should occur only on rare occasions. One of these is as follows. Your opponent's ball appears out and you so call, but return the ball to his court. Inspection reveals that your out call, which stopped play, is in error. Since you actually returned the ball a let is authorized. Had you not returned the ball the point would have been your opponent's.

19. Once an out or let call is made, play stops, regardless of what happens thereafter. This policy is sound, though sometimes maddening. For example, with you at the net your partner serves a bullet that the receiver barely gets to the net for an easy setup which you whack away, but the receiver has yelled out as he was returning the service. Inspection reveals that the service was good. You first feel that your putaway shot should count for the point. But suppose that you had missed the putaway. Your immediate cry would have been for a let because the out call distracted you and made you miss. A rule can't work one way one time and work another way another time. It is unfortunate that a miscall was made on such a good service but you must trust your opponents' intentions to be fair, remember that since they are human they are going to make some mistakes, and realize that since they actually returned the service a let should be called.

20. All points in a match should be treated with the same importance, and there is no justification for considering a match point any differently than the first point. Also, some players will insist that on occasion even though a ball is good they *want* it to be out so badly that they will unconsciously call it out; this reasoning is difficult for a strong-willed, fair-minded player to accept.

21. As a driven ball — in contrast to a ball dropping vertically — strikes the ground (or asphalt or cement, but *not* grass) it will leave a mark in the shape of an ellipse. If this ellipse is near a line and you cannot see court surface *between* the ellipse and the line, the ball is good. If you can see only part of an ellipse on the ground this means that the missing part is on the line or tape, and possibly not visible. Some players will call a ball of this kind out on the basis that all of the mark they can see is outside the line; this thinking is fallacious. An ellipse tangent to a line (literally, touching the line at only one point) still represents a good ball; this is tantamount to saying that a ball 99% out is still good.

22. Notwithstanding the ellipse theory, on courts which have tapes for lines, occasionally a ball will strike the tape, jump an inch, then leave a full ellipse. This is frequently the case with a hard service when the server will see a clear white spot appear on the service tape, only to have the receiver call "out" and point to an ellipse an inch back of the line. To obtain accuracy in such situations is most difficult. The best that the receiver can do is to listen for the sound of the ball touching the tape and look for a clean spot on the tape directly between the server

and the ellipse; if these conditions exist he should give the point to his opponent, the out ellipse notwithstanding. Unless it is a very typical and distinct noise, sound alone can be misleading, particularly when the hearer is some distance — across the net or otherwise — from the sound. Also, an inch and a half is about the maximum that a ball will jump off the tape.

23. In returning service in doubles the receiver's partner must call the service for him, with the receiver aiding his partner in calling the center line and the alley line. If a receiver has to watch the ball, the tapes, and the opponent at the net, his problems are compounded somewhat over his having to watch just the netman and the ball.

24. Returning a service that is obviously out (accompanied by an out call) is a form of rudeness, and when the receiver knows that in making these returns he bothers the server it is gamesmanship. At the same time it must be expected that a fast service that just misses the tape will frequently with justification be returned as a matter of self-protection, even though an out call is made. The speed of some deliveries is such that if the receiver waited for a call before he started to make a return he would be over-powered. Probably the most difficult shot in tennis to call accurately is a hard flat service, aimed directly at the receiver, that hits within an inch of the service line in a grass court singles match.

25. Your opponent's foot-faulting can be irritating, particularly if he goes quite a few inches over the line and rushes the net after he serves. Since there is no traditional basis for your calling a foot-fault either against yourself or your opponent, compliance with the foot-fault is strictly a function of your personal honor system. The plea that you go only four inches over the line and don't rush the net is not acceptable. If you don't foot-fault when there is an umpire but do when there is not one, the time has come for you to examine your own sense of fair play to see if you are the type of person who will cheat provided he thinks he can go undetected or unpunished, and, if you are, try to make a change. Foot-faulting is just as surely cheating as is making a deliberate bad line call.

26. Even if no ethics were involved, from the practical view it behooves a player to avoid foot-faults. It is not uncommon in a match having officials for a chronic foot-faulter to become so upset by the frequent foot-fault calls against him that his whole game disintegrates.

27. A player who hits a weak shot and then, before the ball has crossed the net, utters an exclamation such as "lousy shot" has violated the ethics of good play. His opponent is clearly entitled to a let. However, if the opponent goes ahead and plays the ball and misses, the "two chance" rule holds. There is such a thing as the exclamation being timed so as to come forth just as the opponent is making the shot. It is then properly a matter for the opponent to determine whether or not he is entitled to a let, for *only* he can judge if the hindrance came before his shot or simultaneously with it. If he is going to request a let he should try to make the claim before he sees the outcome of his shot, though this is not always possible. The main thing is that if the opponent was

hindered, then had a chance to stop or to make the shot, then attempted the shot, whether he missed or not is immaterial, for he is considered to have played the ball.

28. In general, any conversion between partners while the ball is in play on *their opponents' side of the net is taboo.* Even when a ball in play is on their own side of the net conversation between partners should be minimized with about the only words permitted being such exhortations as to try hard for a ball ("run!") or to let one pass ("out"), etc. Incidentally, "out," meaning to let a ball drop, does not suffice for the normal call necessary if the ball goes out.

29. With respect to a player moving when a ball is in play or about to be in play, in general he is entitled to feint with *his body* as he wishes. He may change position on the court at any time including while the server is tossing the ball to serve. He may not wave his racket or his arms nor may he talk or make noise in an attempt to create a distraction.

30. A ball from your court going into an adjoining court or a ball from an adjoining court coming into your court can provide the basis for a let. In handling these balls here are some things to remember. When play is in progress don't go behind another court to retrieve a ball or hit a loose ball to that court; this may mean holding a ball for several seconds while a point is being finished. Don't ask for one of your balls until the point in play on the adjoining court has stopped. *In returning a loose ball to another court don't hit it aimlessly as if you didn't care where it goes as long as it leaves your court.* Instead, pick up the ball and hit it so that it goes directly to one of the players on the other court *on the first bounce;* this might be termed "rule One" of court etiquette.

31. In the general area of common courtesy and consideration for others violations are too frequent. Some players in loud tones have a post mortem on each point to the dismay of the players on the adjoining courts. Some players complain of the type of shots an opponent hits (i.e., too many lobs); what he hits are his business as long as they are legal. Don't embarrass a weak opponent by being overly gracious or condescending. Don't spoil the game for your partner or opponents by losing your temper and using vile language or throwing your racket. After losing a point don't slam a ball in anger; a ball boy once lost an eye from this sort of action. And don't sulk when you are losing; instead, praise your opponent's good shots. Above all, try to make tennis a fun game for all participants.

32. As mentioned in paragraph 17, the server's net man should not make an out call on his partner's *first* service even though he thinks it is out, because the receiver may think the service to be good and hit it for a placement. In this instance the net man should not invade the prerogatives of the receiver. However, the net man should volunteer a call on any second service he clearly sees to be out, for in this instance his call terminates the point. The net man is usually in the best position to hear a service touch the net, though custom supports the making of a let call by any player who hears an otherwise good serve touch the net.

33. Calls involving a ball touching a player, a player touching the

net, a double hit, a carry, hitting the ball before it reaches the net, or a double bounce can be very difficult to make. Usually either the player involved or his partner is best qualified to make these calls, and he should volunteer them instantly. The "benefit of the doubt" rule prohibits playing a let in such situations, and an opponent should not raise a question concerning one of these calls either during play or after he has lost the point.

34. Many players want to practice their serves just before they serve the first time, even though the match is then one game or more old. Once a match has started there is no basis for practice of any sort. It would be just as logical to hit practice serves before the tenth game as it would be to hit them before the second game.

35. If you feel that you as a receiver are being victimized by a quick server (frequently, a server who serves when you are getting ready rather than when you *are* ready) the person to blame is most likely yourself. This is true because in any discussion over whether a receiver was ready or not the sole criterion is the receiver's own statement, and if he wasn't ready a let is in order. Obviously, the receiver can't signal by word or position that he is ready, and then just as the server delivers become "unready" and claim a let.

36. The receiver should make no effort to return a serve when he is not ready if he wishes to maintain valid his right to claim a let. On the other hand the server is protected from the "two chances" receiver under the same rule; this rule states that if a receiver makes any attempt to return a service he is *presumed* to have been ready.

37. Some receivers indicate they are ready and then, as the server tosses the ball, become "unready" in an attempt to upset him. This is gamesmanship at its worst. The remedy is for the server to ask "ready" before each serve, a practice (particularly on a second serve) which detracts from the game and can become annoying.

38. When the receiver has indicated that he is ready and the server serves an ace, the receiver's partner cannot then come forward and claim a let because he (the partner of the receiver) was not ready. The receiver's indication of being ready is tantamount to indicating that his team is ready. While no server should serve if he sees either of his opponents is not ready, he is not expected to check both opponents before each serve. It is the receiver's responsibility to protect his partner and to signal ready only when *both* he and his partner are ready.

39. When a server requests three balls to be in his hand prior to each point he is to serve, the receiver should comply with this wish when the third ball is readily available. Since only two balls are normally needed for a service, the receiver should not be required to get the third when it is some distance away, nor, under the continuous play rule, should a server during a game be permitted to retrieve a distant third ball himself. The distant balls should be retrieved at the end of a game.

40. In any argument about facts it should be remembered that each

side has a vote, and one vote equals one vote. Regardless of how sure you are that the score is thirty–fifteen your opponents may be equally sure that it is fifteen–thirty. If no agreement can be reached then the question should be settled by the toss of a racket. Certainly, it would be undesirable to have both teams walk off the court in a huff. Incidentally, arguments about the score can usually be avoided if the server will announce the score before each point.

41. You have had contact with the primary form of stalling when your opponent in an official match purposely arrives 25 minutes late, hoping that those 25 minutes will have provided you with ample opportunity to tense up. Some opponents use an excessively long warmup to achieve the same result. Another form of stalling is provided by the player who walks and plays at about one-third his normal pace, thereby, among other things, taking much of the fun out of the match. Another form is the excess time taken between games when the authorized one minute turns into three due to extra toweling, drinking, taking of pills, and sitting down. Another form is the taking of time at the end of a 6–4 first set; the rules say play shall be continuous except for specified breaks, which do not include one at the end of a first set that ends on an even number of games. Another form is the server's waiting at the net — instead of going to the baseline — while the receiver is retrieving a ball to give him. Another form is the time beyond the authorized ten minute break a player takes at the end of the second set in a three set match. Another is the starting of a discussion to permit a player to catch his breath. Another is the action of the receiver in clearing an out first service that doesn't need to be cleared, such as one that ends up six inches from the backstop. These are some of the more common forms of stalling, a type of gamesmanship aimed at upsetting an opponent. What is the answer to the problem? Again, like foot-faulting, it is a matter of your personal honor system. From a practical view, if you try to outstall a staller you may upset yourself even more, and from an ethical view, you may damage your own reputation. With it all, you can be firm in waiting only reasonable (as you interpret the meaning of the word under the circumstances involved) periods before departing, and in other cases refusing to continue play without an official. The best players are not known as stallers.

42. When your serve hits your partner stationed at the net, is it a let, fault, or loss of point? Likewise, what is the ruling when your serve before touching the ground hits an opponent who is standing *back* of the baseline? The answers to these questions are obvious to anyone who knows the fundamentals of tennis, but it is surprising the number of players who don't know these fundamentals. All players have the responsibility of being familiar with the basic rules. Further, it can be distressing to your opponent when he makes a decision in accordance with a rule and you protest with the remark: "Well, I never heard of that rule before!" Ignorance of the rules constitutes a delinquency on the part of a player and often spoils an otherwise good match.

43. What has been written here constitutes the essentials of "The Code," the summarization of procedures and unwritten rules which custom and tradition dictate all players should follow. If you and your opponents will abide by them you will help in establishing a pattern which will make tennis more fun and a better game for all concerned.

TENNIS BIBLIOGRAPHY

BOOKS AND JOURNALS

Addie, Pauline Betz. *Tennis for Teenagers*. Washington, D.C.: Acropolis Books, 1966.
American Association for Health, Physical Education, and Recreation. *Ideas for Tennis Instruction* (Lifetime Sports Project: Idea Booklets). Washington, D.C.: AAHPER, 1966.
Barnaby, John. *Racket Work, the Key to Tennis*. Boston: Allyn and Bacon, 1969.
Dewhurst, Evelyn. *A Handbook for Coaching Tennis*. London: Carey and Claridge, Ltd., 1963.
Donnally, Mary Jane. *Net Results: A Picture Book of Tennis Fundamentals*. New York: Pageant Press, 1961.
Driver, Helen I. *Tennis for Teachers* (rev. ed.). Madison, Wisconsin: Monona-Driver Book Co., 1966.
Driver, Helen I. *Tennis Self-Instructor*. Madison, Wisconsin: Monona-Driver Book Co., 1960.
Everett, Peter, and Dumas, Virginia. *Beginning Tennis*. Belmont, California: Wadsworth Publishing Co., Inc., 1962.
Faulkner, Edwin. *Teaching and Learning the Four Basic Strokes*. Narberth, Pennsylvania: Middle States Junior Development Program.
Faulkner, Edwin, and Weymuller, Frederick. *Ed Faulkner's Tennis: How to Play It, How to Teach It*. New York: The Dial Press, 1970.
Fogleman, Harry. *Tennis—for the Coach, Teacher, and Player*. Davidson, North Carolina: Davidson Printing Co., 1963.
Gensemer, Robert. *Tennis* (2nd ed.). Philadelphia: W. B. Saunders Company, 1975.
Gonzales, Pancho, and Hawk, Dick. *Tennis*. New York: Fleet Publishing Co., 1962.
Gould, Dick. *Tennis Anyone?* Palo Alto: The National Press, 1964.
Harman, Bob, and Monroe, Keith. *Use Your Head in Tennis*. Port Washington, N.Y.: Kennicott Press, 1966.
Hendrix, John W. "Teaching in the Gymnasium." *Journal of Health, Physical Education, and Recreation,* February, 1962, Vol. 33, no. 2.
Hillas, Marjorie, and La Fevre, J. R. *Tennis*. Dubuque, Iowa: W. C. Brown, 1955.
Jaeger, Eloise M., and Leighton, Harry. *Teaching of Tennis* (rev. ed.). Minneapolis, Minnesota: Burgess Publishing Co., 1963.
Johnson, Joan, and Xanthos, Paul. *Tennis*. Dubuque, Iowa: W. C. Brown Co., 1967.
Kenfield, John F., Jr. *Teaching and Coaching Tennis*. Dubuque, Iowa: W. C. Brown Co., 1964.
King, Billie Jean, and Chapin, Kim. *Tennis to Win*. New York: Harper and Row, 1970.
Kraft, Eve. *The Tennis Workbook*. Princeton: The Princeton Community Tennis Program, 1963.
Kramer, Jack. *How to Win at Tennis*. Englewood Cliffs, New Jersey: Prentice-Hall, Inc.
Laver, Rod. *How to Play Championship Tennis*. New York: Macmillan Co., 1965.
Leighton, Harry. *How to Improve Your Tennis*. Chicago: The Athletic Institute, 1958.
Leighton, Harry ("Cap"). "Introducing Tennis to Youngsters: Teaching Ball Handling Skills." *Journal of Health Physical Education, and Recreation,* February, 1962, vol. 33, no. 2.
Leighton, Harry ("Cap"). *Tennis Instructor's Guide*. Chicago: The Athletic Institute, 1963.
Leighton, James. *Techniques of Winning*. Englewood Cliffs, New Jersey: Prentice-Hall, 1969.
Mace, Wynn, and Tyler, Nicoleau. *Tennis Techniques Illustrated*. New York: Ronald Press, 1962.
Metzler, Paul. *Advanced Tennis*. New York: Sterling Publishing Co., 1968.
Mottram, Tony, and Mottram, Joy. *Modern Lawn Tennis*. London: Nicholas Kaye, 1957.

Mottram, Tony. *Improve your Tennis*. London: Penguin Books, Ltd., 1966.

Murphy, Chet. *Advanced Tennis*. Dubuque, Iowa: W. C. Brown Co., 1970.

Murphy, Chet. "Principles of Learning with Implications for Teaching Tennis." *Journal of Health, Physical Education, and Recreation*, February, 1962, vol. 33, no. 2.

Murphy, William, and Murphy, Chet. *Tennis for Beginners*. New York: Ronald Press, 1958.

Murphy, William, and Murphy, Chet. *Tennis Handbook*. New York: Ronald Press, 1962.

Murphy, William, and Helms, William G. "Developing Simple Tennis Skills through Relays." *Journal of Health, Physical Education, and Recreation*. February, 1962, vol. 33, no. 2.

Palfrey, Sarah. *Tennis for Anyone*. New York: Hawthorne Books, Inc., 1966.

Ploegenman, Stan. *Fundamentals of Tennis*. Englewood Cliffs, New Jersey: Prentice-Hall, 1970.

Staff of *Sports Illustrated*. *The Sports Illustrated Book of Tennis*. Philadelphia: J. B. Lippincott Co., 1961.

Stowe, Tom. *Teaching Tennis System and Stroke Developer*. Napa, California: Silvarado Country Club, 1962.

Talbert, William, and Old, Bruce. *The Game of Singles in Tennis*. Philadelphia: J. B. Lippincott Co., 1962.

Talbert, William, and Old, Bruce. *The Game of Doubles in Tennis*. New York: Henry Holt and Co., 1956.

Tilden, William T. *How to Play Better Tennis*. New York: Simon and Schuster, 1964.

Trengove, Alan, ed. *How to Play Tennis the Professional Way*. New York: Simon and Schuster, 1964.

The United States Lawn Tennis Association. *Umpire's Manual and Rules of Lawn Tennis*. New York: USLTA.

United States Lawn Tennis Association. *USLTA Official Yearbook*. New York: USLTA.

The United States Lawn Tennis Association and the American Association for Health, Physical Education, and Recreation. *Tennis Group Instruction*. Washington, D.C.: AAHPER, 1963.

Wolbers, Charles P. "Creating Enthusiasm," *Journal of Health, Physical Education and Recreation*, February 1962, vol. 33, no. 2.

Xanthos, Paul J. *Tennis, A Pictorial Guide for Teachers*. Paul J. Xanthos Enterprises, 1253 S. Federal Ave., West Los Angeles, Calif., 1963.

MAGAZINES

Tennis, The Magazine of the Racket Sports, Ravinia Station, Highland Park, Illinois.

Tennis, U.S.A., 51 East 42nd Street, New York, New York, 10017 (published by USLTA).

World Tennis Magazine, Book 3, Gracie Station, New York.

AUDIOVISUAL MATERIALS

"Anyone for Tennis," color, 16 mm, USLTA.

"Approach to Tennis," color, sound, Association Films, Inc., 600 Grand Avenue, Ridgefield, N.J. (1970).

"Beginning Tennis," b & w or color, 16 mm, All-American Productions, P.O. Box 801, Riverside, California (1960).

"Beginning Tennis," color, The Athletic Institute, 209 S. State Street, Chicago, Ill.

"Fundamentals of Tennis," b & w, 16 mm, Arizona University (1958).

"Fundamental of Tennis," b & w, 16 mm, produced in association with the AAHPER and USLTA by Transfilms, Inc. (1952).

"Intermediate and Advanced Tennis," b & w, 16 mm, T. N. Rogers Productions, 2808-10 E. Slauson Ave., Huntington Park, Calif.

"Let's Take a Trip to Forrest Hills," b & w, free loan, National Education Films, Inc., 165 W. 46th Street, New York (1957).

"1954 USLTA Singles Championship," film, USLTA, 51 E. 42nd St., New York.

"1956 Davis Cup Challenge Round," b & w, 16 mm, National Educational Films, Inc. (1957).

"Slow Motion Long Films for Tennis Instruction," loop film, USLTA, 51 E. 42nd St., New York.

"Stroke Analysis," b & w, six reels, 16 mm, USLTA, 51 E. 42nd St., New York.

"Tennis," color, super-8, six cartridged loops, Ealing Studios, 2225 Massachusetts, Boston, Mass. (1970).

"Tennis by Contract," color, 16 mm, Audio-Visual Education Films, 7934 Santa Monica Blvd., Santa Monica, Calif. (1962).

"Tennis Class Organization," color, 16 mm, sound, 25 min. This film is a demonstration of successful methods of large class tennis instruction. Available from the USLTA, 51 E. 42nd St., New York.

"Tennis for Beginners," b & w, 16 mm, National Educational Films, Inc., 165 W. 46th Street, New York (1959).

"Tennis for Beginners," b & w, 16 mm, sound, 16 min. The film features some slow motion. Owen Murphy Productions, Inc., 666 5th Avenue, New York, 10009.

"Tennis for Everybody," b & w and color, 16 mm, sound, 13 min. Allegro Film Productions, 201 W. 52nd Street, New York, 10019.

"Tennis Matches from United States and Europe," b & w, 16 mm, National Educational Films, Inc., 165 W. 46th St., New York.

"Tennis—Sports of a Lifetime; Part One: Class Organization," color, 16 mm, Youth Tennis Foundation of Southern California, 609 W. Cahuenga Blvd., Los Angeles, Calif. (1962).

"Tennis Techniques," color, 16 mm, Rogers Productions (1947).

"Tony Trabert 'Loop' Films," b & w, 16 mm, USLTA (1955).

INDEX

Numbers in *italics* refer to glossary entries.